Turkey's New European Era

DATE DUE

NOV 1 4 2008	
SEP 1 2 2011	

Turkey's New European Era

Foreign Policy on the Road to EU Membership

Burak Akçapar

ROWMAN & LITTLEFIELD PUBLISHERS, INC.
Lanham • Boulder • New York • Toronto • Plymouth, UK

10224567

ROWMAN & LITTLEFIELD PUBLISHERS, INC.

Published in the United States of America
by Rowman & Littlefield Publishers, Inc.
A wholly owned subsidiary of The Rowman & Littlefield Publishing Group, Inc.
4501 Forbes Boulevard, Suite 200, Lanham, Maryland 20706
www.rowmanlittlefield.com

Estover Road, Plymouth PL6 7PY, United Kingdom

British Library Cataloguing in Publication Information Available

Library of Congress Cataloging-in-Publication Data
Akçapar, Burak.
  Turkey's new European era : foreign policy on the road to EU
  membership / Burak Akçapar.
    p. cm.
  Includes bibliographical references and index.
  ISBN-13: 978-0-7425-5400-9 (cloth : alk. paper)
  ISBN-10: 0-7425-5400-7 (cloth : alk. paper)
  ISBN-13: 978-0-7425-5401-6 (pbk. : alk. paper)
  ISBN-10: 0-7425-5401-5 (pbk. : alk. paper)
  1. European Union—Turkey. 2. Turkey—Foreign relations—European
Union countries. 3. European Union countries—Foreign relations
—Turkey.   I. Title.
HC240.25.T8A423 2007
341.242'209561—dc22
                                                        2006012204

Printed in the United States of America

⊗™ The paper used in this publication meets the minimum requirements of American
National Standard for Information Sciences—Permanence of Paper for Printed Library
Materials, ANSI/NISO Z39.48-1992.

Contents

	Abbreviations	vii
	Acknowledgments	ix
Introduction	The Sublime Project	1
Chapter 1	The Odyssey	11
Chapter 2	A Tale of Many Reports	41
Chapter 3	Europeanization	57
Chapter 4	The Regional Imperative	77
Chapter 5	Of Europe and America	117
Chapter 6	America as Partner	145
Chapter 7	Negotiating Accession	163
Conclusion	The Coming Age of Janus	185
	Selected Bibliography	193
	Index	203
	About the Author	211

Abbreviations

AU	*African Union*
BLACKSEAFOR	*Black Sea Naval Task Force*
BMENA	*Broader Middle East and North Africa*
BSECO	*Black Sea Economic Cooperation Organization*
CFSP	*Common Foreign and Security Policy*
DAD	*Democracy Assistance Dialogue*
EAPC	*Euro-Atlantic Partnership Council*
EC	*European Communities*
EEC	*European Economic Community*
ENP	*European Neighborhood Policy*
ESDI	*European Security and Defense Initiative*
ESDP	*European Security and Defense Policy*
ESS	*European Security Strategy*
EU	*European Union*
ISAF	*International Security Assistance Force*
NATO	*North Atlantic Treaty Organization*
OECD	*Organization for Economic Cooperation and Development*
OIC	*Organization of the Islamic Conference*
OSCE	*Organization for Security and Cooperation in Europe*
PfP	*Partnership for Peace*
SAP	*Stabilization and Association Process of the EU*

TRNC	*Turkish Republic of Northern Cyprus*
WEU	*Western European Union*
WMD	*Weapons of Mass Destruction*
UN	*United Nations*

Acknowledgments

I am grateful to Dr. Mensur Akgün for the initial idea to write this book. The contents of the book evolved from a speech I gave at the Middle East Technical University in Ankara prior to the launch of the accession negotiations between Turkey and the European Union.

Since then many people have provided essential contributions to further develop my thinking on various subjects covered in this book. I should thank particularly Nabi Şensoy, Mehmet Akat, Reha Keskintepe, Ali Tuygan, Dr. O.Faruk Loğoğlu, and Engin Soysal. Many thanks to Dr. Soner Çağaptay, Dr. Ömer Taşpınar, Dr. Şebnem Akçapar, and Dr. David Cuthell for their valuable comments on the draft of the text. I should also thank Mark Leonard for the idea for the title of the book.

I owe a profound debt of gratitude to my parents, Gürten and Ziya Akçapar, and my son, Z. Onat Akçapar, for always encouraging me.

Rowman and Littlefield's editorial team have been immaculate in their attention and care in producing this book. I extend my heartfelt thanks to assistant editor Jessica Gribble, production editor Bridgette Moore, copyeditor Gary J. Hamel, proofreader Judy Fernow, and the anonymous reviewer.

Needless to say, the responsibility for the contents and any shortcomings of this manuscript is solely mine.

INTRODUCTION

The Sublime Project

The outcome of several hovering consequential questions will have profound implications for our global futures. A partial list would include inquiries like: Will societies be able to come to grips with the powerful economic, social, and political influences of globalization; will the growing rift between the rich and the poor be stemmed; will that rift create a violent backlash, a new wave of violence, a new nihilist ideology; will there be a global clash of civilizations that will eliminate the moderate middle ground and force everyone to take sides; will our habitat be able to adjust to reckless exploitation; will the advent of information societies ironically engender a return to conscience or even to dogma; what will be the implications of the arriving technologies on our economies, nation-states, social networks, political choices, moral lives, and global power balances; will liberal societies preserve and expand their democratic gains or succumb to pressure from asymmetric threats; will currently illiberal societies succeed in proceeding to the camp of human rights and liberties; will China and India continue their ascendancy and with what ramifications for them and the rest of the world; will the international law and organizations manage to adjust to the new requirements and dynamics of international life? We will not have the answers to those questions for decades to come, even if by then. If the new economic, political, social world order comes peacefully, it will come unintroduced; the chances are that most of us will not recognize it. Future is a forbidding concept, not only in that it never comes, but in that it is really a continuum of endless eras. But future can be whittled down to

1

specific visions and outcomes. For any concept of future, its attainment is conditional upon the relationship between sublime projects and the grave errors that may prevent them. Vision and decision is core to progress.

In the endless list of hyperdeterminants of our global future, the membership process of Turkey to the European Union may appear down in the weeds, if not utterly irrelevant. In a sense it is, too. This is not the fall of Byzantium, the invention of the printing press, the discovery of the Americas, the Atatürk revolution. Perhaps it is not even akin to the establishment of the European Coal and Steel Community, NATO, or the UN, nor to the fall of the Berlin Wall. The course of political history has changed in these and many other such critical turning points in history.

Yet if potential impact of the future course of history is the yardstick, then Turkey's EU bid is not irrelevant to our global futures. The future of the European integration project, the Euro-Atlantic project, global energy security, Muslim-Christian relations, Eurasian futures, and greater Middle Eastern evolution are no trivial questions. Nor are American, Western, or another existing or future constellation's engagements in the key geographical expanse centered around Turkey issues for the fainthearted. Whether you are in the Far East, Africa, Australia, or South America, not to mention North America, Europe, Eurasia, or the greater Middle East, you will be influenced in one way or another by these issues rippling out from Europe.

Turkey's membership in the EU is only one of alternative futures for their relationship. Whether that future is attained or missed will have ramifications beyond the EU and Turkey. Membership in the EU will be as fateful as nonmembership, not only for Turkey, but obviously for Europe, the greater Middle East, and Eurasia, if not a wider world. While Turkey or Turkey's relationship with the EU will not singlehandedly determine the future evolution of these regions, any course that they take shall have a fairly substantial Turkish element in it. That puts the topic of a Turkey-EU merger under a very different spotlight indeed.

Turkey's prospective membership in the European Union will not be like any previous accession to that society of nations. Turkey is not like any previous candidate, and the EU is not like any other international body. And the merger between the two promises to create a particular chemistry.

The European Union ranks third in the world in terms of its population, after China and India, and has a gross domestic product that is roughly equal to the United States, the world's leading economic, political, and military power. This is a community of the prosperous who have top living standards, live long, work on average less than many others in the world yet produce much, study a lot, learn foreign languages, and travel extensively. The EU is also the biggest donor of development aid in the world. When asked, 80 percent of EU citizens replied that they were fairly or very satisfied with their lives, and most are optimistic about the future.[1] The EU also has gargantuan problems and challenges, which I will return to later.

As Mark Leonard has so wittily exaggerated, the EU may run the twenty-first century.[2] While that may be an overstatement, the Union will be in the lead in upholding and spreading the values of commitment to multilateral action, democracy, human rights and the international rule of the law, and negotiation and engagement rather than military force. The EU will affix its stamp on international affairs, not by dealing punishing military attacks on supposed enemies but by employing "passive aggression," where its greatest threat will be to have nothing to do with a particular country.[3] It will exert a transformative influence over its sympathizers, as it has been doing until now vis-à-vis the countries that want to join the Union, in ways that will change their societies in an irreversible manner. The countries under the spell of the Union will redraw every aspect of their governance, from economic policies and the way their democracies function to the recipes for their sausage. This is a Union whose highest court has the power to rule that non-Greek European producers will not be allowed to call their cheese "feta."[4] In the military field, of course the North Atlantic Treaty Organization (NATO) has been setting standards for decades, including through the so-called Standardization Agreements, or STANAGs. But the EU's umbrella of rules, standards, and agreements is not limited to military matters nor to any other single issue. This nearly all-pervasive standardization in the EU is also not intended merely for general reference but for strict implementation. While it is not enforced by a centralized European police, surveillance and pressure by the peers is effective. The European image and leadership, Leonard is convinced, will define institutions in the current age of globalization. As the United States designed NATO, the United Nations, the International Monetary Fund, and the World Bank for the previous major period of global uncertainty, for the future, the Europeans have pioneered the creation of the World Trade Organization, the Kyoto Treaty, and the International Criminal Court. All over the world, countries will draw inspiration from the European model and form their own versions. Richard Cooper says this is the best account of the political history of the EU,[5] and Stanley Hoffman appears to agree[6]; I take their word for it. For Europe to fulfill its promise of setting the standards of commitment to laws, universal values, and cooperation, however, it will have to honor these commitments itself. Turkey's membership process will be one witness to that effect.

As the other side of this prospective marriage, Turkey is important in its own right. It does not compare to the European Union in power and influence, including in terms of Mark Leonard's "transformative" power or Joseph Nye's "soft" power.[7] But Turkey has its own strengths. It is considerable in terms of military weight. And though it lags in economic prosperity, it dazzles in potential. Turkey is the unique European, Middle Eastern, Mediterranean, Aegean, Black Sea, Caucasian, Central Asian, Eurasian, Transatlantic, secular, Muslim, democratic nation, with a population of over seventy million and an economy that is already among the top twenty in the world and rapidly growing. And having already felt the transformative power of the EU, Turkey is also an increasingly effective conduit for such influence in the EU's broader neighborhood. In fact, from the U.S., European, or any other great-power perspective, Turkey is a potential facilitator—or hindrance.

Naturally, this does not mean that Turkey always wields significant influence on issues that are of concern. In fact, Turks believe, in utter frustration, that almost always the opposite is true. Take for instance the Cyprus issue. Turks are resentful of the fact that although the first brutal ethnic warfare in post–World War II Europe was prevented by Turkey's action in Cyprus against all odds in 1974, there was no appreciation. And they also resent that the Greek Cypriots, who flatly rejected the deal offered by the United Nations for the resolution of the problem they created in the first instance—by not committing to the arrangement that established the independent Republic of Cyprus in 1960 and by toppling their legitimate government and menacing the Turkish Cypriots until 1974—have entered the EU irrespective of their recalcitrance.

Turkey's own thinkers define the country as a strategic medium power.[8] A country that is neither big nor small, Turkey is neither in the driver's seat nor just riding in the trailer. They are probably right. Turkey's statistical facts and the country's history both validate this premise. All of this tells part of the story.

The chemistry of the relationship between Turkey and the EU is of the greatest significance, and it implies something greater than the addition of the particular qualities of each. The accession of a country the size of Turkey is by itself noteworthy. However, the special chemistry involved comes more directly from the fact that at the end of the current accession process Turkey's standing will help determine the future of Europe, its neighborhood, and Christian-Muslim relations, not to mention the overall tenor of regional affairs. If this large, democratic, secular, Muslim nation succeeds in joining the European Union, the reach of the EU's transformative power will extend deep into Eurasia and indeed into the Muslim world. Turkey's own social, cultural, political, and economic networks will carry the message, interpret and amplify it. And a Europe that can be taken at its word will be even more potent a source of inspiration. The institutions that the EU will espouse for the coming order of the globalized world, as well as the ones that currently undergird the global order, require a Europe and a European model that are for real. But a rule-based global order can only be sustained if the composite American power is behind it. And the United States, or anyone else for that matter, will buy into this vision of global order only if that model remains attractive. Europe can maintain and enhance its luster by wooing and integrating Turkey, thus coalescing and co-opting Turkey's strengths and continuing to look outward as much as inside.

The EU has brought its citizens unsurpassed living standards and economic prowess. It is the only single market that compares to the world's largest, the United States, and it has the potential to surpass it in the not so distant future. The EU has served as a rapid elevator for any country that has joined it. Thus, when asked, many Turks cite economic gains as the number one reason for supporting Turkey's membership drive. Yet, economic success and prosperity mask what has been an even greater achievement and indeed the initial raison d'être of the EU, namely anchoring its members in peace and security. Once the bloodiest of all continents, the "incubator of world wars,"[9] the nest of empires with global reach, Europe has now turned into a security community, almost a Kantian space of perpetual peace. War is not just unlikely among the EU countries, it is also inconceivable.

Although the EU has eradicated the prospect of war among its members and contained insecurity outside its borders, this was not its own success alone. The EU's ability to sustain European security, stability, and prosperity has been contingent on a number of external factors, including foremost the cooperation of the United States and, more recently, of Europe's neighbors. Under U.S. and NATO protection, not only have Europeans felt secure with regard to outsiders, but also with regard to each other. Thus, Europeans can afford to invest less on their security and channel their money into more productive sectors of their economy. European giants have achieved their economic expansion without offending others, without creating hostile contenders trying to engage in balance-of-power politics. What was once seen as a zero-sum struggle for wealth and power came instead to be regarded as a win-win cooperative deal. The idea of a European Coal and Steel Community that began it all in 1952 may have been the product of the genius of Jean Monet, Robert Schuman, and Walter Hallstein, but what made European integration possible was the protected environment furnished by NATO and the United States. There, the name list is not any less significant. European integration, all the way to the reunification of Germany and the fall of the Warsaw Pact, has been as much a U.S. and transatlantic vision and achievement as anything else. Today, countries in the EU's proximity are also taking part in the effort to maintain European stability, security, and prosperity. Without such cooperation, Europe would be a much tenser and more insecure community, with more acrimonious disputes due to the increased stakes. At the very least, there is an unavoidable interdependence between the EU and its neighborhood that requires the EU to coexist with a benign proximity. The EU's enlargement strategy and its European Neighborhood Policy are built on the understanding of this very fact of interdependence. As Andreas Marchetti indicates, "The European Union still seems in a process of discovery just like it has discovered the relevance of 'other vicinities' in the previous past. This cognitive process has always been particularly observable either in the aftermath of enlarging the Community's or later the Union's own geographic scope or as a development at its periphery that had caused direct repercussions on Europe itself."[10] The policy dovetails with European Security Strategy, which acknowledges the need for a ring of well-governed countries to the east of the Union and on the borders of the Mediterranean. The emphasis on well-governed countries is based on a will "to create good neighbors."[11] The beauty of the EU will continue to need the benevolence and cooperation of its neighbors and the engagement of the United States.

Meanwhile, the greatest challenge to the EU may come from within. The calls to stop Europe's enlargement and to have it turn inward, as well as all the energy spent trying to rewind Europe's multicultural gains and attribute Europe's progress in the last five decades to its Christian identity are ultimately self-defeating. Although the United States may be currently leading in the race for the bad image hall of fame, Europe is not too far behind, and its cumulative historical points may give it the edge. By advancing their self-centric ideas, Europe's primary benefactors are rapidly becoming Europe's worst encumbrance.

That said, one should have faith in Europe. The decision to open accession talks with Turkey, taken in the absence of an outpouring of popular demand and affection, which itself has resulted from relentless misinformation, has rested on sound political vision and judgment on the part of the EU leaders.

In their histories, many European states have been both the aggressors and the violated. But the EU has been foremost a peace project. It started as one, and in that spirit it took in the nascent democracies of Eastern Europe. For Turkey, as it has been for the existing members, joining the EU is a leap into a peaceful and prosperous space. And for the EU, Turkey's membership will amount to a quintessential peace and security project.

If Turkey and the EU fail, however, then the credibility and appeal of the EU in the world at large will be shrunk to that of a mere commercial partner and money lender. Universal values, multicultural societies, unity in diversity, primacy of international law, all this will be seen as a smoke screen if doors are slammed shut when a Muslim (albeit staunchly secular and democratic) nation comes seeking entry. The Gambian auto dealer in Baltimore, Maryland, the Pakistani taxi driver in Oslo, Norway, the Chinese translator in Beijing, the Moroccan migrant in Paris, France, the Qatari merchant, the Palestinian teacher are all watching the EU's treatment of the Turkish membership bid.

The comfort of the United States with regard to the effectiveness of multilateral solutions, slow yet thorough transformations, and soft but resilient power will be essential for the European transformative model's influence, hitherto mostly localized, to take hold all over the globe. But should Europe choose to define itself as a Christian club by excluding Turkey, in the uneasy regional and global scene that would follow, the United States, too, would be distracted. Who, then, would be ready to believe that Europe is about universal values and has a global message of a rule-based peaceful world order?

For the reader, all these are lofty thoughts and words, to be sure. Yet ideas do shape the world. Perceptions move the masses. Indeed, wrong ideas have been moving the people in Europe in all the wrong directions about the Turks and Turkey's membership. So let us set the idea right first.

As right as the idea is, achieving Turkey's membership to the European Union will not be a walk in the park. The relationship between Turkey and the EU has always been a wearisome, frustrating enterprise. It takes only a deep breath and a few keystrokes, altogether a mere few seconds, to type the words: "Turkey and the European Union have started negotiations toward full membership." But such ease for the typist belies over four decades of Turkey's trying to gain membership as well as the impending tumult of the times ahead. It has taken a generation of Turks and Europeans to start their merger under the European Union, and even as they have begun treading down a negotiation path that has brought scores of candidate countries to full membership, the future of their relationship is as contentious as ever. Even on the day the accession talks formally began, the EU leaders were still discussing the ultimate objective and the content of the accession process, which had already been applied numerous times before for several other candidates. Every day since, there have been speculations galore regarding when the negotiations would be disrupted and for what reason. Forecasts of impending crises between Turkey and the EU are part and parcel of Turkey's membership bid.

The EU has been an expanding enterprise. What started with six countries in 1957 became twenty-five in 2004 in several waves of enlargement. EU nations that were NATO allies were first joined by neutrals, then by former adversaries, despite the occasional chagrin of Russia. Before the turn of the decade, the EU will admit two more members, Bulgaria and Romania. Croatia is also not far behind. By then, twenty-two countries will have joined the six original founders of the European Economic Community who signed the Treaties of Rome in 1957.

Each enlargement was a challenge. Hardly any of the enlargements were conducted with unanimous public support by all the EU nations. Some countries were more interested and supportive to specific candidates than others. The British joined after having been rejected by France for a decade. And leaders in the United Kingdom are still forced by their constituents to deliver speeches every year on why they should remain in the EU. A divided Cyprus was admitted, carrying the island's problems but only one of its protagonists into the EU. Poland, following the United Kingdom and Spain, broke through the fear threshold of a large nation joining the Union. The Danes came in but remained outside several key arrangements, such as the Euro or the Schengen zone. The Norwegians simply voted down their EU membership. The Swiss were not much interested in the first place. Several EU nations entered the Union as feeble postdictatorial regimes and then flourished as democracies, including Greece, Spain, and Portugal. Ireland entered as a poor backwater and has risen up to become a vanguard globalist economy. Each enlargement was a package of a few candidates, but in 2004 a record ten countries joined the EU in one swing. While all this was happening, Turkey, whose membership in NATO dates back to 1952 and EU Associate Membership to 1963, was always there observing, half in, half out, at first curiously but with increasing nervousness.

Turkey's politicians and diplomats traditionally rate the country's bid to join the European Union as the number one foreign-policy priority. But given the nature of the accession process, the issues involve more than foreign policy. Transposing the entirety of the EU's prolific legislation into a national legal system and implementing it is an arduous task by any standard. The EU's founding treaties, regulations, directives, case law, and other documents have to be translated and adopted. In the meantime, the bureaucratic and judicial authorities must be retrained to implement and enforce the newly internalized EU legislation. Thus, when a candidate country starts negotiating, the accession process is about domestic policy, not only foreign policy. In fact politics among the EU members is not foreign policy in the traditional sense. EU politics is partly domestic politics of the unique European sort.

Negotiations prepare the candidate country for a uniquely intrusive and pervasive alignment with the rest of the EU. Foreign policy is, obviously, part of the negotiation process. The candidate country's foreign policy must conform to the European Common Foreign and Security Policy. This negotiation forms one of nearly three dozen such chapters of negotiation between the candidate country and the EU. But in a grossly contested enlargement path, and in a geography of enormous challenges and opportunities, foreign and security policy constitutes much more than a thirty-fifth of a negotiation. It is rather a crucial area of cooperation, of solidarity, and ultimately of the confidence needed to achieve the merger. Foreign policy is also the playground of the opponents of Turkey's membership.

The time frame of the Turkey-EU full-membership negotiations will define, as the previous forty years could not, the denouement of the Turkish-EU saga. Foreign policy will be somewhere around the core of this episode.

The chapters of this book will take the reader from the past to the present and forward to the optimal future of Turkey's EU membership process. They will ask the reader to put together various dimensions of the relationship between Turkey, Europe, the United States, and a host of nations in Turkey's broad and diverse neighborhood. The book will try to merge into one cohesive whole the historical and present duality of thinking on Turkey, the positively evolving regional profile of Turkey in a geography that it once ruled, the painstaking Europeanization of the country's governance, the impact of Turkey's evolution in Europe's proximity, the context of the transatlantic debate, and the role of the United States. The book will not prescribe specific policies. Instead, it will attempt to form what I believe is the right mind-set to engender the right policies for Turkey, Europe, the United States, and Europe's neighbors.

Andrew Mango writes perceptively that Turkey is avid for modernity and respect as a member of the family of advanced nations; those who "show this respect will soon learn to understand Turkey."[12] For his part, Stephen Kinzer notes that for centuries Turks "shaped world history, and the not so distant memory of Ottoman glory allows them to believe they can again."[13]

This book is not about a distant past glory or ambitions to shape the world. Rather, it is a rejoinder for the recognition that Turkey does present the potential to make a positive impact on aspirations to maintain and develop peace in a challenging world, particularly in a multitude of critical geographies surrounding Turkey, on the spread of freedom, democracy, and prosperity and on regional dreams to forge a just, stable, and progressive order in defiance of more recent history.

Turkish accession to the EU is the next fundamental peace project to be undersigned by Europe and promoted by the United States. At the same time, it is the natural extension of the idea of an integrated Europe. The EU, having transformed age-old antagonisms among its existing members, will not only include Turkey into its peaceful fold but at the same time will construct a sturdy bridge into the Muslim world and Eurasia. A secular, democratic, prosperous, and progressive Turkey, as a member of the European Union, will inspire its Muslim and non-Muslim neighbors. An EU that takes this step will have delivered a defeat to the threatening conundrum of a clash of civilizations.

Such are the stakes in Turkey's journey toward the EU. The Roman mythological figure Janus promoted beginnings that ensured good endings. Turks vie for such a role in the twenty-first century in the vortex and confluence of the west and the east, the north and the south.

Notes

1. Detailed statistics on the EU can be found at the http://epp.eurostat.cec.eu .int/. For a more accessible presentation of EU facts and figures, see: http://europa.eu/ abc/keyfigures/index_en.htm.

2. In fact, he argued, in his very compelling book, that the EU "will" run this century. Mark Leonard, *Why Europe Will Run the 21st Century* (New York: Public Affairs, 2005).

3. Leonard, *Why Europe*, 51.

4. Melissa Block, "EU Court Ruling Protects Greek Feta," *All Things Considered,* NPR, October 26, 2005.

5. Richard Cooper, "Europe: *Why Europe Will Run the 21st Century* by Mark Leonard" [review], *Sunday Times*, February 27, 2005.

6. Stanley Hoffman, "*Why Europe Will Run the 21st Century* by Mark Leonard" [review], *Foreign Affairs* 84, no. 3 (May/June 2005).

7. The concept of "soft power" has been articulated by Dr. Nye in several texts and speeches. See, in particular: Joseph S. Nye Jr., *Soft Power: The Means to Succeed in World Politics* (New York: Public Affairs, 2004).

8. Baskın Oran, *Türk Dış Politikası (Cilt-1 1919–1980) [Turkish Foreign Policy, Volume 1: 1919–1980]* (İstanbul: İletişim Yayınları, 2004). See also Meliha Benli Altunişik and Özlem Tur Kavlı, *Turkey: Themes and Challenges* (London and New York: RoutledgeCurzon, 2004).

9. Leonard, *Why Europe*, 36.

10. Andreas Marchetti, *The European Neighborhood Policy: Foreign Policy at the EU's Periphery* (Bonn: University of Bonn Center for European Integration Studies (ZEI) Publication, 2006), 1–2.

11. Karen Smith, "The Outsiders: The European Neighborhood Policy," *International Affairs* 81, no. 4 (2005): 763.

12. Andrew Mango, *The Turks Today* (Woodstock, NY: Overlook, 2004), 11.

13. Stephen Kinzer, *Crescent and Star: Turkey Between Two Worlds* (New York: Farrar, Straus & Giroux: 2001).

CHAPTER ONE

The Odyssey

The debate concerning Turkey's bid to join the European Union may recall the characterization of the Schleswig-Holstein question in the nineteenth century by the British prime minister Lord Palmerston. When asked what he thought of that problem, the cunning politician responded that there were only three people who ever understood it: one was dead, the second one was in the lunatic asylum, and he himself was the third person, but had forgotten it. Many of the leaders who have put Turkey on the road to EU membership have long been deceased. The whole debate is imbued with such obsession on the part of both the proponents and the opponents that for a casual on-looker the situation might well be perceived as insane. And there is a constant need to recap and summon the big picture lest the significance of this Herculean project be forgotten. At the same time, who remembers today that a seemingly intractable Schleswig-Holstein problem did once bedevil Europe? Whether the current debate about Turkey's membership in the EU will similarly become superfluous, even forgotten one day is anyone's guess.

For the time being, at least, Turkey's bid to accede to the European Union amounts to much more than a footnote in current history. It has been creating political divisions not only in the EU and Turkey, but also across the Atlantic and across cultural divides for a full generation. It is thus hardly possible to overstate the sheer importance of the start of negotiations regarding Turkey's entry into the most dramatic voluntary integration process in modern times. Turkey is a sizable and hyperdynamic secularly and democratically governed Muslim nation that sits atop multiple geostrategic and cultural fault lines and is moving determinedly closer to integration with core Europe and the West at a time when the menace of a clash of civilizations is said to loom over global society. Having once marched on Europe with legions of janissaries, this country now promises to be a Janus, who in Roman mythology was the god of doors, gateways, and beginnings ensuring good endings. Turkey will be bridging or even concentering the different worlds of the west and east, north and south. Such may be the promise and stake of Turkish membership in the European Union.

Thus, seized by the momentousness of opening the Union's doors to a complex and arguably dissimilar country like Turkey, the Dutch prime minister, Jan Peter Balkenende, who himself had been feeling the brunt of opposition in his own country, declared in unequivocal terms that a historic step had been taken at the European Council, the EU's top political organ, by setting a date for negotiations in December 2004. In his words, the EU decision had sent a powerful message that would resound even beyond Turkey's borders, that "there is no breach or unbridgeable chasm between people who have their roots in the Christian tradition and those who see the world through the eyes of Islam."[1] Since then almost everyone involved has been going to great lengths to restate that the negotiations imply a new beginning and not the end of an odyssey. This is a long saga in the making.

The December 2004 summit was a turning point. The EU leaders, acting on the European Commission's evaluation, agreed that Turkey had sufficiently met the qualities of a European democracy and decided to open accession negotiations. Although the opening of the actual negotiations would require a few further steps, both on the part of Turkey and the EU, such as drawing up the terms of the negotiations, it was at this summit that the road was cleared for Turkey to transform from a candidate to a negotiating party. Since every country that has ever started negotiations has been admitted to the Union, this was a quantum leap. Turks were happy, but nonetheless still wary. Subsequent events would vindicate their caution.

The decisions of the December 2004 summit were a mixed blessing for Turkey, granting its strategic objective of opening accession talks on a firm date while burying several expectations. Such halfway satisfaction was perhaps business as usual in the EU, where compromise is the name of the game. Perhaps the result should have increased the optimistic Turks' confidence in the "system" by demonstrating that not only Turkey but the EU leaders too would have to compromise. And they did compromise to some extent, given the widespread opposition to Turkish membership by several EU members. However, satisfaction with the decision to open accession negotiations was quickly tempered by a superfluous reference to the open-ended nature of the negotiations, which would not necessarily culminate in Turkey's full membership in the EU.

The last moments before the decision also heralded the shape of things to come: Turkey would face vagarious pressures from individual EU countries and would be expected to satisfy all member states in foreign and security policy, even if some of the member states were part of the problem. The EU was a kind of karaoke machine, and every member was now to be a star, whatever the tune and the quality of voice. Moreover, Turkey would run this gauntlet in darkness and without a reasonable assurance that it would be allowed into the Union in the end. Samuel Huntington, for one, had the suspicion, as did many Turks, that despite the progress in its membership bid, Turkey would still not end up joining the Union.[2] Thus, the EU, while agreeing to open accession talks, in effect postponed Turkish membership again for the indefinite future.

The discussions at the EU summit on December 17, 2004, almost ended with the Turkish leadership leaving Brussels on a sour note, criticizing what they perceived as unwarranted conditions and demands. The question of Cyprus posed the biggest threat of disruption. In the end Turkey did not recognize the EU member Cyprus as representing the whole island but did agree to sign a document before October 3, 2005, extending the existing Turkey-EU Customs Union to all EU members with a declaration confirming no change of policy vis-à-vis the Cyprus dispute.

Nonetheless, the negotiations between Turkey and the European Union were formally kicked off as scheduled. The drama that unfolded on that day was reminiscent of a Hollywood political thriller. Even the December 2004 experience was overshadowed by what transpired in October 2005.[3] History will record that the accession talks were launched on October 3, 2005, as foreseen. This date had been put on the calendar by the EU and Turkish leaders less than a year earlier. Actually, the negotiations formally began early in the morning on October 4. The clocks were symbolically stopped at the conference a few minutes before midnight as the EU foreign ministers waited for the plane carrying their Turkish counterparts to land in Luxembourg. Foreign Minister Abdullah Gül and the chief negotiator, Minister Ali Babacan, made it to the conference before midnight, not according to local time but rather UK time. By then the British foreign secretary, Jack Straw, was exhausted, having brought to fruition an intra-EU agreement on the framework for the accession negotiations only a few hours before. It had then taken Turkey a few hours and telephone calls to concur with the document. This essential framework, setting out the scope and procedures of the accession negotiations, was to have been agreed to within the EU, and ultimately by Turkey, in advance of the October appointment. But as the date of October 3 approached, it became publicly known that the framework document could not be agreed upon within the EU. The British EU presidency called emergency talks of the EU foreign ministers, warning that the parties stood on the edge of a precipice.

This diplomatic melodrama involved every possible player, but the key actor appeared to be the Austrian government. The international press reported that the Austrians were calling into question the ultimate objective of the accession talks. They insisted on proposing a privileged partnership instead of a full membership for Turkey. Austria appeared isolated in this regard within the EU, not even joined by the Greek Cypriots. Nevertheless, the Austrian foreign minister hung on to this position, due to pressure emanating from the local elections taking place in her country. The Austrians also insisted on the opening of negotiations with Croatia, which depended on a report from the International Criminal Tribunal on the War Crimes in Former Yugoslavia that the country was cooperating with the tribunal. The chief prosecutor, Carla Del Ponte, produced that report just in time for the Austrians to find a face-saving exit out of the impasse.

On their part, the Greek Cypriots, although not eager to push Turkey off the negotiating table, were scrambling to force Turkey to "recognize" Cyprus, which in effect meant recognizing that the Greek Cypriot government represented the Turkish Cypriots as well—not at all the reality. They were also aiming to insert a sentence into the framework document requiring Turkey to relinquish its prerogative to veto Greek Cypriot accession to any international organization, notably NATO. The Greek Cypriot president, Tasos Papadopoulos, who had successfully campaigned against the UN-brokered reunification of the island a year earlier and was nonetheless rewarded by EU membership, was emboldened by a sense of impunity to also adamantly press to see in advance the speech to be delivered by the Turkish foreign minister at the opening ceremony of the negotiations.

Meanwhile, the clock was ticking, and the United States was called into the equation, reportedly by the British. Secretary of State Condoleezza Rice ruled out short-track NATO membership for Cyprus, reaffirming that this issue is a prerogative of NATO, not the EU.

As this diplomatic drama was playing out, a group of diaspora Armenians were outside the conference hall in Luxembourg cheering the Austrians for their hardheaded stand against Turkey's EU membership, carrying banners that referenced the Viennese defense against the Ottoman Muslim siege in 1683. They were oblivious to the interests and indeed the wishes of Armenians inside Armenia, who extended support to Turkey's EU bid, anticipating the benefits of bordering an EU country.[4] Elsewhere, of course, other skeptics in Europe, Turkey, and even the United States were also hoping the Austrians would not budge.[5]

Turkish protesters in turn were turning up in sizable numbers in Istanbul and Ankara, demonstrating against the EU. For the Turks, the Negotiating Framework document, even without these last-minute assertions, was already a profound shock. The Austrian and Greek Cypriot demands were not only unacceptable but also unabashedly abusive. The crisis was quickly turning acute, with an angry Turkish walkout becoming more imminent every passing second. Turkish leaders remained in Ankara, insisting that they would not go to Luxembourg until they saw and endorsed the final Negotiating Framework. A veteran American observer of Turkey, Mark Parris, was to conclude later that if the Austrian and Greek Cypriot demands had not been dropped and Minister Gül ended up not flying to Luxembourg, he would have received broad support among the Turkish public for his decision.[6] The situation was tough enough even in the absence of these last-ditch demands.

Jack Straw and his team were caught in the middle of it all, trying to sort out the mess. In the end, Austrians and Greek Cypriots agreed to drop their points of insistence, at least for the moment.

Only a few months later the same drama was lived again when the Greek Cypriots tried to impose similar demands and threatened to veto the opening of the actual negotiations on the first chapter, related to science and research. Again the compromise was found literally close to midnight on June 12, 2006. The actual negotiations were opened on science and research and immediately closed as Turkey had already complied with the EU legislation on that chapter. But the fact remained, if not revalidated, that not even the easiest of chapters could be negotiated without harangue and squabble on issues that were extrinsic to the subject matter of the negotiations.

As things now stand, EU and Turkish leaders have launched the accession negotiations with the stated objective of Turkey's full membership. All leaders and commentators agree that this will not happen before 2014, if even by then. This does not mean that Turkey has won. The document was hard to swallow for Turkey, given the ferociously stringent parameters that no other EU candidate has had to endure. Repeated statements from French, German, and other politicians continue to cast doubts on the prospects for Turkish accession to the EU, and polls show weak support for Turkey's membership. In addition, the Greek Cypriots seem determined to abuse their position in the EU. The leaders of those countries where public resistance to Turkish membership appears strong emphasize in their public discourse the drawn-out nature of the accession process. Even then, the people will have the final say, whether through a referendum such as in France and Austria or through the parliaments, including the European Parliament. Just about everyone emphasizes the virtues of the process and the expectation that Turkey and the EU will be better off during and hopefully at the end of the accession negotiations. At least this is what the publics have been promised, both in the EU and in Turkey.

But the process can go wrong. And if recent experience to date is any guide, there is much to be worried about, as well as encouraged by. At the end of the turmoil leading up to the formal launch of the accession talks in October 2005 and the actual negotiations in June 2006, the message inferred by the Turkish citizens was that no effort would be spared to convince the Turks to settle on their own for a separate deal well short of membership. As the *Times* of London noted:

> The conditions, as provocative as they are politically disingenuous, pander to an increasingly hostile EU opinion by citing issues that appear reasonable but are calculated to anger Ankara. The same is true of those European politicians . . . who are now talking of "privileged partnership" as a substitute for full EU membership. . . . What politicians in Strasbourg, Paris and Berlin are hoping is that a piqued Turkey will herself flounce out of the talks. For what they fear has, at heart, little to do with agricultural costs, Turkey's human rights record or the tortuous Cyprus negotiations. It is, more crudely, the atavistic clash of civilizations—the contention that a Europe based on Christian values and culture has no place in its midst for a Muslim nation. Beneath the rumblings in France, Germany, Austria and the Netherlands also lie popular hostility to Islam and a rejection of any more Muslim immigration.[7]

If the purpose was indeed to provoke Turkey's walkout, it failed for now. A voluntary self-disqualification would be ideal for Turkey's opponents in Europe and Europe's opponents in Turkey. But the process that would produce such a rupture can only be a harbinger of a profoundly damaged relationship, which even the skeptics on both sides appear willing to avoid.

This is not the moment for acrimony. It is instead the time to expend maximum efforts to make the process work in the best way possible. The launch of the accession talks required resolute diplomacy to defeat debilitating prejudice and brinkmanship. Nonetheless, at the end of the day it was all smiles and handshakes. British Foreign Secretary Straw was unequivocal about the result at the joint conference with the Turkish minister, Abdullah Gül, and the EU commissioner, Olli Rehn, when he stated: "We have just made history."

Except for the drained faces of everyone in the room, the last-minute diplomatic maelstrom was not apparent to those who had not stayed up to

watch the television broadcast of the late-night launch of the accession negotiations. Reading the opening speeches, which unanimously announced to
the world that something momentous had been achieved, one could easily be
fooled by the serenity that followed the storm. Feelings were bruised and future landmines well planted, but the result was nonetheless historic. The
Economist wrote:

> When the countries of the European Union agreed last December to grant
> Turkey her fondest dream and begin formal talks on admitting the big, predom-
> inantly Muslim nation as a member, it was no doubt envisaged, or at least
> hoped, that the date pencilled in the diary for the start of the process would be
> a time of ceremony and celebrations, not bickering and brinkmanship. But the
> EU wouldn't be the EU without those last-minute panics, replete with desper-
> ate horse-trading and just-good-enough fudges, and in this respect Monday Oc-
> tober 3rd did not disappoint. For much of the day, it looked like the love affair
> was in real danger of ending in acrimony. But thanks to some frenzied diplo-
> matic activity, it ended instead in a firm—though hardly warm—embrace.[8]

It remains to be seen whether the *Economist* was right to qualify the embrace as firm. Doubts remain on both sides of the negotiating table augmented by the travails encountered on the day the first chapter was negotiated. Unmistakably, a bad taste remained from the circumstances
surrounding the launch of the negotiations. And much more of this drama is
likely to revisit Turkey's accession process.

The commissioner responsible for EU enlargement, Olli Rehn, was no
doubt guided by this background of mutual unease when he flew to Ankara
only two days after the negotiations were formally declared open in 2005. He
would discuss the start of practical and technical phases of the actual negotiation process. His premise was correct: the only way to know what will happen between the EU and Turkey is not to ponder behind a desk or a camera,
but to actually walk the distance.

On the long road ahead, a lengthy process of negotiations between a
global economic power and an ascendant regional player will take place.
There seems to be sufficient language inserted in the documents governing
the negotiations to guarantee continued strain going forward. The agreed-on
framework for the negotiations confirmed and even planted more road-side
bombs for Turkey. The last ten candidates to join the EU in May 2004, and
the two set to join by 2007, namely Bulgaria and Romania, were not subject
to the same conditions that Turkey will have to meet. Actually, no one in the
expanding enterprise of the EU has ever been expected to meet as high standards as Turkey. The argument is that the previous negotiations' faults and

shortcomings have been proven so great that they need to be amended in view of the negative experience. This explanation was given some credibility by also submitting toughened—but not as tough—conditions for the other remaining negotiating candidate country, Croatia. The fact of the matter remains, however, that Turkey will be negotiating under the most stringent framework any EU candidate country has had since the very inception of the European integration project.

As many have rushed to assert, accession to the EU will require a thorough overhauling of almost every aspect of Turkish governance, requiring reforms that are hard to digest. And they will have to be effected without commensurate financial compensation by the EU. The negotiations, being intergovernmental, will not be politically sterile. The beginning of the negotiations coincides with the political crisis that has engulfed the EU project due to the French and Dutch votes against the proposed European Constitution. To further complicate things, several of the EU's members are themselves in economic, social, and consequently political difficulty. The EU's enlargement and Turkey's membership prospects are providing an easy target in the associated political polemic.

The debate on Turkey was carried into national domestic politics in several countries, including France and Germany, not only on its own merits but as a proxy in national power struggles. The proposed Constitutional Treaty of the EU, which Turkey helped to prepare alongside all the EU member and candidate countries, received an overwhelming no vote in the French and Dutch spring 2005 referenda. The political campaigns in the lead-up to the referenda, more so than the results of the referenda itself, provided the anticlimax to the celebrated December 2004 EU summit that had seemed to open the doors to Turkey. In both these political campaigns the worst of political attitudes against Muslim minorities, Turks, and Turkish membership to the EU were manifested. The French referendum on May 29, 2005, which produced a 55 percent vote against the EU's draft Constitutional Treaty, was not about Turkish membership to the EU; neither was the Dutch referendum, which produced an even stronger no on the heels of the French. However, the issue of Turkish accession to the EU was made part of the successful campaign for a no vote in a way that exploited popular misperceptions about the Turks.

One could not help being appalled by the intensity of the anti-Turkish feelings, by the fact that so much negativity can exist in one society for another. Irrespective of the question of the Turkish membership, it appears that Europe may be rushing toward a serious social crisis. The rising intensity of xenophobia cannot be ignored and should not be understated. Given Europe's history, this problem must be openly confronted and addressed. As a positive note, however, the October elections in 2005 in Germany and Austria have demonstrated, paradoxically, that anti-Turkish discourse does not necessarily pay off decisively at the ballot box. At least for now.

Thus, the road ahead in Turkey's journey toward the EU remains perilous, the map unreliable. From the Turkish point of view this was expected. The Turks have been told by their leaders that the road to the EU will be no illuminated modern boulevard neatly marked and well maintained by gas stations and hotels and restaurants. President Turgut Özal, for one, had warned that instead Turks shall walk a long and winding path. Since that warning over a decade ago, Turks have managed to take some steps on the path. However, it has been a march of two steps forward and one step back, as the Ottoman military band used to march. Or as some might suggest, it is like a walk on the steps depicted in M. C. Escher's drawing *Ascending and Descending*, where no matter how many steps you climb, you end up where you first started. Yet this may not be so bad anyway, others would suggest, since after all, this is like a jog on the treadmill: you are better off afterward despite not having traveled anywhere. The fact is, most if not all of the reforms that Turkey has enacted to get into the EU have made life better for Turkey and the Turks.

Many official commentators would underscore that these reforms are what the Turks wanted anyway. Support for EU membership has remained high in Turkey over the last decades, although it was no secret what reforms the EU was demanding. The EU representatives have never been shy, or even diplomatic, in their open pronouncements of Turkey's shortcomings and what the country had to do to overcome them. Nevertheless, public and political discourse in Turkey remains in favor of EU membership.

To be accurate, among the panoply of reforms asked for and fulfilled, some have been more controversial within Turkey than others. Abrogating capital punishment was not controversial on its own merits. For the preceding fifteen years Turkey had not carried out a single execution. Every execution was subject to parliamentary endorsement, and Parliament never endorsed a verdict of capital punishment in that entire time. But lifting capital punishment after the capture and conviction of the ringleader of the Kurdistan Workers' Party (PKK) terrorist organization—which had cost Turkey some forty thousand lives, over $100 billion in resources, and immeasurable loss of prestige and even self-esteem—was surely not easy. Yet it was done. At any rate, the mainstream debate has been about the extent to which Turkey had to bend over backwards in fulfilling incessant EU requirements, not whether Turkey should join the EU or comply with its fundamental terms. EU membership remained a goal despite the EU.

For the EU's part, it is as hard for them to give a definite yes as a definite no to Turkey. Even for the culturally unbiased, it is proving tricky to embrace Turkey wholeheartedly due to a number of factors. Above all, Turkey remains poorer than the other EU nations in terms of per-capita income. According to the EU's statistical office, Eurostat, based on the estimates of purchasing-power parities for 2004, Turkey's per-person income was about 30 percent of the EU average. While this is the lowest among all twenty-five EU member countries and four candidates, it is neck-and-neck with the figures for Bulgaria and Romania, who are slated to join the EU in 2007. Furthermore, there are thirteen current EU members who are also below the Union's average, three of them being longtime members.[9] What is more, Turkey registers the highest actual economic growth rates, not only among EU member and candidate countries but in fact also among the entire membership of the Organization for Economic Cooperation and Development (OECD). The GNP growth over the past three years has been a striking 26 percent. In other words, Turkey's real economic growth is three times higher than the EU average. That Turkey has a robust economy is not lost on the European press, but somehow it has not yet dawned on the European publics.[10] As Anne Krueger, first deputy managing director of the International Monetary Fund said, "These are striking achievements and underline the enormous potential of the Turkish economy."[11] The potential is surely there and it is real.

If Turkey's dynamism continues, the chances are that Turkey would in fact contribute significantly to the economic vitality of the EU. Given the significant and sustained trade deficits in the EU over the decades, Turkey has already been financing a chunk of European economic prosperity. Already among the twenty largest economies in the world, with a service sector constituting 65 percent of GDP and a public procurement market of over $40 billion and growing, Turkey offers high economic potential for the EU. Turkey also boasts a young, dynamic, and entrepreneurial population; an export-oriented economy; and a rapidly developing information society. Turkey's accession will increase the size and competitiveness of the European internal market.

The fulfillment of this tremendous economic potential will depend on whether Turkey is able to realize structural upgrades to its economy. Krueger, as well as Turkish and international economists, also states that Turkey will have to carry out significant structural reforms to make the recent gains irreversible. But Turkey has shown a capacity to leap ahead in economic performance, and the Turks are beginning to see that reforms do pay off. The inflation rate, which was 70 percent in 2002, has come down to 8 percent, its lowest level in thirty-five years. Therefore, the economic argument that is currently leveled against Turkish membership can be transformed into one that is rather in support. Chances are that by the time the European publics are confronted with the final decision on Turkey's membership, the "impoverished country" argument may well have become only relative and polemical.

There are other arguments that have been put forth against Turkey's membership to the Union. Valéry Giscard d'Estaing, former French president and the dignitary who had led the European Convention to draft the EU's Constitutional Treaty, which was ironically voted down by the French people, summarized these views in an article in the *Financial Times* where he invoked the fact that

> five-sixths of Turkey's territory, and her capital city, are located outside Europe, the size of her population, the economic and social consequences of the arrival of the poorest country in the Union, the existence of a huge Turkish-speaking community outside Turkish territory, and the strangeness for Europe of suddenly sharing its borders with Syria, Iraq and Iran.[12]

Most, if not all, of those arguments do not stand up to serious scrutiny. Regarding the small portion of Turkish territories lying within geographical Europe, the contention that this disqualifies Turkey's membership lacks sincerity. To start with, it overlooks the fact that the entirety of Cyprus lies outside of that geographical delineation, which is rather arbitrary in any case. Furthermore, this debate should in fact be obsolete. The question about geography has been addressed before in Turkey's long relationship with the European community. Turkey has consistently been confirmed as being eligible for EU membership, including on geographical considerations. And the territory that lies within that geographical conception, comprising an area about the size of Massachusetts, is larger than a number of EU member states. The geographical argument has thus been suggested rather to give the impression that there are concrete grounds to opposing Turkey's membership to the EU. But it is not in the least convincing.

A more serious point is raised with regard to the size of Turkey's population. Indeed, Turkey currently has a population of about seventy million and is expected to reach eighty-five million by 2030. That will likely be the approximate level at which Turkey's population would stabilize. Currently, only Germany is more populous among the EU nations. With negative demographic pressures all over the EU, the European labor market would probably be a magnet for young laborers from outside the Union. There are various ways to look at this issue. The prevailing and much abused popular view seems to underscore an alien invasion of youthful strangers replacing the aging European workforce. Accordingly, this would upset the social cohesion of European societies, increase criminality, and take away the jobs of the remaining European youth.

One cannot ignore the possible adverse social effects of uncontrolled migration, such as a number of societies in and outside Europe have been witnessing. Where this argument breaks down is that it is the least relevant in Turkey's case. To start with, currently around 30 percent of Turkey's population is below the age of fifteen, and these young people are living through a period of close alignment with European standards and norms, including in the educational sector. There is already an increasing scale of congruity and compatibility. In the decade ahead, with the further intensification of links between the EU and Turkey, this youthful population will be raised as a Turkish-European generation. They will be more naturally EU compatible than those who do not benefit from the opportunities of an accession candidate. Europe will need labor, and the Turkish supply will be the least problematic to integrate.

At the same time, an empirical study conducted by Bogazici University has concluded that the migrational pressure on the EU from Turkey would not be as alarming as some suggest. The study forecast that EU membership would instead dampen such pressure:

> If Turkey loses the membership perspective, the EU may end up having more immigrants than a free movement of labour regime with Turkey. And the composition of this migration would be less conducive for the EU labour markets—and—for integration in the host societies. The experiences of Greece, Portugal and Spain indicate that a successful accession period with high growth and effective implementation of the reforms reduces and gradually eliminates the migration pressures. There is no a priori reason why Turkey would not go through a similar experience.[13]

The problem for the EU could be not that there would be too many but too few Turks to migrate to the EU markets, where youthful and skilled Turkish labor will be increasingly needed under the current demographic trends in Europe. Turkish youth travel to Europe for employment mostly for lack of employment at home, and this scenario may be more likely to continue if Turkey does not join the EU.

It is well to remember, too, that the negotiation process will produce grace periods in a number of areas, including in the movement of persons and labor. In the latest round of accessions, a seven-year transition period was negotiated. In Turkey's case that would mean seven years on top of the ten that is the anticipated period for the negotiation process. Given the current European demographic trends, most of those who now object to Turkish membership or the Turks' free movement in Europe could by then be vying for Turkish labor and the contributions of Turkish wage earners into whatever type of social security network the EU countries come to implement.

In any case, to insist on permanent restrictions on the mobility of the Turks would definitely raise the concern that the EU is pushing Turkey into a second-class membership status and violating the principle of four freedoms on which the European community is built.

In the current EU system of Union-wide political governance, population size also has political ramifications. States are attributed seats and voting power in accordance with their population strengths. In that regard, Turkey would be one of the major nations of the EU. However, even if the spirit of the current arrangements struck in the Nice Treaty were maintained, Turkey would not dramatically alter the extant power balances within the EU. As Kirsty Hughes asserts:

> On an individual country basis, there is nothing in the inclusion of Turkey in the EU's voting system that dramatically shifts the relative power of different countries—even with the new double-majority voting system. While today Germany has 18.1% of the population share of votes in an EU of 25, France 13.2% and the UK 13.0%, looking to 2015, in an EU of 28 including Turkey, then Germany would have 14.5% of the population vote, Turkey 14.4%, France and the UK almost 11.0%. Indeed with the reduction in Germany's voting weight, the system could be said to be more evenly balanced.[14]

A similar conclusion is reached also with regard to the effect of Turkey on the European Parliament. With Turkey and Germany both having eighty-four seats, the size of the largest country's share will somewhat diminish, thus obviating "a situation of unbalanced dominance by one or two larger countries."[15] That said, France will retract from the second power in the EU to the third, a point that may hint at a strand of the French elite's narrow-minded opposition to Turkey's membership.

Therefore, in the aggregate, the population argument, although more objective than the others, is still largely flawed in terms of a presumed negative impact on the EU. The arguments about the economic and social consequences of a new poor member also enjoy an aura of objectivity, yet they are circumstantial and transient. The decade ahead will show whether they are resilient in the face of Turkey's dynamic circumstance.

Another point raised by Giscard d'Estaing, namely that a huge Turkish-speaking community exists outside Turkish territory, is more difficult to comment on. That is because it is not clear what this means or even whether it is meant to be meaningful in any sense. Or worse still, it may mean something that could be more self-damaging for the EU than Giscard d'Estaing and others who share his views seem to realize.

A huge Turkish-speaking population does exist outside Turkey. In fact, Turkey's population houses just about half of the Turkish-speaking world. In his groundbreaking study of the Turkic nations, Hugh Pope asserts that there is indeed a Turkic world.[16] Twenty countries have significant Turkic communities, six with a Turkic majority. They total some 140 million people. There is cultural affinity among the Turks of Turkey and the Azeris, Turkmens, Kyrgiz, Uzbek, Kazakh, Uigurs, and several other Turkic-speaking groups.

The fact is that to the occasional dismay of Turkish nationalists, these peoples have their own countries and are not looking for a patron. Yet it is also true that there is an ethnic bond that unites them, whether this is demonstrated in political terms or not. The opportunities of ethnic and cultural kinship among the various components of the Turkic world are not lost on the international—including European—business community. Istanbul provides an opportune venue to base commercial operations toward this prolific community of Turkic speakers. And the Turks of Turkey are already visibly active in the Turkic world. As Hugh Pope writes:

> Many Turkish businesses, based in Istanbul, are working in these former Soviet countries. In each of the Turkic states, the biggest single community of businessmen is usually one of the Turks. They are not dominant, but they are there building schools, restaurants, and hotels. They are running hotels, they are building pipelines. They are also very busy in Bulgaria, Romania, and Russia. But because the old Iron Curtain has dropped away, you suddenly feel that the last hundred years has been an aberration.[17]

Turkey also offers significant strategic assets to the EU and indeed to the United States in reaching out to the Turkic world. As Michael Emerson and Nathalie Tocci point out:

> Turkey's accession process could offer the potential to strengthen both the EU and Turkish roles in Central Asia. The EU could benefit from Turkey's bilateral ties. The deficiencies of technical assistance due to the lack of necessary language skills could be rectified to some extent through Turkish participation. At the same time, these initiatives would not be tainted by pan-Turkic undertones.[18]

An EU that includes Turkey among its members will be a natural bridge to the Central Asian steppes and its peoples as well as to their significant resources. Giscard d'Estaing's complaint about Turkish speakers outside Turkish territories ignores these benefits. The Spanish speakers of Latin America have not been a disadvantage for the EU. To the contrary, Spain's accession to the EU benefited from the Hispanic world. And the EU has benefited from Spain's Latin American connections.

However, in reality the argument was probably about the sizable Turkish community, numbering more than three million people, residing in the EU countries. Many of them are already citizens of their host countries. The largest concentration resides in Germany, which has become the adopted home to more than two million people of Turkish origin. It doesn't take much imagination to see Giscard d'Estaing's reference as targeting the ethnic Turks living in the EU countries. And this gives rise to a troubling premonition for Europe. The Turks are a fraction of the migrants in Europe, Muslim or otherwise. They are caught up in a bigger storm that concerns immigration, integration, and xenophobia.

Two Dutch murder cases are indicative of the malaise developing in Europe. One is the murder of Theo van Gogh, a controversial filmmaker who focused on the abuse of women by Muslim men and who, the killer thought, expressed hostility to Islam. He was murdered by a Moroccan Muslim immigrant with Dutch citizenship. The Dutch population reacted to the heinous crime understandably with abomination. But subsequently the reaction went overboard, extending to opposition to Turkey's EU membership.

The second murder case involved Pim Fortuyn, an anti-immigrant politician who called for the repeal of the article of the Dutch constitution that bans discrimination.[19] His murderer was Dutch and was allegedly motivated by the idea of stopping the rise of a neo-Nazi to power. Fortuyn's appeal was particularly strong with the Dutch youth, as "nearly one half of 18–30-year-olds recently polled want to see zero Muslim immigration, and said they would be voting for Fortuyn" in 2002 elections.[20] Fortuyn's followers continue to oppose Turkey's EU membership. At the same time, some want to ease the expulsion of naturalized Muslim immigrants from their adopted country, stripping them of their Dutch citizenship. There is hardly any more effective way of seeding hostility and counteracting integration than suggesting that race and religion must forever set citizens apart.

The integration of immigrants is a difficult question in every host society. EU countries facing difficulty in coming to grips with the "alien" element are slowly realizing that this is a permanent addition to their population. This creates resentment on the part of those who aspire toward ethnic and religious homogeneity. The resentment also exposes the fragility of multiculturalism in Europe. Indeed, as Graham Bowley reported in the *International Herald Tribune*, it was "Turkey's misfortune that it is seeking to enter this exclusive, mainly Christian, club at a time when many Europeans believe they are witnessing the failure of multicultural society in Europe."[21]

It is too late to challenge and try to reverse multiethnicity in Europe. Individual EU countries may be more or less homogeneous, but at the continental level, heterogeneity is inherent in the fact that Europe is composed of distinct nations. Thus, a Europe that does not see itself as a mosaic is not Europe as we know it. This is particularly true given that after decades of migratory flow and free movement of peoples, the individual countries, too, have come to reflect increasing heterogeneity in terms of ethnicity, religion, and social and cultural backgrounds. The only universally binding identity in such a European mosaic is the identity of "Europeanness," and that can only be defined in terms of what is binding, not dividing, what is inclusive, not exclusive. Furthermore, this Europeanness cannot be static; it must be adequately dynamic to evolve in a bid to attract and hold together different identities that cohabit the European social sphere.

Several countries, including Germany, tried to promote returns of the Turkish *gastarbeiter* and put in place obstacles to more Turks entering for work and settlement. The plan did not really work, as spouses and children of the families split by labor migration arrived. Those who did not come legally found ways of ending up in Germany and other prosperous European countries illegally. Crime networks were established to smuggle immigrants into Europe. Criminal and terrorist organizations exploited the demand for entry into prosperous labor markets. Countless political-asylum applications were filed, frequently on faked grounds, to try out this path to immigration. The freedoms provided in European countries were exploited to the extent that there was reaction and backlash in a security-conscious world. The political fights in host countries, including Turkey, were imported to European streets, disturbing the peace of the countries receiving immigrants. All this happened when Germany, for one, had tried to slam the door shut to immigration.

Against this background, rejection of Turkey's EU membership is probably the second worst possible remedy one could use to address the question of immigration. The worst, of course, is trying to expel them or cave in to the racism that existed in several societies long before the arrival of the Turks or the Muslims. The Turkish settlement in Western Europe proved resilient, including against occasionally violent, even lethal, racist attacks. Any leeway given to racism promises to create explosive consequences, not to mention moral degradation, in Europe.

That said, obviously there is a fair argument to be made in favor of seeking the integration of the immigrant populations in their adopted countries. Short of assimilation, this would mean adjustment on the part of both the immigrants and the indigenous populace. With the first and second generation there have been few success stories. However, the third generation of Turkish immigrants in Europe is full of promise for becoming a bridge between their acquired nation and their ancestral country. Already in 2005, politicians of Turkish origin represent Germany at the European Parliament. Whatever integration problems the first and the second generations have experienced in Germany, France, Belgium, the Netherlands, or elsewhere in the EU will dissipate as they assume a respectable position in these countries. As a cross-check, a much smaller number of Turkish-origin Americans are fully integrated. Revered and successful in the United States, they prove that integration of the Turks is not a universal but rather a European challenge. The U.S. example also disproves the contention that the integration of Turks in Europe is difficult due to religion, as Christian identity is arguably more expressed in America than in Europe.

On the other hand, some commentators, including arguably Giscard d'Estaing, may be fearful that their citizens of Turkish origin might form a permanent extension of Turkey within their polities, a source of influence for Turkey. In the information age, Turkey's media networks reach Turkish speakers around the world, including in Europe, and keep alive the cultural if not political connection with Turkey. Turkey's issues are communicated in real time to Turkish migrants through these media. Given Europe's history of usurping Christian minorities in the later Ottoman times, exploiting them as leverage against the state, there may be a phobia that Turkey would now turn the tables. This reflects an irrational fear that nonetheless can better be addressed by integrating rather than alienating Turkey within a multiethnic EU based on unity in diversity.

Despite its inescapably atavistic tune, the cultural-religious argument inhabits a more serious, although hardly justified, domain than most other viewpoints opposing Turkey's EU membership. This is because this argument concerns the fundamental nature of the European experience and the future evolution of European values. It is more serious also because it is unavoidably offensive not only to the Turks but to a billion Muslims around the world and in Europe. Also, while issues like the free movement of people or economic development—the presumed "burden" of Turkey—would be subject to evolution and at any rate negotiation in the decade ahead, such would not be the case for religious convictions.

The views against Turkish membership based on a Muslim-Christian divide clash openly with the achievements of the pluralistic nature of the European integration project. As David L. Phillips indicates, the doubt about whether Turkey could ever become truly "European" ignores the fact that "today's Europe is a rich mosaic of cultures, ethnicities, and religions.

It is a community of values, in which democracy is strengthened by diversity. More than a political and economic bloc, the union is a dynamic democracy-building project."[22] Many in Europe would agree, but many others do not. Europeans appear divided and disoriented, especially after the French and Dutch referenda. The confusion and disagreement relates most concretely to the quintessential questions of "Who are we?" and "What is Europe?" Turkey cannot answer these questions for the rest of Europe, but the case of Turkish membership will allow Europe to look at itself in the mirror. Turkey's membership in the EU is not only about Turkey. It is also about where Europe wants to go. In this regard, except for those who would be complacent about the European gains in establishing secular peace after centuries of ferocious religious infighting, why Muslim Turks should impact negatively on Europe is a point that remains fundamentally unanswered.

First of all, Turkey is staunchly secular with absolutely no intentions for a religious agenda for Europe. Given that Turkish secularism has its roots in the French *laicitee*, the model in itself is not incompatible. That answers the concern raised regarding Europeans fearing a future Turkish government "that wants to influence the educational system or believes that the Holy Book of Islam is above democratic debate."[23] A religious political agenda is inconceivable under the Turkish constitution and social consensus, and Turkey would not want to be part of an EU that would harm its secular regime.

On the other hand, ironically, the religious-oriented politicians in Turkey and in the EU are likely to become natural allies in a Europe that is brave enough to host them both. Their social, political, even cultural agendas converge to a significant degree. Both espouse conservative ideals, and both complain about their societies' declining moral values and devoutness. Many who think they are following a Christian or a Muslim social or cultural idea would be surprised to see that many such ideas are in fact shared across these religions. To the extent that mutual suspicion and hostility toward the other religionists are avoided, it is not inconceivable that Christian and Muslim conservative democrats would coalesce to push conservative agendas for Europe. Was it not part of the idea of Europe that Europeans should ultimately gather around ideas, not ethnicities or religious beliefs? Christianity and Islam on their own merits are not in contradiction or opposition. It is the politics that brings about antagonism. Extremists exist on both sides and arguably always will. They are not and need not represent the overwhelming majority. As history has painfully shown, such politics bode ill for respective societies and the world at large.

Whether in Europe or indeed many other places, extremism is already taking its toll. The social strain is already visible, even quantifiable, in terms of violent occurrences. Muslim communities in Western Europe and North America, observes Ömur Orhun, the OSCE chairman's personal representative on combating intolerance and discrimination against Muslims, "are experiencing an increasingly hostile environment towards them, coupled with discrimination and intolerance in various forms."[24] The phenomenon of Islamophobia is "more pronounced in the post–September 11 period" and includes "stereotyping all Muslims as 'terrorist, violent or otherwise unfit;' lack of provision, recognition and respect for Muslims in public institutions; and attacks, abuse, harassment and violence against persons perceived to be Muslim and against their property and prayer places."[25] The Islamophobia is also intellectually legitimized and the attacks are directed not only at the Muslims but also at their faith. Having lived through the scourge of anti-Semitism, Islamophobia now emerges as another moral bankruptcy with virulent potentials. Thus, the personal representative asserts, in order to be able to manage the challenges of increasingly diverse and multicultural societies in religious, cultural, racial, and linguistic aspects, we must identify our shared values and commonalities and "strive towards creating strong and 'cohesive communities' where every individual has a sense of belonging to his/her community and State, as well as a stake in its well-being."[26]

Stephen Schwartz is partially correct when he indicates that Muslims in Europe should recognize their responsibilities and live up to the norms of Western Europe.[27] Muslims everywhere must condemn and distance themselves from terror, while revealing the true tolerant nature of their faith. In no lesser degree, they should strive to integrate into mainstream society and politics. Integration cannot be seen as assimilation or imposed or self-inflicted ghettoization. However, this is only one part of the story. The mainstream European societies must also be amenable and encouraging toward the integration of the Muslim communities, and Islamophobia is not the way to do that.

The OSCE representative points out that "While freedom of expression and freedom of speech are core values in democratic societies, we must be careful not to exploit them intentionally and deliberately provoke groups whose values we do not understand or share."[28] Dialogue based on the understanding of the diversity that marks Western societies, and rejection of violence, is the only way to a peaceful coexistence.

This is a complex debate that is likely to remain on the agenda for an indefinite period. It involves more than clear-cut categories of Muslims and Christians. Instead, this is a debate among the concerned and between the moderate and extremist worldviews. The Turkish input is of fundamental importance. As Stephen Schwartz himself recognizes, both the OSCE representative quoted above and the secretary general of the Organization of the

Islamic Conference, who puts emphasis on dialogue, mutual recognition, and respect, are Turkish, pointing in no small degree to the role of the Turks in building bridges within Europe and the West and across different faiths.

However, as far as Turkey's membership bid is concerned, obviously the debate is not only about Europe and Islam. Rather, it is also about Europe and Christianity. Norman Davies observed that "while the separation of church and state—a Christian doctrine—has been a core principle for the development of European constitutionalism, the modern decline in religious practice in Europe has left many churches deserted, and Christian Europe is now more a myth than a reality."[29] In a way, this may indeed be the problem itself. The debate about Muslim Turks' admission to an ostensibly Christian Europe can be used and abused by those who want to promote greater Christian devoutness in Europe by creating or rekindling an adversarial Muslim Turkish image. The Turks, Turkey, and Turkish membership to the EU might well become the targets for such ill-conceived exploitation. The poison apple for Europe in this regard is not Turkey's EU membership but rather the hostility of such designs.

The final argument opposing Turkey's membership to the EU invokes Turkey's borders with Iran, Syria, and Iraq, troubled countries with which Europeans do not want to be neighbors. But this region will continue to be in the EU's close proximity irrespective of whether Turkey joins the EU. The argument inherently presumes that Turkey would accept being a buffer zone between its neighborhood and the EU countries even if its membership drive was thwarted.

Similar premises are found in the calls for a "privileged partnership" between the EU and Turkey. Thus, a leading parliamentarian in the German Bundestag was arguing:

> [EU's] borders should create a close and comprehensive bond between Europe and its neighbors. This can be done successfully on the EU's border with Turkey—but not on along Turkey's other borders. At the same time, the EU cannot shy away from security challenges posed by instability in what is usually referred to as the Greater Middle East. Many of the objectives upheld by advocates of Turkey's EU membership deserve our support. . . . However, one might ask whether these objectives should only be achieved by pursuing full EU membership for Turkey."[30]

The answer to this question is obviously that full membership is indeed the only way the security objectives can be achieved: First, various formulas to keep Turkey awkwardly and partially within defense and economic structures and outside political decision making have been tried before, each ending up in increasing Turkey's distaste. Second, Europe's insistence on half measures that are only in its own presumed interest promote a negative influence on regional and global politics.

If it is possible to take novel steps to integrate Turkey into the framework of European foreign, security, and defense policies as an equal partner even before Turkey becomes a full member, then these should be taken. For instance, the same German parliamentarian was proposing that "Turkey should be offered the prospect of membership in European foreign, security and defense policy structures on an equal basis."[31] There is no reason why this should not be offered during the accession negotiation period without attaching strings like Turkey's giving up its full membership bid. After all, foreign, security, and defense policies are subjects of high politics that concern peace, security, and sustainability of prosperity. If that can be done later for barter, one should be able to do it earlier without strings for the common good.

The complexity of Turkey's accession process to the European Union is matched only by the density of its strategic value in terms of geographic location as well as national political, military, social, and cultural assets. The importance of Turkey for Europe is so vast, and its extant fusion with the rest of Europe is so impossible to disentangle, that the opponents of full EU membership in Europe cannot muster a definite no. Even if EU leaders blunder into saying no, it will not hold—as was the case in 1997 when the Luxembourg Summit thought it had produced a rejection of Turkey's membership; it lasted only two years. Roughly a decade earlier, in 1988, a similar note was played when the European Commission thought it had buried Turkey's European bid by issuing a negative opinion on Turkey's membership. It did not fly. Each generation of leaders may try their hand in resisting historical, political, regional, and global dynamics that long preceded them and shall in all likelihood also supersede them. But Turkey always ends up being part and parcel of the European equation, and eventually it will also be inseparable from its institutions.

The anticipated ten-year span of Turkey's EU membership talks will coincide with a time of upheaval and change in its general neighborhood. It is easy to forecast that the coming decade will be momentous in regional and international affairs. The European Security Strategy (ESS), approved by the European leaders in December 2003, acknowledges that Europe, while it has never been as prosperous and as secure in its history, nonetheless faces challenges, threats, and risks that are both global and regional. The strategy document observed that:

> the post Cold War environment is one of increasingly open borders in which the internal and external aspects of security are indissolubly linked. Flows of trade and investment, the development of technology and the spread of democracy have

brought freedom and prosperity to many people. Others have perceived globalization as a cause of frustration and injustice. These developments have also increased the scope for non-state groups to play a part in international affairs. And they have increased European dependence—and so vulnerability—on an interconnected infrastructure in transport, energy, information and other fields.[32]

Turkey is a key actor but also a partner for Europe and the United States in addressing the contemporary challenges and threats. The foreign and security policies that this regional power will pursue will make an impact on the evolution of the regional and global order in the next decade. In view of this anticipated impact, Turkey has been attracting heightened attention as a foreign-policy actor in its region and the world. The fate of Turkey's bid for membership to the European Union is closely watched in Europe, the United States, the broader Middle East, the Muslim world, and Eurasia.

This interest has been augmented by the decision of the European Union to open accession negotiations with Turkey after over four decades of a difficult relationship. Given the myriad roles that Turkey is assigned to play directly or indirectly, the interest in the policies that it will follow in the next ten years of negotiations with the EU will thus persist. Turkey has been referred to as a model for democracy and modernization in the Muslim world, a catalyst for conciliation between Christians and Muslims, an architect of regional cooperation in a multitude of regions, an emerging major market, a secure energy corridor, an increasingly assertive regional power, a pivotal actor in international affairs, and a key ally for the United States in a difficult geography.

The swell of both popular opposition and support in Europe for Turkey's eventual EU membership is indicative of the passionate dichotomy that has become a permanent feature of the Turks' reception in Europe. Europeans are admittedly not alone in their confusion of what to make of the Turks. In a sense, Turkey remains an enigma and a marvel to Europe and the world. Jan Morris exposes such sentiment, stating that "neither quite this nor altogether that, terrifically itself yet perpetually ambiguous, Turkey stands alone among the nations. For centuries it was the terror of Christianity; for generations it was the Sick Man of Europe; today it stands formidably on the edge of Asia surrounded in the universal mind, as always, by an aura of mingled respect, resentment, and fear."[33] As early as 1979, Dankwart A. Rustow observed that "no nation that has maintained close relations with the United States for the last generation is so little understood by well-informed Americans as is Turkey."[34] He cautioned that "it requires a larger effort of the imagination than most of us are accustomed to making to grasp the seeming contradictions of a country that is part in Europe, part in Asia, bordering on the Soviet Union in the north and the Arab countries in the south; a developing nation that is a dedicated and vociferous democracy; a Muslim population in a secular state; not to mention a country with a Central Asian language written in the Roman alphabet."[35] Delete the reference to the Soviet Union and the message would be valid even today. Confusion and dearth of understanding about Turkey is common in Europe, the United States, and indeed elsewhere.

If the issue were only lack of clarity, that would not necessarily pose a problem for the Turks on their journey toward the European Union. But as Mary Lee Settle observed, of the countries she has known, Turkey had "the worst and most ill-drawn public image."[36] That is an image created mainly by those who have psychological fixations against a former colonial master and those who have never been to Turkey. "The Turks I saw in *Lawrence of Arabia* and *Midnight Express*" protests Settle, "were ogrelike cartoon caricatures compared to the people I had known and lived among for three of the happiest years of my life."[37] "You do not look like a Turk!" is a remark many Turks remember from their encounters with Western Europeans and Americans. What the Turks have not been able to do in terms of explaining themselves and publicizing their views, their adversaries have been doing effectively for centuries. For someone who has not had the opportunity to know Turkey and the Turks, it is easy to get carried away by the abundant negative literature. In the words of Jan Morris, "The echoes of historical quarrels, old and new, still swirl around the name of Turkey."[38]

The anti-Turkish prejudice is not only widespread but also deep, going as far back into history as the Crusades. The ill-fated Crusades have laid the ground for the enemy image created in Christian Europe for the Muslim Turks. The legacy of the Crusades was bad enough for Europe—they "contributed enormously to strengthening a tradition of martial intolerance in Christian Europe to heretics, pagans and above all, to Muslims."[39] But they also engrained a deep prejudice against the Turks in particular. Turkish military advances in the ensuing centuries only aggravated these perceptions. As Stephen Kinzer notes, since then, "what made [the Turks] such an awful thing to contemplate was that their forces were battering down across Europe itself."[40]

At its peak, the Ottoman Empire, which preceded the modern Turkish Republic, created a duality in the "Western" mind about the Turk. On one side was the persistent and largely religious-based demonization of Turks and indeed Muslims. British Prime Minister Gladstone wrote, "They were upon the whole, from the black day when they first entered Europe, the one great anti-human specimen of humanity."[41] Needless to say, he earned himself eternal contempt for his rash words, which were not only disgraceful but also revealed a self-serving ignorance. The Ottoman empire, like any other, had its good as well as its bad deeds. Stanley Kurtz repeats what is a common assessment of most scholars of Ottoman history: "The Ottoman Empire's tolerance for its many minority communities—and the high degree of self-government granted them—were among its greatest strengths. Nowadays we're used to seeing migrations from East to West, but in the fifteenth, sixteenth, and seventeenth centuries, immigrants flowed freely from Europe to live in the tolerant and prosperous lands of the Ottomans."[42]

The empire was, at the least, "no worse than the boasted civilized nations of Europe."[43] The Ottomans, however, were not in the business of mingling socially with the rest of the Europeans or promoting their image. Even diplomatic contacts with the world outside were sporadic until the Ottomans' fateful final century of painful collapse. The basic source of wisdom for the Europeans regarding the Ottomans were the so-called early "orientalists." Edward Said exposed the often highly distorted and prejudiced accounts of Western travelers to the Muslim Middle East ruled by the Ottomans. Said also contended that even the contemporary scholarship was infected by similar distortions, biases, and imperial ambition.[44]

However, there has also been concurrent fascination with the Turks, notably at the heyday of the Ottoman Empire. As Mark Mazower noted, "For all the religious antipathy between Christian and Muslim, sixteenth-century Europeans respected and feared the power, reach and efficiency of the Turks."[45] Thomas Fuller wrote in the seventeenth century that the Ottoman Empire was "the greatest and best-compacted that the sunne ever saw . . . commanding the most fruitful countreys of Europe, Asia and Africa . . . its magnificence overshadowed its squabling neighbors in Christendom."[46] But as the Ottoman power declined and European states rose from backwardness and religious bigotry to military, economic, technological, and gradually political superiority, the fascination was overshadowed again by scorn for the Turk. Since then, views about Turkey and the Turks have jumped to and fro in European minds. The duality of admiration and contempt continues to reign over the image of Turkey in Europe. A matter taken less seriously until recently, the question of image has become a central one in Turkey's EU bid. The Turks will now have to learn an art that has long escaped them: public relations.

The history of the Turkish quest for membership in the European Union has been long and arduous. Turkey first filed an application to join in July 1959, shortly after the European Economic Community was created. The Community responded by proposing Associate Membership until Turkey's circumstances permitted accession as a full member. Consequently, the "Agreement Creating an Association between the Republic of Turkey and the European Economic Community" was signed on September 12, 1963. The Ankara Association Agreement aimed at Turkey's full membership in the European Communities (EC) in phases. That agreement envisaged the progressive establishment of a Customs Union allowing free circulation of goods, people, services, and capital between the parties as a step toward membership.

The Ankara Agreement thus constituted the legal basis of the association between Turkey and the EC with the clear objective of Turkey's eventual full membership. Since then progress toward this goal has been incoherent. First, Turkey's import substitution–based economy constituted an obstacle, only to be overcome in the 1980s when the country shifted to a free market economy. Then, the military intervention of 1980 brought relations to a virtual freeze. This too was overcome as Turkish democracy returned to full vigor with the multiparty elections of 1983. Encouraged by developments at home on the economic and political fronts, Turkey applied directly for full membership in 1987. While the EC responded by underlining Turkey's eligibility for membership as a European country, it deferred the in-depth analysis of Turkey's application until the emergence of "a more favorable environment."[47]

This decision came at a time when the EC was completing its Single Market and, as the excuse went, was not prepared to contemplate enlargement. However, Turkey and the EC continued to progress toward the envisaged Customs Union, despite recurrent Greek vetoes of financial aid packages to Turkey. The Customs Union entered into force on the first day of 1996. Since then, Turkey has abolished all duties and equivalent charges on imports of industrial goods from the EU and set out to progressively adapt itself to the EU's commercial policy and preferential trade arrangements with specific third countries. In time, basic agricultural products came also to be covered by a preferential trade regime. However, the Customs Union did not go as far as to include Turkey in the EU's decision-making mechanisms. And the Association Council that was to oversee the Customs Union proved largely ineffective in giving Turkey any reasonable say.

While Turkey has maintained its focus on membership in the EU, successive EU decisions barred tangible progress to that effect while repeatedly confirming Turkey's eligibility. A breakthrough was achieved in December 1999 when the Helsinki Summit officially recognized Turkey without any precondition as an accession candidate on an equal footing with the other candidate states. Another leap forward was achieved on December 17, 2004, when the EU decided that Turkey met the political criteria for a pluralistic democracy and agreed to open accession negotiations.

Since Turkey first applied for membership, the Union has successfully completed several rounds of enlargement, at the last of which ten nations joined the Union. In the many decades of this relationship, Turkey's own woes have contributed to retarding the process of membership to the EU. Most notably, Turkish democracy has had its share of ups and downs. But the advances in Turkish governance and democracy, at a pace that hardly any student had anticipated, have now broken the ranks of opposition to Turkish membership. Those for whom democratic deficits had formed the basis of rejection have virtually no argument.

Turkey's place in Europe has been a recurrent debate that seems to have been resolved almost always in its favor. The Ottomans were not represented in the 1815 Congress of Vienna and were excluded by the scholars of international law from "the Christian family of nations." Yet, at the end of the Crimean War, the Turks were admitted in the mid-nineteenth century to participate in the advantages of Public Law and System of Europe in return for reforms regarding property, justice, and the rights of Christians. And although Turkey's bid to join NATO in the wake of World War II was strongly disputed and resisted, Turkey has become a critical ally in NATO. Over fifty years down the road since 1952, when Turkey and Greece joined the alliance, the arguments against their accession now look silly.

The Turks have become an intrinsic part of every imaginable type of European framework. In sports, Turks compete in European cup competitions. The European soccer titles, Union of European Football Associations (UEFA) Cup and the Super Cup were won by a Turkish team, Galatasaray, in 2000, which defeated Arsenal of the United Kingdom and Real Madrid of Spain, respectively. The European Champions League final match in 2005 was played in an Istanbul stadium. In every other sport you will find a Turkish athlete in the European halls of fame. In music, Sertap Erener, a Turkish singer, won the European song contest (Eurovision) in 2003, after which Turkey hosted the event broadcast live all over Europe. Turks have won European beauty contests. Istanbul has been designated as the 2010 European Capital of Culture alongside Essen of Germany and Pecs of Hungary. In global politics, Turkey has put in its bid for the UN Security Council term membership for the years 2009–2010 in the Western European and Others group. The list is virtually endless. The fact of the matter is that Turkey and Europe have become inseparable over the centuries. This will grow, not diminish, over the next ten years in the course of the EU negotiation process. Turks will take part in all aspects of the evolution of Europe from science and education to agriculture and defense. The problem lies mainly in reckoning and closure.

This is not to suggest that Turkey's acceptance as a full-fledged component tile in the European mosaic will be smooth. The duality in European minds about the Turks and Turkey again marks the debate about Turkish membership in the EU. Beyond Turkey's size and complexity, this duality of mind about the Muslim faith forms the background as to why Turkish membership to the EU is intrinsically different from the other accessions. The coming lengthy accession period will require sensitive management and adept leadership. Unless the relationship is built on sound grounds, future strains are to be expected. The odyssey is ongoing, and the end will not be known until it has been reached.

Notes

1. Jan Peter Balkenende, "Address to the European Parliament," December 21, 2004. The full text can be found at www.eu2004.nl.

2. See: Şükran Pakkan, "Turkiye AB üyesi olamayacak" [Turkey Will Not Be Able to Be a Member of the EU], Milliyet, May 25, 2005.

3. The following account of the last-ditch diplomatic efforts leading to the start of the accession negotiations is summarized from the detailed coverage by various news media. Not surprisingly, the most detail was to be found in the live broadcasts of the Turkish television channels, although national newspapers around Europe, the United States, the broader Middle East, and Asia have not been too far behind their Turkish colleagues. For U.S. coverage, see for instance: CBS News, "Turkey, EU Reach Deal," October 3, 2005, from www.cbsnews.com; or CNN, "Relief as Turkey EU Talks Begin," October 4, 2005, from www.cnn.com. See also Craig Smith, "European Union Formally Opens Talks on Turkey's Joining," New York Times, October 4, 2005.

4. "Unexpected Support for Turkey's EU Prospects," Economist, October 6, 2005.

5. For one such skeptic in the United States, see Frank J. Gaffney Jr., "'No' to Islamist Turkey," Washington Times, September 27, 2005.

6. Retired U.S. ambassador to Ankara Mark Parris made this observation at a presentation marking the launch of a report (Policy Focus No. 48) at the Washington Institute for Near East Policy in October 2005.

7. "Eastern Promise," Times of London, September 29, 2005.

8. "Better Late Than Never," Economist, October 4, 2005.

9. Eurostat, press release: 75/2005, June 3, 2005.

10. Several of the statistics cited here are in fact repeated in various European news media. See, for instance, Guillaume Perrier, "L'economie turque emerge aux portes de l'Europe," Le Monde, October 12, 2005.

11. Anne O. Krueger, "Turkey's Economy: A Future Full of Promise" (speech at Istanbul Forum, May 5, 2005).

12. Valéry Giscard d'Estaing, "A Better European Bridge to Turkey," Financial Times, November 24, 2004.

13. Refik Erzan, Umut Kuzubaş, and Nilüfer Yıldız, "Growth and Immigration Scenarios: Turkey-EU," CEPS: Turkey in Europe Monitor, no. 12 (December 2004):124.

14. Kirsty Hughes, "The Political Dynamics of Turkish Accession to the EU: A European Success Story or the EU's Most Contested Enlargement?" (Swedish Institute for European Policy Studies, Report No. 9, December, 2004), p. 13.

15. Hughes, "The Political Dynamics of Turkish Accession," p. 13.

16. Hugh Pope, *Sons of the Conquerors: The Rise of the Turkic World* (New York: Overlook Press, 2005).

17. Pope, *Sons of the Conquerors.*

18. Michael Emerson and Nathalie Tocci, "Integrating EU and Turkish Foreign Policy," *CEPS: Turkey in Europe Monitor*, no. 7 (July 2004): 60.

19. "Obituary: Pim Fortuyn," *Economist*, May 6, 2002.

20. "Obituary: Pim Fortuyn."

21. Graham Bowley, "Wary Public May Hurt Ankara's Dreams: Turkey Offers a Test of EU Multiculturism," *International Herald Tribune*, December 15, 2004.

22. David L. Phillip, response to Wolfgang Schäuble in Wolfgang Schäuble and David L. Phillips "Talking Turkey," *Foreign Affairs* 83, no. 6 (November–December 2004). www.foreignaffairs.org/20041101faresponse83613/wolfgang-schauble-david-l-phillips/talking-turkey.html.

23. Bowley, "Wary Public."

24. Ömur Orhun, "Challenges to Tolerance in a Multicultural Society" (speech at the Madrid Seminar jointly organized by Helsinki, Espana, and the Dutch Embassy, February 15, 2006).

25. Orhun, "Challenges to Tolerance."

26. Orhun, "Challenges to Tolerance."

27. Stephen Schwartz, "More Fallout from the Cartoon Jihad? Euro-Muslims Show a Surprising New Moderation," *The Weekly Standard*, May 29, 2006.

28. Orhun, "Challenges to Tolerance."

29. Norman Davies made this statement at the conference entitled "Is Europe for Christians Only" at the American Enterprise Institute, April 2004.

30. Karl-Theodor zu Guttenberg, "Offer Turkey a 'Privileged Partnership' Instead," *International Herald Tribune*, December 15, 2004.

31. Guttenberg, "Offer Turkey."

32. "A Secure Europe in a Better World—The European Security Strategy," approved by the European Council held in Brussels on December 12, 2003, and drafted under the responsibilities of EU High Representative Javier Solana. For full text, see: http://ue.eu.int/uedocs/cmsUpload/78367.pdf.

33. Jan Morris, introduction to Mary Lee Settle, *Turkish Reflections* (New York: Touchstone, 1991), ix.

34. Dankwart A. Rustow, "Turkey's Travails," Foreign Affairs 58, no. 1 (Fall 1979): 82.

35. Rustow, "Turkey's Travails," 82.

36. Settle, *Turkish Reflections*, xi.

37. Settle, *Turkish Reflections*, xii.

38. Morris, introduction to *Turkish Reflections*, ix.

39. Mark Mazower, *The Balkans* (London: Phoenix, 2001), 6.

40. Stephen Kinzer, *Crescent and Star: Turkey between Two Worlds* (New York: Farrar, Straus & Giroux, 2001).

41. William Ewart Gladstone, *Bulgarian Horrors and the Question of the East* (London: J. Murray, 1876), 9.

42. Stanley Kurtz, "Root Causes," *Policy Review*, no. 112 (April–May 2002). www.policyreview.org/apr02/kurtz.html.

43. Thomas Adolphus, *The English in Ireland: A Reply to "The Turks in Europe" by Edward A. Freeman* (Philadelphia: Edward A. Freeman, 1878), vi.

44. Edward Said, *Orientalism* (New York: Vintage, 1979).

45. Mazower, *The Balkans*, 7.

46. Quoted in Mazower, *The Balkans*, 7.

47. The European Commission's Opinion on Turkish Membership, endorsed by the European Council in February 1990.

CHAPTER TWO

A Tale of Many Reports

As Turkey, Europe, and the United States were bracing in 2004 for the impending decision on Turkey's European future, two reports published within days of each other on two shores of the Atlantic were separately reminding the European Union leaders of the import of their decision. The results reached by these two reports were characteristic of most other reports assessing the value of Turkey's membership for the EU. The Independent Commission on Turkey[1] and the Atlantic Council of the United States[2] rallied eminent personalities in Europe and the United States, respectively, to address the critical issue of the future course of European integration and Turkey's place in it. They were unanimous in calling for the opening of the accession talks at the summit of the EU leaders in Brussels on December 17, 2004. Whereas the United States has consistently supported Turkey's accession to the EU on strategic grounds, until very recently voices of support from the EU side have been harder to register.

The report produced by the Independent Commission on Turkey was an influential part of the growing chorus of voices supporting Turkey in the EU. Against folkloric arguments based on historic, religious, and cultural stereotypes and prejudices, there were strategic realities and vision.

The positive decision to launch accession talks with Turkey was no doubt foremost due to the dramatic reforms in Turkey that have taken everyone, including the Turks, by surprise. Coinciding with the improved internal and external security environment after the capture of the leader of the PKK terrorist organization, Turkey's recognition in 1999 as a candidate country by the EU was conducive to reforms that basically redefined Turkish democracy in the European image. The reforms that had already started during the coalition rule of the social democratic, nationalistic, and center-right parties were accelerated to heart-stopping speeds when the Justice and Development Party swept into power on its own.

The consequent successive constitutional reform packages removed military officers as judges in the State Security Courts, amended political parties law to make judicial closure of parties more difficult, allowed broadcasting and education in mother tongues other than Turkish, eliminated the political role of the National Security Council, abolished the death penalty, and improved freedom of thought and expression. The packages also expanded the right to association; imposed stricter penalties on human traffickers; allowed non-Muslim minority communities greater rights over religious properties; strengthened the fight against torture; broadened the scope of freedoms of association, demonstration, and peaceful assembly; expanded the freedom to use Kurdish in broadcasting and election campaign periods; removed specific antidemocratic elements in the Turkish Penal Code; introduced measures to improve police conduct; provided prisoners and detainees immediate access to lawyers; lifted restrictions on the press; and allowed greater parliamentary scrutiny over military expenses. The government declared a zero-tolerance policy on human rights abuses and launched extensive retraining programs for security officials. The Turkish state radio and television (TRT) started broadcasting in Bosnian, Arabic, Circassian, and two common Kurdish dialects. Human rights committees were created in each province and district.[3] And these were only part of the reforms that were carried out in a period of less than four years. As the Turkish Parliament and government worked relentlessly, with the public and the press firmly at their backs, to fundamentally overhaul the legal system, the question being asked even as far away as Australia was "What more must Turkey do before Europe says yes?"[4]

Against this backdrop, the European Commission, which was tasked by the European Council in Copenhagen in 2002 to suggest whether Turkey met the necessary political criteria and thus could start accession talks with the EU, came up with an affirmative recommendation.[5] The EU leaders meeting in Brussels on December 17, 2004, endorsed this assessment and agreed to launch accession negotiations with Turkey, which they did in the fall of 2005.

Turkey's reforms have eliminated the political incompatibility between the EU and Turkey. In terms of the model of democracy, Turkey had clearly opted for the EU example and acted determinedly to simulate it. Against this background, serious attention could be given to integrating Turkey to the EU, not just tentatively anchoring Turkey to the West. Special limited relationships between the EU and others can only be pertinent in cases where more cannot be achieved. For Turkey, more is not only achievable but also desirable, if not necessary, for both Turkey and the EU.

It is desirable because both the EU and Turkey will reap significant benefits from Turkey's membership. In addition, full membership is perhaps necessary because of Turkey's strategic value for Europe and Europe's strategic value for Turkey. Indeed, as Niall Ferguson concluded, "The strategic arguments for binding Turkey to the West by new institutional ties are compelling."[6]

The European Commission elaborated this judgment in a study assessing the likely impact of Turkey's accession to the EU, and under the section entitled "geopolitical dimension" that "Turkey's accession would be different from previous enlargements because of the combined impact of Turkey's population, size, geographical location, economic, security and military potential, as well as cultural and religious characteristics. These factors give Turkey the capacity to contribute to regional and international stability. Expectations regarding EU policies towards these regions will grow as well, taking into account Turkey's existing political and economic links to her neighbours."[7]

Heather Grabbe observed that "Turkey's membership aspirations are widely seen as a threat to European integration, but they are really an astonishing opportunity for the EU. Turkey is the largest and strategically most important country ever to apply for membership. It is a valuable partner for the EU in the Black Sea region and the Middle East."[8] And Michael Emerson and Nathalie Tocci in Brussels add that Turkey's membership offers a structural potential to enhance the credibility of EU policies toward the Middle East, the Balkans, the Caucasus, and the Mediterranean regions and would affect the credibility of the EU as a foreign policy actor.[9] In their words, "Turkey offers a number of specific potential assets for helping the EU address these concerns, ranging from the concrete realities of location and logistics, through to matters of culture and ideology and the search for a harmony rather than clash of civilizations."[10]

The European Commission did obviously pose the essential question of whether the EU would want to be a geopolitical player, stating that "much will depend on how the EU itself will take on the challenge to become a fully fledged foreign policy player in the medium term in regions traditionally characterised by instability and tensions, including the Middle East and the Caucasus."[11] On this question, Emerson and Tocci argue that should the EU get serious about playing a greater role in the world, then Turkey's member-ship would help the EU to play a genuinely stabilizing, pacifying, and mod-ernizing role in its neighborhood, beyond token actions. Joschka Fischer commented to the *Süddeutsche Zeitung* that Europe did not really have an op-tion: "We can neither bid farewell to the Balkans nor can we turn our back on the Middle East—a dangerous region and one which defines our security. The world and its problems are not going to wait for Europe. And if the door is slammed in Turkey's face even though we have been making promises since Adenauer's day, we will end up regretting it."[12]

At any rate, the Independent Commission on Turkey, chaired by the for-mer president of Finland, Marti Ahtisaari, was particularly forthright on the geopolitical importance of Turkey for the European Union. Their baseline observation was that "for the Union, the unique geopolitical position of Turkey at the crossroads of the Balkans, the wider Middle East, South Cau-casus, Central Asia and beyond, its importance for the security of Europe's energy supplies and her political, economic and military weight would be great assets."[13] This observation in effect points to Turkey's geopolitical weight with or without EU membership.

The emphasis put on Turkey's strategic value for Europe and the United States is easy to understand. In several categories of power, Turkey's strengths are not superficial. Its population, territory, resources, economy, military ca-pability, and strategic location make it a valuable partner in world affairs. De-mographically, the country is home to some seventy million people. About 60 percent of the population is at a productive age. Turks are state-builders known throughout their history for a natural tendency to organize into co-hesive social and political units. The Turkish society benefits from a signifi-cant level of linguistic, cultural, and religious harmony among people who have a long history of living together.

Turkey owns the largest territory among European states—excluding, of course, the Russian Federation and Greenland. The country has negligible oil and gas resources, but is in possession of rich chromium and borium re-serves. Although not a water-rich country, it has nonetheless sufficient water and an advanced technical base for efficient water use. Turkey also has a largely self-sufficient agricultural potential. The Turkish economy ranks sixth in Europe in terms of purchasing power and among the top twenty in the world in GNP rating. It also registers very high rates of growth. Barring ma-jor upsets, if the recent levels of growth can be maintained over the next decade, the GNP is estimated to double.

Turkey is also a significant military power. It maintains the eighth largest armed force and sixteenth largest defense budget in the world. The level of training and equipment is high, assuring Turkey a credible defensive capability. The Turkish armed forces are particularly well proven in fighting terrorist operations and in low-intensity warfare. The country also offers significant assets as a base for projecting security and stability. As Şadi Ergüvenç notes, "Turkey's proximity to active and potential crisis areas renders it a suitable place for force projection and logistic basing. As a result, Turkey becomes a competitive strategic partner for all actors having an interest in the region."[14] However, this is both a blessing and a curse. Again quoting Ergüvenç: "[Turkey's] strategic location, at times, creates sensitivities and puts Turkey under stress between competing pressures."[15] The Turkish parliament wants to be convinced before the bases on Turkish territory can be used for projecting military power.

Turkey also is an experienced actor in international peacekeeping and peace support operations and able to deploy a good number of troops for international contingencies. This includes a fifty-thousand-strong quick-response corps, five to six long-range deployable battalions that are able to function day and night, as well as twelve home-security battalions. Overall, Turkey is able to contribute to four different peace operation contingencies with battalion-size units. The Turkish air force owns the second largest number of F-16 fighter jets after the United States. They are able to participate in live-fire exercises thousands of miles away, thanks to airborne refueling capabilities. The air force also has full capability to conduct night missions and is second only to the United States in that regard. Turkey has no nuclear, biological, or chemical weapons and is a party to all associated international legal treaties and arrangements.

Obviously, energy and the security of its production and transfer to markets play a major role in geopolitical calculations. In 2006 the European Union imported half of its energy requirements. However, the European Commission forecasts that in the next twenty to thirty years, some 70 percent of all European energy requirements will be met by imported products, some from regions threatened by insecurity.[16] The hydrocarbon energy sources of oil and natural gas have been a critical input to economic development and growth for well over a century, but the dependence on them has been growing to worrisome levels. The import dependency of the EU would reach 94 percent for oil and 84 percent for natural gas by 2030.[17] The picture is even bleaker when one considers the fact that around half of the EU's gas imports come from Russia, Norway, and Algeria. Energy supply is not only Europe's problem. The energy demand is in fact on the rise globally. Global oil consumption has risen by 20 percent since 1994, and is expected to grow by 1.6 percent per year in the time ahead. Overall world energy demand may rise by some 60 percent in the next twenty-five years.

Not a major producer of either oil or gas, and in fact heavily dependent on imported hydrocarbons itself, Turkey instead capitalizes on its geographical location to put itself on the global energy map. Turkey is geographically in close proximity to two-thirds of the world's proven oil and gas resources. The country is "of strategic importance for the security of energy supplies to the EU, lying at the crossroads of various existing and future pipelines carrying both oil and gas from many core producer regions, namely Russia, the Caspian Sea, the Middle East and Northern Africa."[18] As such, the country is destined to be the fourth main artery of Europe for the supply of hydrocarbons. Turkey achieves this transport hub role by connecting global markets and producers by pipelines that run through Turkey in both east-west and north-south directions. This involves no less than eighteen oil and natural gas pipelines that exist, are currently under construction, or are planned. Altogether, some 7 percent of the global energy supply or one out of every sixteen barrels of oil will be transported through Turkey once all these pipelines are complete.

The Kirkuk-Yumurtalik crude oil twin pipeline was in fact the earliest major pipeline that brought Iraqi crude to a Turkish seaport. These pipelines, built in 1974 and 1987, have a capacity of some 71 million tons annual transport capacity. Once a robust oil conveyor, Kirkuk-Yumurtalik pipelines have been negatively affected by the 1990–1991 Gulf crisis, being closed down due to sanctions until 2000 and then during the 2003 Iraq war. Although technically available for transport, it continues to suffer due to circumstances in Iraq. That said, Turkey is already investing in further projects, including gas,[19] in Iraq, which can be expected to become a major energy player in the next decades, provided, of course, that it manages to stay united as a country and is not consumed by civil wars and chaos. Remaining in the Middle East, Turkey and Egypt have also agreed to establish a gas pipeline between them.

Since the 1990s, with strong U.S. encouragement and support, Turkey has established itself firmly on the so-called "East-West Transportation Corridor," which is an oil and gas export route from the Caspian Region through Georgia and Turkey to Western markets. The East-West corridor forms the modern day Silk Road of hydrocarbon energy, involving trans-Caucasian and trans-Caspian pipelines.

The keystone of the East-West energy corridor is the Baku-Tblisi-Ceyhan oil pipeline, or the BTC. The BTC extends 1,770 kilometers, or 1,100 miles, until it reaches Ceyhan, on Turkey's Mediterranean coast, which has become the primary outlet for some fifty million tons of oil per year from Azerbaijan. The pipeline has become fully operational as of July 2006. In the next stage, the BTC pipeline will be used also to transport oil from Kazakhstan.

The East-West corridor also involves the lesser known Baku-Tblisi-Erzurum (BTE) and Trans-Caspian natural gas pipelines. The BTE will connect the giant offshore Azeri field of Shah Deniz, which has proven reserves of 460 billion cubic meters, to the Turkish gas pipeline system and thence to the European gas networks.

In terms of linking Turkish and European gas pipelines, a number of projects are underway. One is the Nabucco project involving Turkey, Bulgaria, Romania, Hungary, and Austria. Another such project is the Turkey-Greece natural gas pipeline that is slated for completion in 2006. This pipeline will subsequently be extended underneath the Adriatic Sea to Italy. Through these projects, Turkey will connect gas supplies in the Caspian and the Middle East with markets in Europe.

Turkey is also cultivating projects that would engender a North-South corridor. Already, Russia, Turkey, and Italy have built the Blue Stream pipeline that runs for 400 kilometers, or 250 miles, along the bottom of the Black Sea between Izobilnoye in Russia and Ankara. The Blue Stream comprises two parallel pipelines with a capacity of sixteen billion cubic meters per year. There are talks to link Turkey and Israel by an underwater pipeline to supply the Israeli market with Russian gas.

Indeed, every gas or oil project is a bypass line for the extremely endangered Turkish straits and the megapol city of Istanbul. Some seven thousand tankers have carried 140 million tons of crude oil literally through a city of roughly fourteen million. Given that the propensity is for this unbearable risk to increase over the coming years, Turks have been emphasizing hydrocarbon transport means that avoid the Turkish straits. A number of pipelines are being considered, including some that avoid Turkey altogether. However, there are others that still go through Turkish territory. One increasingly popular project involves ferrying oil from Novorossisk in Russia to Samsun at the Turkish Black Sea and thence to Ceyhan via pipelines.

Overall, it is estimated that Turkey will carry two hundred billion barrels of crude oil and eighteen trillion cubic meters of natural gas just from the Caspian to Europe and other markets. Various gas and oil pipelines running through Turkey will enable the European countries to diversify and secure their energy supply.[20] Already in 2000, the Green Paper of the European Commission entitled "Towards a European Strategy for the Security of Energy Supply" underscored that "particular attention should be given to transit states such as Turkey in the context of transport routes that will be necessary for the full exploitation of the resources of the Caspian Sea."[21] Turkey alone cannot ensure stability of supply from the source nations. The case of the Kirkuk-Yumurtalik pipeline, which have been beleaguered for more than a decade due to Iraq's own problems, is a case in point. However, Turkey itself provides a stable terminal for both oil and gas, which increasingly converge in Turkey before being redistributed to Western buyers. This is a geopolitical asset. When mixed with Turkey's other assets, the energy corridors produce a major trump card for Turkey going beyond geopolitics. Thus, Zeyno Baran observes that "a Turkey that is an EU member, a close partner of Russia, and a strategic ally of the U.S. would, with the realization of these projects, have enormous political and economic pull for the South Caucasus and Central Asian countries that also want to be closely associated with the transatlantic alliance."[22]

Obviously, figures such as those cited above are taken into account by strategic analysts, who undoubtedly see the significance of a nation-state able to garner and maintain attributes of power such as these. And there is a bonus value in having them in a key geographical location. Yet strategic importance must be seen in a much broader and deeper context.

Turkey's strategic value has always had a strong ideological component. During the Cold War, Turkey was a stalwart against expansionist Communism. In the current environment, Turkey is again on the side of democracies. Turkey is governed by a constitutional order that is based on the fundamental principles of secularism, democracy, and the rule of law. Its population being predominantly Muslim, Turkey is a living example that there is no reason why democracy, secularism, and Islam should be incompatible. Turkey has additional strategic value because it is a voice for moderation in both the Muslim and Western worlds. It is a leader in the alliance of civilizations. The West in Turkey's presence cannot be defined on the basis of religion or race but instead by the commitment to freedom and democracy.

This point has not been lost in the report of the Independent Commission on Turkey, which argued that "as a large Muslim country firmly embedded in the European Union, Turkey could play a significant role in Europe's relations with the Islamic world."[23] Jack Straw described Turkey's candidacy as the "acid test" of whether Europe could defeat terrorist attempts to sow division between Islam and the West. He said that granting Turkey membership would prove that the EU was committed to "combating the notion that Islam and Europe are separate entities which are doomed to conflict."[24] And even beyond the Muslim world, Turkey is also a candidate for providing interface among the EU; the United States; and the cultural, linguistic, historical, or geographical kinsmen in the Caucasus and Central Asia.

Thus, concludes Meltem Müftüler-Bac, "Turkey's inclusion into the EU orbit brings numerous benefits for the Union's foreign and security policies through Turkey's capabilities and its ties in the regions around it."[25] Numerous other analysts concur in their reports that Turkey's candidacy and eventual membership may give the EU more weight in world affairs by enhancing the political, cultural, and military capabilities of the European allies.

The official Turkish discourse also emphasizes that Turkey's accession would promote the goal of a stronger EU involvement in regional and global foreign and security-policy affairs. For instance, Foreign Minister Abdullah Gül argued at the Royal Institute for International Affairs:

> The EU needs to play a more significant role for international peace and security. Would Turkey's geostrategic importance or her associations and relations in the Caucasus, Central Asia and the Middle East weaken or strengthen the Common Foreign and Security Policy? The answer is in the dynamism of the multi-dimensional Turkish foreign policy, which is promising, result oriented and respected in Europe, the Middle East, the Caucasus and Central Asia. A European Union that includes Turkey will be a Union that is better equipped across the board.[26]

Since 1991 the United States has not wavered in its support for Turkey's EU membership. In return, (some) Europeans complained that just as the EU will not tell the United States what to do with Mexico, the United States should not interfere in the EU's business. But while Turkey's accession to the EU is European and Turkish business, the ripple effects of Turkey's alienation from Europe will be hard to ignore for the United States, or anyone else for that matter. Nonetheless, the authors of the report by the U.S. Atlantic Council, led by the former U.S. ambassador to Turkey Morton Abramowitz and the former ambassador to Germany Richard Burt, sensed a dilemma. They were concerned about potential disagreements between the United States and Turkey. They thought it would create challenges for U.S. foreign policy: "As Turkey must prove her willingness to adhere to common European positions, the United States may well find Turkey on the other side of the transatlantic fence on some key issues."[27] Of particular concern were such issues as the Israeli-Palestinian conflict, the International Criminal Court, and perhaps over Iran and the need for reform in the broader Middle Eastern region. They recommended nevertheless that the United States continue to support Turkey's EU membership because "it will be important to recall that the alternative to Turkish accession would be a Turkey less anchored in the West and more susceptible to domestic and regional pressures that could lead to instability—an outcome that would benefit no one."[28]

Renewed awareness of Turkey's value seems to have strengthened Turkey's hand in the EU membership process. However, notwithstanding the hitherto consistent U.S. support for Turkey's EU bid, there is at least some concern of losing Turkey. A poll by the German Marshall Fund[29] indicated that the warmth of feelings toward the United States is significantly lower in Turkey than even in France. This led the *Economist* to ask whether Turkish membership in the EU would really suit America, suggesting: "French global ambitions, bolstered by Turkish troops: now that could be an interesting combination."[30]

In fact, the results of the poll by the German Marshall Fund might have surprised the skeptics in Europe who were deriding Turkey rather as a prospective U.S. trojan horse in Europe. It turned out instead that the majority of Turks stated that they disapproved of U.S. foreign policy, focusing obviously on the U.S. invasion of Iraq, which they believed reopened a can of worms in this troubled geographical region.

But beware. Many apparently foregone conclusions about Turkish foreign and security policy may well fall victim to the country's almost unique distinctiveness. One can easily misjudge the Turks' responses to questions about how much of the EU, how much of the United States, and how much of everything else should be reflected in Turkey's foreign and security policies.

The same population that demonstrated unease with U.S. policies also showed warmth toward the American people and culture. A scientific poll initiated by the ARI movement, an Istanbul-based NGO, established in 2005 that 41 percent of Turks had positive feelings toward Americans and American culture. While 46 percent wanted their children to study in the United States, 56 percent thought Turks living in the United States had better living standards. Those who had negative views of both American policies and the Americans remained low at 16 percent. Some even thought that the United States would attack Turkey; those who maintained coldness toward the Americans were mostly those who subscribed to that theory. The pollster, Emre Erdogan, concluded that the validity of the anti-Americanism hypothesis was questionable.[31] At the same time, the poll also confirmed strong resentment regarding the detention of Turkish soldiers by U.S. NATO allies in July 2004 and the U.S. policy vis-à-vis the PKK terrorist presence in northern Iraq. Overall, a whopping 73 percent thought the United States has treated Turkey unjustly in recent years. Perceptions shaped by recent developments in Iraq went a long way in defining attitudes toward the United States. Those perceptions can nonetheless be corrected through cooperation and mutual effort, which is not lacking in Turkish-U.S. relations.

Graham Fuller, for one, does not seem to be comfortable with easy dichotomies. He describes the complexity of the remarkable realities of Turkey's evolution during recent years by referring to "serious utilization of democratic process; a willingness to act not just as a Western power but as an Eastern power as well; a greater exercise of national sovereignty supported by the people; a greater independence of action that no longer clings insecurely to the United States or any other power in implementing its foreign policies; considerable progress toward the solution of a burning internal ethnic minority (the Kurdish) issue; and a demonstrated capability to resolve the leading challenge to the Muslim world today: the management and political integration of Islam."[32]

The new realities post– and post-post–Cold War have forced Turkey's hand with regard to specific regional policies in terms that are not immediately overlapping with the U.S. approach and its short-term expectations. This was not due to the influence of a different EU position or pressure. Rather, Turkey has been developing a new appreciation of its neighborhood. The region, which so far has only been seen as producing unbearable difficulties and risks for the country, is now gradually being seen as providing opportunities as well.

The Turks are painfully aware that their security and prosperity are inextricably linked with stability in the neighborhood. There is also a higher appreciation that passive policies concerning the outstanding problems in Turkey's vicinity are tenable only at a high cost. On top of this, add Turkish sensibilities toward neighboring Russia; the Turkic world; and other rising powers further afield such as China, India, and Pakistan, as well as transregional groups like the Organization of the Islamic Conference (OIC). This is not identity politics but a more sophisticated understanding of geopolitics in the age of globalization.

Turkey and its predecessor, the Ottoman Empire, have been for centuries at the epicenter of geopolitics, benefiting and suffering at the same time from its geostrategic location. However, as important as it is, geopolitics alone does not explain Turkey's multipronged foreign policy. In a world of receding boundaries among the domestic, international, political, economic, and cultural spheres, policy making is infinitely complex, albeit not immune to realism. Policy makers are not isolated and faceless actors; national policies are not determined exclusively by the political, civilian, and military bureaucracies; and the states are not the only actors in the international field. The power or weakness of a country is not defined solely in terms of relatively concrete attributes such as military hardware and training, population size, and material wealth. States are rational actors only to the extent permitted by other intervening factors, including the ideological zeal of its leaders. The information age and globalization impose strong influences on any state, but particularly on nations that have opened up politically and economically to close interaction with the world. Those who resist are also not immune to globalization. To the contrary, countries that adjust fare better than those who do not. The resisters fight a losing battle against globalization, as even the forces that threaten our societies seize its benefits. Turkey does not yet ride on top of the wave, but it is increasingly aware of the bright side and not only the dark side of globalization.

On the other hand, as Thomas Friedman's dichotomy of the Lexus and the Olive Tree suggests, even as we are compelled to take a global and fairly reformist view, at the same time, the olive tree that "represent[s] everything that roots us, anchors us, identifies us and locates us in this world"[33] continues to be important in how we perceive the world outside us. Thus, geographical, cultural, communal, and traditional proximities continue to impose themselves as an essential concern. Turkey is no exception.

The cumulative effect of Turkey's sensitivities toward its neighborhood, the process of accession to the EU, and the constant importance of the United States vis-à-vis all of Turkey's foreign and security policy priorities point to a need for creative thinking and perhaps an attempt at harmonization. Several factors are likely to complicate things further for Turkish policy makers, including who holds power in Turkey, how well the EU accession process progresses, how the respective positions of the United States and the EU evolve, and how regional developments take shape, in addition to, of course, how the EU's Common Foreign and Security Policy develops.

The future of the relationship among the EU, the candidate Turkey, and the United States carries well beyond trilateral impact on the individual parties. This triangular relationship could in fact help shape in part the contemporary definition of transatlantic cooperation, particularly with respect to the broader Middle East, the Caucasus, and Central Asia.

The most glaring argument in favor of Turkish membership to the EU has been furnished by Turkey's strategic value, both in figurative hardware and software terms. Indeed, Turkey offers increasingly vigorous foreign and security policy capabilities, strengthened by its energetic regional roles in diverse geostrategic basins. As a vibrant secular democracy, Turkey also embodies a global political message and is becoming increasingly adept in articulating it, as was seen, for instance, in its initiative to host a joint forum between the EU and the OIC promptly after the September 11 terrorist atrocities. In the words of Paul Wolfowitz, "It is the great good fortune of NATO and the West, indeed of the world, that Turkey, one of our strongest, most reliable and most self-reliant allies, occupies one of the most important strategic crossroads in the world."[34] Or, as Charles Hill noted, "The EU is in a strange way lucky to have Turkey as a candidate."[35] It is important that Turkey continues to be seen that way even when it disagrees with a specific policy that was prescribed by others.

Unlike in the past, Turkey's strategic value is no longer determined by geographic location alone. Nor is it only about providing territorial facilities to great powers. Rather, Turkey is strategic because of its human resources, system of government, tradition of statecraft including diplomatic and military skills, and bustling free market economy, which is also an outlet for Caspian and Central Asian energy. While there is much to be done to build on and sharpen extant attributes, these already imbue Turkey with a unique clout.

Turkey is more significant than its GNP, natural resources, or even military power alone would suggest. But ultimately it is more necessary to put Turkey's assets to use in resolving issues and addressing challenges than to merely pay lip service to Turkey's significance for Europe, the United States, and the region. Utilizing Turkey's assets in the optimum way may be foremost a Turkish task, but it is also a European and U.S. task to produce the appropriate framework to encourage greater Turkish contributions to resolving regional and global challenges. When Turkey's figurative telephone rings it is usually about a complaint or a call for some flexibility on Turkey's part, which leaves its potential to address the core problems untouched. Where Turkey's help is needed, it should be included in the core groups, contact groups, cochairmen, or whatever format may be used to address the issue.

Mind-set and attitude as much as traditional and soft-power attributes, constraints, and the dictates of globalization affect how we comprehend the foreign policy and security values of an EU candidate and the member countries. Therefore, being able to make the best use of Turkey's assets, capabilities, and potential in the interests of the common good is partly a question of mind-set and attitude on the part of Turkey, the EU, and the United States, not to mention Turkey's neighbors. On one side, it is about how Turkey is perceived. On the other side, it is about how Turkey sees itself.

The summary of many reports is that something important and positive is in store for Turkey, both in its region and in the wider world, and EU membership will help unleash its great potential, benefiting the EU and the United States as well as Turkey itself. The question is whether the parties will have the right mind-set and attitude to make the most of it.

Notes

1. Independent Commission on Turkey, "Turkey in Europe: More Than a Promise?" The Independent Commission is chaired by Marti Ahtisaari, former president of Finland, and includes a group of eminent personalities from a variety of EU member countries. The full text of the report can be found at: www.independent commissiononturkey.org/.

2. Atlantic Council of the United States Program on Transatlantic Relations, Morton Abramowitz and Richard Burt, co-chairs, "Turkey on the Threshold: Europe's Decision and U.S. Interests." www.acus.org/docs/0408-Turkey_Threshold_Europe_Decision_U.S._Interests.pdf.

3. ABIG, Factsheet: "A Brief Glance at the Democratic Reform in Turkey," September 3, 2004. www.abig.org.tr.

4. Tony Parkinson, "What More Must Turkey Do before Europe Says Yes?" *Age* (Melbourne), December 20, 2002.

5. Communication from the Commission to the Council and the European Parliament: "Recommendaton of the European Commission on Turkey's Progress Towards Accession," Brussels, June 10, 2004, Com(2004) 656 Final.

6. Niall Ferguson, *Colossus: The Rise and Fall of the American Empire* (New York: Penguin, 2005), 253.

7. Commission of the European Communities, "Issues Arising from Turkey's Membership Perspective," Commission Staff Working Document, Brussels, June 10, 2004, Sec(2004)1202, Com(2004) 656 Final, 4.

8. Heather Grabbe, *From Drift to Strategy: Why the EU Should Start Accession Talks with Turkey* (London: Centre for European Reform, 2004), 6.

9. Michael Emerson and Nathalie Tocci, "Turkey as a Bridgehead and Spearhead: Integrating EU and Turkish Foreign Policy" (EU-Turkey Working Papers No. 1, Brussels: Center for European Policy Studies, August 2004), 8.

10. Emerson and Tocci, "Turkey as a Bridgehead," 4.

11. Commission of the European Communities, "Issues Arising," 4.

12. Joschka Fischer, "Interview von Bundesaußenminister Fischer mit der *Süddeutschen Zeitung* am 6.8.2005 zu den Themen Iran, Europa, VN-Reform." www.auswaertiges-amt.de.

13. Independent Commission on Turkey, "Turkey in Europe," 43.

14. Şadi Ergüvenç, "The New Security Environment and Turkey's Contribution to European Security," in *Contemporary Issues in International Politics: Essays in Honour of Seyfi Taşhan*, ed. Foreign Policy Institute (Ankara: Dış Politika Enstitüsü, 2004), 150.

15. Ergüvenç, "New Security Environment," 150.

16. The European Commission, "Green Paper: A European Strategy for Sustainable, Competitive and Secure Energy," [SEC(2006) 317], March 8, 2006, 3.

17. The European Commission, "Annex to the Green Paper: A European Strategy for Sustainable, Competitive and Secure Energy What Is at Stake—Background Document," [COM(2006) 105 final], 11.

18. European Commission, "Annex to the Green Paper," 37.

19. See: Nüzhet Cem Orekli, "Turkey's Energy Strategy in a New Era: Time to Re-look South," www.tusiad.us/Content/uploaded/CEM%20OREKLI-TURKEY'S %20 ENERGY%20STRATEGY.PDF

20. Selma Stern, "Turkey's Energy and Foreign Policy," *Globalization* 3, no. 1 (2003), globalization.icaap.org/content/v3.1/03_stern.html. See also Brent Sasley,

"Turkey Energy's Politics," in *Turkey in World Politics: An Emerging Multiregional Power*, ed. Barry Rubin and Kemal Kirişçi (Boulder, CO: Lynne Rienner Publishers, 2001).

21. The European Commission, "Green Paper: Towards a European Strategy for the Security of Energy Supply," November 29, 2000.

22. Zeyno Baran, "The Baku-Tbilisi-Ceyhan Pipeline: Implications for Turkey," in *The Baku-Tbilisi-Ceyhan Pipeline: Oil Window to the West*, ed. S. Frederick Starr and Svante E. Cornell (Washington DC: Johns Hopkins University Central Asia-Caucasus Institute & Silk Road Studies Program, 2005), p. 118.

23. Independent Commission on Turkey, "Turkey in Europe," 43.

24. Tom Happold, "Straw: Turkey Is EU 'Acid Test,'" *The Guardian* (Manchester), March 23, 2004.

25. Meltem Müftüler-Bac, "Turkey's Role in the EU's Security and Foreign Policies," *Security Dialogue* 31, no. 4 (2000): 498.

26. Abdullah Gül, "Turkish Perspectives towards a New Environment in the European Union and the Middle East" (address to the Royal Institute of International Affairs, London, July 3, 2003).

27. Atlantic Council of the United States, "Turkey on the Threshold," viii.

28. Atlantic Council of the United States, "Turkey on the Threshold," viii.

29. German Marshall Fund of the United States, "Transatlantic Trends," 2004 and 2005, www.transatlantictrends.org.

30. "Turkish Tales: Would Turkish Membership of the EU Really Suit America?" *Economist*, September 9, 2004.

31. For the findings of the poll, see www.ari.org.tr/arastirma/research.htm.

32. Graham Fuller, "Turkey's Strategic Model: Myths and Realities," *Washington Quarterly* 27, no. 3 (2004): 51.

33. Thomas Friedman, *The Lexus and the Olive Tree* (New York: Farrar, Strauss & Giroux, 2000), p. 31.

34. Paul Wolfowitz, speech at the International Institute for Strategic Studies, (London, December 2, 2002).

35. The veteran American diplomat and professor made this remark during a commentary on my speech at Yale University, November 4, 2005.

CHAPTER THREE

Europeanization

No state's self-image is immune to refractions created by the collective perceptions of its society. Phillip Zelikow argued that all national security and foreign policy strategies start with a mental image of the world.[1] This suggestion should be expanded to include the mental image of the self as well. Indeed, foreign policy as a distinct area of public policy is a factor of "a shared sense of national identity, of a nation-state's place in the world, its friends and enemies, its interests and aspirations. These underlying assumptions are embedded in national history and myth, changing slowly over time as political leaders reinterpret them and external and internal developments shape them."[2] Although states in the international legal order are sovereign, national choices are only part of their foreign policy decision making. How big a part may depend on how powerful a state is vis-à-vis the outer world, how coherent and effective it is domestically, and the particulars of the international environment. The regional and transregional security situation exerts influence on national decision making. Similarly, globalization and its impact on the economy and even society affect the choices available to the state beyond questions of identity and perception. The fact of the matter is that no state is exempt from the unwieldy influences of living in an international community.

Whether big or small, a state's ability to comprehend, use, and manipulate these influences is critical to its survival and development. Nations are social entities both domestically and externally, and the global society they live in favors the better public speaker, the better groomed, the wealthier and healthier, and yes, the stronger.

Obviously, both foreign and security policies are influenced strongly by existing capabilities and available instruments. This argument restates in a way the importance of the power factor, which traditionally involves geography, demographics, technology, armed forces, and wealth. Alliances, too, would be considered in this framework. Robert Kagan believes that power conceived in conventional terms defines foreign policy's tenor. Mark Leonard thinks, in contrast, that there may be a strength in weakness, which creates less antagonism. At any rate, following Joseph Nye's concept of soft power, all the various factors that contribute to the image of and perceptions about a particular state and nation must be recognized as part of a state's foreign policy and security policy capabilities.[3]

Moral high ground is almost universally part and parcel of soft power. International law, whether codified treaty law or universal principles that are recognized over and above the words on paper, provide guidance but do not self-implement. As the only practical judge in international conscience seems to be the general consensus of the many, building up the power of weakness, or soft power, but also traditional power over the longer term requires restraints on purely national policy making and action.

All these factors affect the aspirations, choices, and actions of a state's foreign and security policies. Such a broad framework applies to all states partaking in the global society, regulating their interaction and constraining them in various sorts of ways.

However, in the case of countries that are members or candidates to the EU there is an additional factor in play. One could write a few hundred pages describing it, or call it loosely and vaguely *Europeanization*.

The term is loose indeed. For those states on the periphery of the European Union, it is about resembling the ones that are at the center of it. However, for those that are members of the EU, the term has a narrower and more specific connotation. Largely unknown or ignored outside Europe, most of the scholarly literature on the concept of Europeanization defines it in a number of ways as a variety of phenomena and processes of change within the EU.[4]

The starting point for the scholarly use of "Europeanization" is the integration in post–World War II Europe that culminated in the European Union. The underlying logic of European integration has been the shifting of activities and loyalties of national actors toward a supranational center.[5] In the process, the European Union has emerged as a distinct international actor sufficiently different from either states or international organizations. Mark Leonard conveniently terms this sui generis international actor a "network of centers of power united by common policies and goals."[6]

This network has a foreign policy that "emerges from and is contextualized by a unique experiment in political integration in Europe."[7] EU foreign policy activity "refers to the universe of concrete civilian actions, policies, positions, relations, commitments and choices of the EC (and EU) in international politics which have come to cover nearly all areas and issues of international politics."[8] One note of clarification may be needed here. The EU has conventionally defined its economic foreign policy, covering mainly trade and development aid relations with third parties, as "external relations" and has distinguished it from political and security-based foreign policies.

In the words of Brian White, whichever way European foreign policy is defined, "it cannot easily be contained within a traditional state-centred analysis with relatively clear boundaries between internal and external policy environments."[9] This increases the validity of Christopher Hill's conceptualization of EU foreign policy incorporating "the sum of what the EU *and* its member states do in international relations."[10] This conception is important because it correctly identifies the interaction between the national and supranational layers of EU foreign policy. In this context, the difficulty of delimiting internal versus external policy environments is particularly pertinent in the case of the foreign policies of the specific member states.

Claudio Radaelli has offered an influential definition of Europeanization as consisting of "processes of construction, diffusion, institutionalization of formal and informal rules, procedures, policy paradigms, styles, 'ways of doing things,' and shared beliefs and norms which are first defined and consolidated in the making of EU decisions and then incorporated in the logic of domestic discourse, identities, political structures and public policies."[11] However, in the area of foreign policy this definition may prove problematic due to its reference to the primacy of the EU policy process.

Technically, unlike almost all other aspects of EU governance, foreign and security policy continues to reflect predominantly intergovernmental decision making where the primacy rests with national capitals, not the Commission. The only comparably intergovernmental area seems to be Justice and Home Affairs.

Instead, it may be more accurate to argue that Europeanization occurs as a result of "the processes of foreign policy change at the national level originated by the adaptation pressures and the new opportunities generated by the European integration process."[12] Indeed, for all the intergovernmental nature of foreign policy, a wide common ground and incentives to forge that common ground exist, despite the resilience of broad individual tracks. Iraq was an example of failed policy convergence for the EU. While the United Kingdom and several others contributed troops to Iraq, many others did not and objected fiercely. Yet even in this exceptional case, the EU continued to legislate a broad array of common policies on a number of other issues, even as the disagreement over Iraq continued. Beyond that, and several other issues that relate mostly to the particular case of relations with the United States, the national policies of the members have been under constant pressure to adapt and converge within the EU.

There are ample analyses on the extent to which European foreign policy is shaped by national policies or, conversely, national foreign policies are transformed in the EU-level policy environment. Nevertheless, it is important to recognize foremost that there is a two-way relationship between national and EU foreign policies. It may be that Europeanization is conceived as only the top-down flow of policy from the EU to the member states, whereas the opposite directional flow is termed "projection." Yet this is too fine a point and, particularly in the case of foreign policy, perhaps redundant.

The EU's laws and common policies form when members agree on rules and procedures of decision making. The European Council, comprising all member states, is the ultimate legislative organ. In specific minor cases, the Council may decide by simple majority. However, decisions on single market, environment, transportation, research, employment, social exclusion, equal opportunity, and public health matters require a qualified majority vote. Most of the EU's common foreign and security policy (CFSP) is constituted by nonbinding common statements, declarations, and demarches. However, there are also common positions, joint actions, and common strategies that are legally binding under international treaty law. The common strategies, such as the ones agreed to on Russia, the Ukraine, and the Mediterranean, are documents in which the EU member states entertain important common interests and objectives. For these strategy documents unanimity is the rule. As for the common positions and joint actions that provide the means to act collectively, there is the possibility of deciding by a qualified majority.

Once these common positions are established, all members are expected to adhere to them. During the negotiation process, member states influence common policies by uploading aspects of their own national policies. By the time the negotiation and decision process is finalized, the finished product may barely resemble any single member state's original policy. Once the common EU position is thus formed, it reflects back on the national policy, because all members are called to implement it.

As such, the Europeanization impact is generated by both voluntary policy convergence, in which the country chooses to adopt EU policies to the development of which it contributes, and by directed policy transfer or downloading, where the country is expected to adopt and support the agreed EU policies, although it may not have voted in favor of it.

A comparable mutual pull factor can be at play with regard to the accession candidates. Policy flow is from the EU to the candidate state, including in foreign and security policy. Accession candidates, like member states, are expected to give active and unconditional support to the implementation of the CFSP in a spirit of loyalty and mutual solidarity and must conform to the common positions and defend these positions in international forums. But this is often a less imposing requirement in foreign policy than in other areas of European integration such as, for instance, agricultural policies. At the current state of development of the EU, foreign and security policy is an area in which the intergovernmental nature of cooperation and the national prerogative remain the norm, and various CFSP instruments are not part of the European community law but are binding under international law.

Therefore, the field of common foreign and security policy is not based on legal instruments such as directives and regulations, which for instance the European Court of Justice can enforce. In this chapter of the negotiations, no transposition into the national legal order of the candidate countries is necessary.

The candidates do not normally have a say in the formulation of EU common policies. They are, however, accorded political dialogue as well as certain consultation mechanisms. The latter is a product of the Nice Treaty but more accurately of a separate arrangement under a 2002 document on European Security and Defense Policy (ESDP): "ESDP: Implementation of the Nice Provisions on the Involvement of the Non-EU European Allies," also known as the Ankara agreement.

Accordingly, the EU is obligated to have permanent and continuing consultations with the non-EU European allies, including Turkey and not too many others, covering the full range of security, defense, and crisis-management issues. This includes meetings in advance of the EU Political and Security Committee as well as the Military Committee, where decisions may be made on matters affecting the security interests of the non-EU European allies. Notably, the document states explicitly that "the objective of these consultations will be for the European Union and the non-EU European allies to exchange views, and to discuss any concerns and interests raised by these Allies, so as to enable the European Union to take them into consideration. As with CFSP, these consultations will enable the non-EU European Allies to contribute to European Security and Defence Policy and to associate themselves with EU decisions, actions and declarations on ESDP."[13]

It is important to note that this arrangement, the Ankara agreement, has been achieved following a mutually nerve-racking standoff between the EU and Turkey, which lasted between 1999 and 2002 and was resolved only when Turkey's legitimate concerns were met by the EU, with the United States and Great Britain playing a key mediation role.

Therefore, Turkey was able to project or upload some of its policy to the EU although it was not yet a member. This particular experience was tainted by a degree of acrimony. The position of several EU members and the United States vacillated from benign pressure to intimidation and finally to accommodation. Nonetheless, its positive result should make the benefits of mutual accommodation unequivocally obvious.

This example of two-way flow of policy before a candidate becomes a member is not unique to Turkey's case. Such two-way policy transfer is in fact in line with the broad logic of policy transfer in the European context. Thus, as Elisabeth Bomberg and John Peterson argue, "Europeanization is a two-way process: European integration shapes domestic policies, politics and polities, but Member States also project themselves by seeking to shape the trajectory of European integration in ways that suit national interests."[14] Although less evident, a similar logic may apply to candidate countries.

A specific case in point has been documented by Jose Torreblanca's study of the Spanish experience. "Spain has 'exported' parts of its own foreign policy agenda and subsequently managed to have the EU adopt policies on areas, such as Latin America or the Mediterranean, in which the EU had minor or marginal interests of its own."[15] Furthermore, although this uploading of policy occurred after the Spanish accession to the EU, it was already visible during the negotiations of the accession treaty. As the accession negotiations were under way, Spain "obtained a declaration stating the commitment of the EC to help Spain make its accession compatible with the maintaining and promotion of its national interests in Latin America."[16] After its accession to the EU, in the first European Council meeting that Spain attended as a full member of the EU, the Commission was tasked to prepare a strategy to upgrade EU relations with Latin America. The ensuing initial strategy involved an increase in development aid, the coordination of development policies, and the promotion of regional integration and trade exchanges as well as peace processes. As the EU's strategy toward Latin America was updated in the years to follow, it culminated in the signing of association or free trade agreements with the Mercosur group and Mexico, as well as the opening up of EU markets to the Andean and Central American countries.

It is important to recall that Spanish policy was not transferred to the EU without modifications. Instead, the Spanish position also evolved and was justified in terms of European, and not just Spanish, national interests. Torreblanca points out, "Obviously, Spain could not impose its national interests and policies on the EU without changes or adaptations. Even if it could negotiate this policy transfer and exchange it for its support for other member states' policy areas, success could only be based on persuading the other EU members that the EU had a distinct interest in the matter and, therefore, of the need for the EU to have a policy of its own. . . . What Spain offered was a justification for action in terms of "European," not just Spanish national interests."[17]

Accordingly, Spain argued mainly for the economic benefits for the EU in terms of increased trade and investment flows. There was apparently also the argument of "offering some Latin American countries a counterbalance to U.S. influence in the region."[18] Once a member, Spain also was influential in developing the EU's Mediterranean policy.

As the Spanish and the ESDP examples demonstrate, candidates can upload their interests and policies to the EU while the EU simultaneously downloads the basic premises of the collective foreign-policy making to the candidate. Therein lies a fundamental point about the need for mutual accommodation that will be pertinent for Turkish-EU relations.

The importance of this point is in a way linked with Turkey's mental image of the world and of itself, as well as with the background of the relationship between Turkey and its European partners, which perpetuates this mental image. There are fascinating questions to ask regarding Turkey at this point. How does Turkey's mental image of the world, its self-image, its capabilities in both traditional and "soft" power, the constraints and dictates of globalization, and the emerging pull of Europeanization affect the evolution of its foreign and security policies? Where does Turkey currently stand in Robert Kagan's Mars and Venus analogy, and where is it heading?[19] What has been or will likely be the impact of the much referenced "Europeanization" on the accession candidate Turkey in terms of foreign policy? How "Europeanized" is Turkey already in foreign-policy thinking and action? What will determine the extent to which Europeanization will proceed? And what can be done to ensure success? A perceptive approach in response to these questions may help design an appropriate framework of thinking and action to promote Turkey's EU journey for those who want to promote it. Furthermore, that framework might hold the analytical key to interpreting Turkish thinking and actions, while helping to unleash Turkey's potential as a credible positive actor in regional and world politics. In this regard, one could provide several pointers for reflection.

"Transatlantic Trends" is an annual public opinion survey examining American and European attitudes, conducted for the German Marshall Fund in the United States and Germany, France, Great Britain, Italy, the Netherlands, Poland, Portugal, Slovakia, Spain, and Turkey. The 1995 surveys revealed significant overlaps between Turkey and the EU on some issues and between Turkey and the United States in others, as well as some differences for both.[20] The most basic summary one can draw from the data provided by the surveys is that Turkish public opinion can be posited somewhere between Mars and Venus, getting closer to Europe but perhaps more accurately situated right here on Earth.

Such a middle-of-the-road security culture can be discerned from a variety of answers given by the Turks. Thus, 71 percent of the Turk respondents agreed that economic power is more important than military power, as opposed to 86 percent in the nine EU countries polled and 66 percent of the U.S. respondents. When asked whether war might be necessary under certain circumstances to achieve justice, 35 percent from the EU countries, 46 percent from Turkey, and 78 percent from the United States responded affirmatively. Turks were significantly ahead of the other European countries in believing that the best way to ensure peace is through military strength. Accordingly, 49 percent of the Turks, 22 percent of the EU respondents, and 44 percent of those in the United States thought this way.

The poll also revealed certain unilateralist tendencies in Turkey, where only 50 percent agreed that when their country acts on a national security issue, it is critical that this be done together with closest allies. The European average on this question was 86 percent and the U.S. an unexpected 89 percent. The question on whether it is justified to bypass the UN when the country's security is threatened evoked an affirmative response from 66 percent of the Turks. The United States respondents agreed with the Turks (62 percent), whereas the percentage of the nine EU countries on the question was a significantly lower 46 percent. This data can be interpreted as a lack of faith that allies or international forums like the UN would show enough solidarity with Turkey to jointly act against a security threat.

One should perhaps put down a contextual marker for the interpretation of Turkish responses to questions about the use of force. For the majority of Turkish respondents, the specific experience of the fight against PKK terrorism defines the context of the use of force. This assumption is supported by the significantly high percentage of agreement in the 2004 survey with the suggestion that military action to eliminate terrorist organizations is the most appropriate way to fight terrorism. In that survey the Turkish percentage was 74 percent, as opposed to 49 percent for other Europeans and 63 percent for Americans. Obviously, experience matters, and it is influential in shaping perceptions and reflexes. Unfortunately, Turkey probably has more experience in the fight against terrorism than anyone would want.

These findings are generally in agreement with Turkey's presumed mental image of the world. That image is largely focused defensively on Turkey's own region, albeit gradually broadening as the country becomes an economic, political, and social player outside its close proximity. Indeed, there is already a discernible expansion of focus. The country is already a member of the G-20 initiative, which may in the future transform beyond the meeting of finance ministers to include foreign ministers and heads of state. Turkey is at the same time a founding member of the D-8 initiative of developing nations.[21] Turkey also has staked its bid to join the United Nations Security Council for 2009–2010. In the meantime, however, its focus on regional issues appears to be pegged to the resilience of the perils stemming from the neighborhood. Yet this focus is conditioned not only by the obvious current state of affairs in this volatile vicinity: there is also the fact that half the population of contemporary Turkey is descended from Muslims who were driven from the Balkans and the Caucasus or the 5.5 million more who perished in those lands, all between 1821 and 1923. In the Turkish heartland, 2.3 million died between 1912 and 1923 as a result of war. And this image is kept alive by the more recent memory of one million Turkish speaking Azeris who were expelled from their homes in and around Nagorno-Karabakh after 1990, not to mention the grievances of the Bosnians or indeed the Turkish Cypriots.

Turkey is seen as the center of this neighborhood, which is subject to the abuses of greater powers over its spoils. A notable observer of Turkish affairs, David Barchard, in his 2002 testimony to the British Parliament reflects a perception that is arguably shared by tens of millions of Turks in their collective conscience:

There still seems to be a Gladstonian tendency to regard Turkey as "different" from its southeastern European neighbours; to focus attention on perceived shortcomings; and to promote separatist or centrifugal ethnic currents, whether actual or potential. A recent British academic study of North-Eastern Turkey for instance questions the lack of separatist nationalist sentiment among its population. It is amusing to note that while hostile attitudes toward Turkey are relatively constant, the grounds offered for them can change dramatically. In the nineteenth century, Turkey was berated by British liberals for being an Islamic theocracy. Today it comes under fire in the same quarters for its secular system and alleged repression of political Islamists. More fundamentally prejudice leads to a tendency—stronger perhaps in parts of continental Europe than in the UK—to underrate Turkey's strengths and potential.[22]

Turkey's self-image, influenced and perpetuated by the image of the world outside, is one of a proud nation that is little understood, frequently threatened or subverted, and almost alone in defending the remarkable gains made during its Republican era. Every involvement of a greater power is met by a degree of popular suspicion, mitigated however by Turkish pragmatism and a penchant for moderation. Turks know their country possesses significant national assets, hindered in their full use by economic shortcomings. The state and the society are increasingly open to the influences of globalism and arguably appreciative of at least certain aspects of it. The national aspiration is to be respected as an advanced and modern democratic member of the global society living in a stable, peaceful, and prosperous neighborhood. The twofold fundamental guidance of the founder of the Republic, Mustafa Kemal Atatürk, remains "peace at home, peace in the world" and "reaching the contemporary level of civilization," statements which hardly need interpretation.

Turkish intellectuals are often resentful but not oblivious to the limits of Turkish power to engender a benign environment for the country. They are also largely protective of Turkish prerogative and sovereignty, as they perceive ill-will, or at best disregard, for Turkish interests by others. While many aspirant countries have joined the EU in relatively short order, the protracted nature of the accession process for Turkey threatens to invoke defensive reflexes in the society while consolidating the Turkish people's widespread skepticism and even cynicism of the great powers, which in today's world include the United States and the European Union. As the 2005 "Transatlantic Trends" poll suggests, the Turks are cautious about either the United States or the EU being a hegemonic power. Although followed closely by those who want the EU to become a superpower like the United States, most Turkish respondents did not want any superpower in the world.[23]

Against this background, two contradictory forces act on Turkish foreign-policy makers. On one side, there is modernization and globalism as well as the drive toward EU membership. On the other side, there is simultaneously a lingering resentment of abrupt coercive change and instability in the neighborhood as well as the actions of great powers that are regarded as defiant of Turkish views and sensitivities. The latter perception may produce occasional outbursts of public anxiety, a relapse to a time not so distant in collective memory when great powers subverted, manipulated, and ultimately invaded Turkey, culminating in the Turkish War of Independence. The notorious treaty designed to partition Turkey signed in 1920 in the French town of Sevres, a fiasco of historic proportions, happily never saw daylight. But it continues to cast a psychological shadow over the Turkish psyche and perceptions, which others ignore at their peril.

Ultimately, the European and Turkish psychologies, if left to their own devices, do not bode well for the kind of integration that is implied by EU membership. From the perspective of the EU and its member countries, admitting Turkey would be giving Turkey a say in the future evolution of the

Union. As grandiose as this sounds, it is however not unqualified. But Turkey will have a say in the evolution of the Union even if it does not join the EU in the end. European security and defense, its markets, its relationships with its neighbors, political clout, even domestic politics will continue to have a Turkish aspect. Furthermore, this Turkish aspect will be a significantly less sympathetic and "Europeanized" one if Turkey does not become an EU member. Therefore, both the Turkish and European skeptics miss the point about each other. And the fact that they do makes it harder.

It is even different from the case of Greece, whose population long maintained similarly cynical views of Europe (and the United States).[24] That attitude was effectively unidirectional from Greece toward Europe. In contrast, on the European side the opposite was true to a fanciful degree, where proponents of Greek membership seemed convinced that the example of ancient Greece and not the more recent Byzantium was being brought into the EU. In Turkey's case the cynical feelings are more or less reciprocal. Yet the solution of the Turkish dilemma can still be inspired by the Greek example. Only a Turkey that is brought into the Union can overcome its cynicism regarding Europe and Europe's cynicism regarding Turkey. And the cynicism will definitely not be overcome by a Turkey that is kept at bay or clumsily docked through mechanisms implied by a "privileged partnership" that Turkey's opponents espouse.

Therefore, presumably, the better that Turkish modernization, globalization, and integration into the EU proceed, the greater will be Turkish and European mutual confidence. The accession talks with the EU can in time help alleviate deep-rooted suspicion on the part of the Turkish people and political establishment that Turkey will never be admitted to the Union.[25] But it is nonetheless worth mentioning that the support for EU membership in Turkey appears to have fallen by no less than 10 percentage points in one year, from 73 percent in 2004 to 63 percent in 2005. The current debate in Europe about Turkish membership to the EU obviously plays a weighty role in this drop. This can change for the better or worse depending on how much more Turks will have to endure in the EU negotiation and accession process—or, indeed, on whether the accession talks will be successful in engendering accession.

The EU gains direct influence in Turkey only when it offers Turkey an open door. Indeed, the mere fact that Turkey's candidate status was recognized at the Helsinki Summit in 1999 amplified the attraction of the EU.[26] The less forthcoming the EU policies were toward Turkey, the more resistance grew in Turkey to foreign policy re-conceptualizations espoused by the EU or its member states. One specific example is the ordeal over the European Security and

Defense Initiative (ESDI), the resolution of which was greatly aided by perceived progress toward EU membership.[27] It is abundantly clear that management of the period of negotiations, through all the anticipated tension, anguish, and even potential ruptures, remains a challenge, and success is nowhere guaranteed.

Pinar Bilgin argues that the process of European integration, which constructed a specific security culture, had two implications for Turkey in the 1990s:

> First, as European integration constituted its own insecurities in the form of "soft security" threats, Turkish policy makers remained rather oblivious to their EU counterparts' sensitivities and failed to realize how these became "existential threats" from an EU perspective. Second, EU policy-makers have tended to view security issues from their own perspective that evolved during the Cold War in a relatively stable environment provided by NATO security guarantee. As a result, EU policy-makers became less sensitive to the security needs and interests of those countries, such as Turkey, that are still faced with military threats that stem from both inside and outside the national boundaries.[28]

As such, while Turkey has taken a greater interest in the EU's insecurities as part of the EU accession process,[29] it is difficult to argue in favor of a position change on the part of the EU toward Turkey's own threat perceptions. The EU was ultimately a negative influence in the fight against terrorism for a long time. At least one EU member was complicit in the training and abetting of PKK terrorists. Several others were disinterested in cutting terrorist finances. Several more had displayed profound confusion, to Turkey's disadvantage, about the difference between the democratic right for free speech and outright incitement for terror. Some of this confusion remains even today, despite the belated recognition of PKK as a terrorist organization. The debate about European Security and Defense Policy and the participation of non-EU NATO allies in the emerging EU military arrangements, in which Turks perceived a clear policy to exclude Turkey, also exacerbated Turkish insecurity about European intentions.[30]

The effective removal of the PKK as a serious threat in 1999 allowed for the *desecuritization* of a number of issues, facilitating further liberalization of the country.[31] It has also helped Turkey to pioneer new diplomatic initiatives to improve relations with neighbors. Desecuritization has facilitated a gradual change in foreign and security policy culture in Turkey. PKK's return as a security threat may create a re-securitization somewhat akin to the impact of September 11 on the United States.

The lack of European support for Turkey's primary security issue and the fact that the war against terrorism had to be waged almost exclusively with

Turkey's national means consolidated the perceived primacy of national security capabilities over multilateral remedies. As such, the early 2000s saw the cohabitation of multilateralist and unilateralist tendencies as well as soft and hard security agendas and capabilities.

In fact, since the celebrated end of the Cold War, Turkey's foreign and security policies have been undergoing significant change, a fact that is not exclusive to Turkey. As the next chapter will explain, Turkey has turned from a spectator of the poor state of affairs of its neighborhood into one that seeks to improve it. It has become an active participant on a series of regional and international developments, resolved or allayed a number of its long-standing bilateral disputes, and used its military crisis-management capabilities extensively in different regions such as Afghanistan and the Balkans. Turkey has started to open up to its region economically, politically, and socially a decade or so after it opened up its economy to global free-market influences. Today, this flowering continues in full swing.

One suggested explanation for this change is the influence of globalization on the state and the public. Whether Turks like it or not, they are living in a country that is already part of the globalization train. Globalization's full-blown political impact was checked in Turkey due to the fight against terrorism, problems with neighbors, and domestic economic and political woes. To an extent these factors also retarded Turkey's participation in European enlargement alongside the ten countries that joined the EU in 2004. Nonetheless, globalization's influence has been discernible not only in the economic field, but in more or less similar terms in the political and security fields, as well.

In terms of foreign and security policies, the impact of globalization implies "multilateralism, interdependence and a shift from active confrontation to cooperative arrangements."[32] Globalization also facilitates "going beyond the national security framework."[33] Both these definitions apply to the Turkish experience. Ali Karaosmanoğlu argues that due to its historical and geopolitical circumstances, Turkey is influenced by the two conflicting trends that characterize the globalizing international system. On the one hand, "its EU candidacy, NATO membership, its active performance in PfP [Partnership for Peace] and participation in peace operations are inspiring internationalization, multilateralism, cooperative security, democratic control of the armed forces, and emphasis on societal and individual security." On the other hand, however, "its regional environment is suggesting security through power politics and the sustained primacy of the nation state."[34] As regards the latter, Karaosmanoğlu observed nonetheless that "despite the adverse regional environment, Turkey has made strides to adapt to the internationalization of security."[35]

Turkey's security culture is evolving. Karaosmanoğlu identified the two constitutive elements of Turkey's security culture as the tradition of realpolitik and the process of Westernization.[36] The Turkish brand of realpolitik was and remains essentially "defensive," emphasizing balance-of-power diplomacy, not the maximization of power through conquest. Obviously, Turkey's foreign and security policy culture has been, in Pinar Bilgin's words, "quintessentially realist" throughout the Cold War, based on a "geographical assumption of givenness."[37] Turkey's foreign and security elite, as well as the public in general, seem to give much credence to the centrality of the predicaments created by Turkey's volatile neighborhood.

However, there are indications that at the policy level Turkey has begun to reconstruct its perception of its neighborhood. Concerns over regional stability have come to reverse the traditional preference for noninvolvement in regional affairs, followed by a spate of assertiveness to address the PKK's collaboration with several neighbors. This evolution has recently brought Turkey to the point of seeking positive change in the region through diplomacy and economic cooperation. The perception of the neighborhood has shifted to emphasize the benefits of active engagement in the region to promote positive change. As a result, Turkish discourse has become particularly reformist in relation to the broader Middle East, backed by concrete bilateral as well as multilateral roles.

Therefore, the evolution of Turkish society and democracy has brought Turkey visibly closer to Western European strategic culture, not necessarily by design but as an outcome of Turkey's military success in the fight against terrorism and the ensuing democratization and desecuritization drives at home. Currently, Turkish foreign policy gives prominence to multilateralism, while providing greater emphasis on regional conflict prevention and crisis management as well as international cooperation. A recent much-publicized example of Turkey's multilateralist emphasis was the Turkish insistence in 2002–2003 on a UN or other multilateral mandate for the invasion of Iraq. Nonetheless, the "Transatlantic Trends" survey shows that the Turkish public continues to display some distrust for external powers, including the allies. This is hardly surprising to a student of Turkish affairs. As Bilge Criss and Ali Karaosmanoğlu argued, "The fear of abandonment and fear of loss of territory became a major aspect of Turkish security culture in the (Ottoman) Empire and the same fears were inherited by the Republic."[38]

Turkey's foreign and security policies, like the underlying culture, thus display the characteristics of both Mars and Venus, to borrow Kagan's terminology again, and the two sides of the mythical god of openings and doors, Janus. On one side is the stipulation of forward defense, which is meant mainly against terrorism. On the other side is the emphasis on multilateralism. These policies were put forth in the 2000 Turkish Defense white paper.[39]

The white paper defines the objective of the national military strategy as "maintaining a military force that will provide a deterrent influence on the centers of risk and threat in the environment of instability and uncertainty surrounding Turkey." Against this background, the military strategy has been built on the four pillars of deterrence, military contribution to crisis management and intervention in crises, forward defense, and collective security. "Forward defense" is defined as determining as early as possible the scope of a probable aggression, and when subjected to an actual external aggression, stopping it. This refers to engagements across borders to fight terrorism. The forward defense concept as such was put to use in Turkey's military operations in northern Iraq against the PKK until a new state of affairs was established after the U.S. invasion of Iraq in 2003.

Regarding the "crises that concern Turkey's security," the white paper gives primacy to "the peaceful resolution of the disagreements in accordance with the diplomatic, economic and other crisis management measures" but also tasks the "Turkish Armed Forces to be ready to contribute to reducing tension, prevent tensions from transforming into armed conflicts and containing the aggressor." The paper also makes direct reference to the contribution of the Turkish armed forces in the international efforts by the United Nations and "alliances of which Turkey is a party" for the resolution of crises that threaten peace and stability. NATO thus continues to occupy a central place in Turkish defense policy, and Turkey has assigned almost all of the Turkish armed forces to NATO.

With the ongoing modernization plans of the Turkish armed forces, there is increasing alignment between strategic objectives and military capabilities, which is likely to increase further as these plans are implemented. Turkey's policy of military modernization should be understood in the context of the challenges it has faced in the recent past, particularly the embargoes that were either officially or de facto levied on Turkey in different instances. The U.S. embargo in the latter half of the 1970s, which ended abruptly with the Iranian revolution, was particularly sobering. As a result, for part of the Cold War the Turkish military—and therefore allied conventional military strength—depreciated. In retrospect, obviously U.S. faith in Iran as an alternative to Turkey was gravely misplaced.

The lesson learned from this embargo, as well as subsequent ones, has been that the Turkish defense industry needed to be bolstered to provide minimum self-sufficiency across the services. There have also been moves to diversify the supplier base as well as joint ventures for production and development of weapons in order to shield the country's defenses from the caprices of domestic politics in the United States and Europe. Although Turkey is still heavily reliant on foreign purchases and will perhaps always remain a net customer, there has been progress in domestic production and in diversity of suppliers even for relatively high-technology equipment.[40]

Turkish security culture may be both Venutian and Martian, thus mostly Earthly, but the strong pull of the EU cannot be denied. Successive progress reports by the European Commission dealing with Turkey's progress toward membership have observed that beyond a doubt Turkey has continued to position its foreign and security policies generally in line with that of the European Union. Yet it is not clear whether this positioning can truly be characterized as deliberate Europeanization in the sense of the downward transfer of policies from the EU to the candidate Turkey. While policy transfer is obvious in several reforms related to the democratization of Turkey and its dramatic and sustained political, economic, and legal reforms, similar influence is not openly discernible in foreign and security policies. This is true even with regard to issues with Greece or the Cyprus problem, which have become part of Turkey's accession process. Despite these issues bearing so much on Turkey's membership, a policy transfer onto Turkey has yet to happen, although Greece was able to upload its policy to the EU. Turkey's accession process does, however, produce an incentive for Turkey to align its policy with the EU. It may be argued that the current broad alignment was due in part to the Turkish foreign policy elite's choosing to broaden the bases of convergence with the EU in order to promote Turkey's bid to open accession talks.

At any rate, there is significant convergence in EU and Turkish positions at multinational forums. Thus, in 2004 Turkey joined some 87 percent of the various EU initiatives at forums such as the UN and the Organization for Security and Cooperation in Europe (OSCE). This figure was 89 percent in 2003, 80 percent in 2002 and 84 percent in 2001. In the specific case of the OSCE, Turkey's participation in EU statements has increased from 78 percent in 2001 to roughly 95 percent in 2004.[41] The European Commission observed in 2005 that "Turkey's record of alignment with EU sanctions and restrictive measures, statements, declarations and demarches continues to demonstrate the significant extent of convergence of EU-Turkey views."[42] Nonetheless, the commission could not refrain from also underscoring that "Turkey's overall record suggests that alignment has been somewhat selective from a geographical point of view with delays or lacunae observed as regards the Balkans, Asia (Burma) and Africa (Darfur)."[43]

While Turkey's alignment should be expected to grow, one should note that in general Turkey's value is precisely due to its differences. The strong geopolitical and strategic arguments that make the case for Turkey's EU membership also demonstrate the value of Turkey's foreign and security policies in the twenty-first century. The EU, while aiming to make use of Turkey's foreign policy assets and strategic weight, cannot reasonably aim to stifle them during the negotiation process. In fact, the EU should rather encourage Turkey to bring its own perspectives, game plans, interests and sensitivities, methods, and assets to the fore and engage in an exercise of policy convergence with Turkey. For instance, to the debate about democratization of the Muslim or Turkic world, Turkey can bring in the contribution of being Muslim and Turkic as well as European and Western. Trying to do that by itself, Turkey's resources and impact may be limited, but coalesced with the EU, the influence would be much greater. The end product may be a different one than what the current EU countries or even Turkey had in mind initially. But the policy outcomes from such an approach can be useful, and this very fact underlies the logic of Turkey's strategic importance as a unique force multiplier.

The current state of far-reaching congruence between the CFSP and Turkey's policies presents only a limited snapshot. If the relationship can be founded on a healthy ground, the potential Turkish-EU complementarities are significantly higher than what meets the eye. Accordingly, Michael Emerson and Nathalie Tocci have identified eleven major theaters of operation representing the core of common foreign and security concerns of both the EU and Turkey.[44] They have deemed that in the Balkans, the Black Sea, Central Asia, the Mediterranean, Russia, Iran, Saudi Arabia, and the Gulf, EU and Turkish foreign policies are convergent. In the Middle East they are increasingly convergent and complementary, whereas in the specific case of Iraq there may be special sensitivities concerning the Kurds and the Turkomans.

Building on these policy convergences, Emerson and Tocci conclude that Turkey and the EU can mutually reinforce each other's assets and capabilities: "Turkey has human resource assets that are complementary to those of the EU, with the cultural links and understanding of Eurasia and the Middle East that could in principle be deployed alongside the financial and technical resources of the EU." Furthermore, "Turkey has both military and police forces that could make major contributions to the headline goals of the EU for its security and defense policy, and especially by way of resources that could be effectively deployed in south-east Europe and the wider Middle East."[45]

The detailed assessment by Emerson and Tocci laying out the potential for further Turkish-EU convergence and synergy concurs with the point made by the president of the European Commission who stated that: "We in the EU are aware of the important benefits that Turkey's membership could bring to the European Union."[46] The fruit of this awareness should be more than launching accession negotiations with Turkey. It should go further and lead to awareness also that the greatest contributions of Turkey to regional and global peace, security, stability, and prosperity have yet to be elaborated.

This is nowhere more relevant than in Turkey's and the EU's own vicinity, a vast and diverse geography of tremendous strategic importance.

Notes

1. Phillip Zelikow, "The Transformation of National Security: Five Redefinitions" *The National Interest*, no. 71 (Spring 2003): 17.

2. Christopher Hill and William Wallace, "Introduction: Actors and Actions" in *The Actors in Europe's Foreign Policy*, ed. Christopher Hill (New York: Routledge, 1996), 8.

3. Mark Leonard, *Why Europe Will Run the 21st Century* (New York: Public Affairs, 2005); Joseph S. Nye Jr., *Soft Power: The Means to Succeed in World Politics* (New York: Public Affairs, 2004); Robert Kagan, *Of Paradise and Power: America and Europe in the New World Order* (New York: Vintage, 2004).

4. Johan P. Olsen, "The Many Faces of Europeanization" (ARENA Working Papers, WP 01/2). www.arena.uio.no/publications/wp02_2.htm.

5. Ernst B. Haas, *The Uniting of Europe: Political Social and Economic Forces, 1950–57* (Stanford, CA: Stanford University Press, 1968).

6. Leonard, *Why Europe*, 6.

7. Brian White, "Foreign Policy Analysis and the New Europe" in *Contemporary European Foreign Policy*, ed. Walter Carlsnaess, Helene Sjursen, and Brian White (London: Sage, 2004), 15.

8. Roy Ginsberg, *The European Union in International Politics: Baptism by Fire* (Lanham, MD: Rowman and Littlefield, 2001), 3.

9. White, "Foreign Policy Analysis," 11.

10. Christopher Hill, "Closing the Capabilities-Expectations Gap?" in *A Common Foreign Policy for Europe? Competing Visions of the CFSP*, ed. John Peterson and Helene Sjursen (London: Routledge, 1998), 18.

11. Claudio M. Radaelli, "The Europeanization of Public Policy," in *The Politics of Europeanisation*, ed. K. Featherstone and C. Radaelli (Oxford: Oxford University Press, 2002), 3.

12. Jordi Vaquer i Fanes, "Europeanisation and Foreign Policy" (Observatori de Politica Exterior Europa, Autonomous University of Barcelona, working paper no. 21, April 2001). http://selene.uab.es/_cs_iuee/catala/obs/m_working.html.

13. The text of the document, entitled "ESDP: Implementation of the Nice Provisions on the Involvement of the Non-EU European Allies" or Annex II of the 2002 Copenhagen Summit Presidency Conclusions can be found at: www.europa.eu.int/abc/doc/off/bull/en/200210/i1015.htm#anch0034.

14. Elizabeth Bomberg and John Peterson, "Policy Transfer and Europeanization: Passing the Heineken Test?" (paper for the Political Studies Association-UK 50th Annual Conference, April 10–13, 2000, London), p. 7.

15. Jose I. Torreblanca, "Ideas, Preferences and Institutions: Explaining the Europeanization of Spanish Foreign Policy" (Arena Working Papers, January 26, 2001). www.arena.uio.no/publications/working-papers2001/papers/wp01_26.htm

16. Torreblanca, "Ideas, Preferences and Institutions."

17. Torreblanca, "Ideas, Preferences and Institutions."

18. Torreblanca, "Ideas, Preferences and Institutions."

19. The analogy of Mars versus Venus was adopted by Kagan in *Of Paradise and Power* (Vintage, 2004), where he argued, among other things, that the United States and Europe have parted ways in terms of setting national priorities, determining threats and challenges, and foreign policy. To embellish his argument Kagan wrote that Europeans are from Venus and Americans from Mars.

20. The German Marshall Fund of the United States, "Transatlantic Trends 2005." www.transatlantictrends.org. The nine EU members that were covered by this survey included France, Germany, UK, Italy, Netherlands, Poland, Portugal, Slovakia, and Spain.

21. The Developing-8 or D-8 was established in Istanbul on June 15, 1997, at a summit of heads of state and government. The initiative aims to improve development cooperation among its members, which include alongside Turkey, Bangladesh, Egypt, Indonesia, Iran, Malaysia, Nigeria, and Pakistan.

22. David Barchard, "Relations between Turkey and the United Kingdom," (Memorandum to the UK Parliament, Select Committee on Foreign Affairs, January 2002).

23. German Marshall Fund, "Transatlantic Trends 2005."

24. A. D. Papagiannidis, "Greece May Slip Back to 1980s Style Euroscepticism," *Europe's World* 1, Autumn (2005).

25. For a discussion of Euro-scepticism in Turkey, see: Ayşe Güneş Ayata, "From Euro-scepticism to Turkey-scepticism: Changing Political Attitudes on the European Union," *Journal of Southern Europe and the Balkans* 5, no. 2 (August, 2003): 205–22.

26. Ziya Öniş, "Domestic Politics, International Norms and Challenges to the State: Turkey-EU Relations in the Post-Helsinki Era," *Turkish Studies* 4, no. 1 (Spring 2003): 9–34.

27. See: Hüseyin Bağcı and Ali Yıldız, "Turkey and the European Security and Defence Policy (ESDP): From Confrontational to Cooperative Relationship," in *The Europeanization of Turkey's Security Policy: Prospects and Pitfalls*, ed. A. L. Karaosmanoğlu and Seyfi Taşhan (Ankara: Dış Politika Enstitüsü, 2004).

28. Pınar Bilgin, "Clash of Cultures? Differences between Turkey and the European Union on Security," in *The Europeanization of Turkey's Security Policy: Prospects and Pitfalls*, ed. A. L. Karaosmanoğlu and Seyfi Taşhan (Ankara: Dış Politika Enstitüsü, 2004), 40.

29. For instance, the EU assessment in the field of Justice and Home Affairs stated that "with regard to corruption, the fight against drugs, organised crime,

money laundering and judicial cooperation in criminal and civil matter, efforts have been made to implement and apply the *acquis*."

30. For a Turkish view on the ESDI debate, see Ömür Orhun, "European Security and Defence Identity—Common European Security and Defence Policy: A Turkish Perspective," *Perceptions* 5, no. 3 (2000): 115–24.

31. For a discussion on the implications of the fight against PKK terrorism on Turkey's liberalization see Ersel Aydınlı, "Security and Liberalization: Decoding Turkey's Struggle with the PKK," *Security Dialogue* 33, no. 2 (2002): 209–25.

32. John D. Steinbrunner, *Principles of Global Security* (Washington, DC: The Brookings Institution, 2002), 146.

33. Christopher Coker, "Globalization and Insecurity in the Twenty-First Century: NATO and the Management of Risk" (Adelphi Paper 345, London: IISS, 2002), 52.

34. Ali L. Karaosmanoğlu, "Globalisation and Its Impact on Turkey's Security" in *The Europeanization of Turkey's Security Policy*, ed. Karaosmanoğlu and Taşhan, 11.

35. Karaosmanoğlu, "Globalisation and Its Impact," 12.

36. Ali L. Karaosmanoğlu, "The Evolution of the National Security Culture and the Military in Turkey," *Journal of International Affairs* 54, no. 1 (Fall 2000).

37. Bilgin, "Clash of Cultures?" 40.

38. Nur Bilge Criss and Ali L. Karaosmanoğlu, "Explaining Turkey's Alignment with NATO" (unpublished manuscript, reported in Bilgin, "Clash of Cultures?").

39. The full English text can be found at the Ministry of National Defense website: www.msb.gov.tr.

40. Concerning the Turkish defense industry strategies, see Namik Kemal Pak, "Changing Concepts of National Security in the Post–Cold War Era and Turkish Defence Industry," *Perceptions* 7, no. 2 (June–August 2002): 102–17.

41. These figures are based on the author's own estimations. However, the author believes they are in the ballpark.

42. The European Commission, "Turkey: Progress Report," Brussels, November 9, 2005, SEC (2005) 1426, 127.

43. European Commission, "Turkey: Progress Report," 127

44. Michael Emerson and Nathalie Tocci, "Turkey as a Bridgehead and Spearhead: Integrating EU and Turkish Foreign Policy" (EU-Turkey Working Papers No. 1, Brussels: Center for European Policy Studies, August 2004).

45. Emerson and Tocci, "Turkey as a Bridgehead," 28–29.

46. Romano Prodi, Speech at the Boğaziçi University in Istanbul, January 16, 2004.

CHAPTER FOUR

The Regional Imperative

The domestic public debates, including among intellectuals, particularly around the issue of Iraq, Lebanon, and the broader Middle East Initiative, have demonstrated that the question of whether Turkey should be more or less engaged in its neighborhood has yet to be fully resolved. Some are in favor of greater involvement to protect interests, while others advocate caution, fearing that Turkey could get entangled in the quagmires that several regional issues have indeed become.

Nonetheless, arguably, this debate is becoming increasingly anachronistic, given the fact that Turkey is already significantly immersed in regional politics and economics. Turkey is an active regional player, and there may be need for even more investment in regional policies.

Turkey's motives in this regard have frequently been questioned. For some, Turkey's historical baggage as the primary successor state of the Ottoman Empire, which ruled most of Turkey's neighborhood for centuries, causes unease. This discomfort presents itself mainly in terms of an ill-defined suspicion that Turkey might reestablish imperial politics. As a corollary, some contended that Turkey might use ethnic kinsmen to gain influence in neighboring countries. For others, as a secular and Western-oriented state, Turkey seems to be an alien element in its neighborhood, allegedly acting as a conduit for Western interests. Still others regard Turkey as a potential impediment to achieving regional leadership or realizing a specific national aspiration. In many cases, all or some of these perceptions coalesce. Whatever the putative reason, Turkey's regional activities have not been without opponents.

But this opposition has been changing dramatically in recent years. The change started in Turkey's western neighbors during the 1990s and was gradually carried into those in the east in the 2000s. Regional public opinion has been rapidly turning positive in recent years, with the media in several countries supporting Turkey's regional policies as well as its EU membership bid. As Ibrahim al-Maraishi observed:

> News media in Egypt has been supportive of Turkish attempts to foster peace between Palestinians and Israelis, a goal that Cairo actively seeks as well. The Iranian media, many agencies of which reflect official opinions in Tehran, has also pointed out that relations have improved between the two countries, especially in terms of trade. While Iraqi views were critical of Turkey's willingness to deploy troops in Iraq, all communities, including Arabs, Kurds and Turkmen, have expressed their desire for cooperation between Baghdad and Ankara in the future. Distrust in the region tends to arise when Turkey is deemed a partner to American initiatives in the Middle East. . . . Turkey can still play a positive role in the region, as long as it encourages reform through domestic dialogue, with local cultural characteristics in mind.[1]

On their part, the Turks have traditionally been expressive of the problems of their tough and volatile neighborhood. They display their own share of discomfort with the regional state of affairs and particularly the Near East. Even during the relatively more stable bipolar global order, Turkish sources were vocal in describing the difficulties faced by the country due to its geographic proximity to zones of confrontation, conflict, or instability.

Nevertheless, Turkish discourse appeared to be driven more by the urge to underscore Turkey's strategic importance to the West than by any activism to address regional problems. This was not surprising, given the confines of the Cold War and Turkey's own domestic problems and limited resources. Throughout the Cold War, Turkey conceptualized its foreign and security policy in tandem with the United States and the transatlantic alliance. The notable exceptions were policies toward Greece and the Cyprus problem, where distinctly national stances were taken by successive Turkish governments, owing to the virtually exclusive representation of the Greek side in international public opinion and organizations.

Turkey was ill prepared for the 1990s. The Cold War order dissipated too quickly, the long-contained but deeply brewing regional security threats and challenges flared too abruptly, and Europe veered away too unexpectedly. Gone in a blitz was almost everything that Turkey had taken for granted in the preceding four decades. The collapse of the Warsaw Pact and the Soviet Union, the first Gulf War, Balkan tragedies, Germany's reunification and

European integration's gallop toward former Warsaw Pact countries, the reemergence of the Caucasus and Central Asia, Azeri-Armenian war, the surge of PKK terrorism, and several other developments produced tectonic shifts in a time frame of little over half a decade.

Following the demise of the more or less stable Cold War framework, Turkey found itself virtually trapped in a difficult geographical location,[2] unaided by increasing disagreements among its NATO allies and its own near solitude in the fight against PKK terrorism. The EU was absorbed by its integration and enlargement in a way that for all intents and purposes excluded Turkey. Europe's security focus was almost exclusively on the raging Balkan conflicts. Turkey noted with deep distaste what it saw as a lack of solidarity displayed by several European allies before, during, and after the first Gulf War. When hundreds of thousands of Kurds fled Iraq toward Turkey in a matter of days and weeks in 1991, Turkey's ability to provide food and shelter was stretched to the limit. Not only that, but Turkey was left out in the cold, with almost no other country taking in refugees and sharing the burden. Instead, the shortcomings of the Turkish relief effort along the Iraqi mountains bordering Turkey was heavy-handedly criticized in European and American media. While no country had done nearly as much to shelter the fleeing Kurds, the shortcomings of the Turkish relief effort were misrepresented as a manifestation of hostility toward the Kurds. Turkey fell short also in the task of explaining its side of the story, thereby contributing to such generalizations taking hold. The work half done in the first Gulf War left Saddam Hussein's government intact and northern Iraq basically turned into a camp for terrorism and secessionism.

Although siding with its traditional Western allies after Iraq's invasion of Kuwait in August 1990, following the war, Turkey's gigantic losses were scarcely compensated. The PKK terror increased in the 1990s due to the power vacuum created in northern Iraq right across Turkey's border. In addition, there were massive economic losses because Iraq had been a major trading partner. As Bill Park explains, "Turkey had enjoyed broadly cooperative economic and political relations with Iraq both before and since the 1990-1 Gulf War. However, as a result of this war, the consequent closure of the Kirkuk-Yumurtalik pipeline to Turkey's Mediterranean coast, and the subsequent sanctions and impoverishment of Iraq, Turkey had lost its major trading partner in the region and a lucrative source of revenue. Downturns in tourism, foreign investment and general economic confidence in the wake of the 1990-1 Gulf War inflicted further (though largely indirect) blows to the already weak national economy. Furthermore, promises of compensation for Turkey's war losses had failed to fully materialize."[3]

Throughout early 1990s the question was asked in and outside Turkey: Why was the country not intervening to protect the Bosnian Muslims from crimes against humanity? As irrational as the expectation was, in retrospect it was not altogether irrelevant. We now learn that Greeks and Russians were aiding fellow Eastern Orthodox Serbs in their massacres. Quoting from the *New York Times*: "During the Bosnian war, Greek companies shipped oil to the Bosnian Serbs and to Serbian dominated Yugoslavia, in violation of the United Nations economic embargo. Greek arms merchants got weapons to the Serbian forces, in violation of the arms embargo. When the Bosnian Serbs attacked the United Nations 'safe area' of Srebrenica . . . Greek mercenaries fought with them and raised the blue and white Greek flag triumphantly when the enclave fell."[4] This was the same Srebrenica where seven thousand Muslim men, women, and children were murdered. In turn, Muslims from various countries were coming in, albeit belatedly, to fight on the side of Bosnian Muslims. All this time, the Turkish policy was restrained and in sync with the West.

Although Turkey followed a policy that was closely aligned with Europe vis-à-vis the Balkan conflicts and the first Gulf War, this appeared to win close to no appreciation and produced no rewards for Turkey in terms of its relations with the EU. It did not prevent the EU from eviscerating earlier arrangements between Turkey and the Western European Union while new EU security and defense structures were being built.

Relieved of Cold War constraints, Europe was dashing ahead in redefining European integration, leaving out Turkey. Therefore, the lessons of the early 1990s implied that Turkey's efforts to maintain the Cold War framework of unqualified subscribing to Western policies would not insulate Turkey from its unstable neighborhood. The visible erosion of cohesion within the NATO alliance and the growing discord among the transatlantic partners also contributed to a growing recognition among the Turks that Turkey must on its own make greater efforts to stabilize its neighborhood in order to cushion its security as well as its economic and political interests.

From the outset it was obvious that Turkey did not have the means to effect conflict resolution or benign change by itself, nor did it have the political clout to organize a coalition effort. Except for the brief spell of euphoria at the reemergence of the Turkic world on the ruins of the Soviet Union, Turks have not been lured by grandiose designs or unrealistic aspirations. Instead, through the 1990s Turkey has redefined its regional policies to complement those of the United States. Whether in the Balkans, the Middle East, or the Caucasus and Central Asia, Turkey and the United States were successful in carving out a collaborative policy framework that appealed to both countries.

This has yielded several concrete strategic products that benefited both the global superpower and the emerging regional power. Probably the best example has been the Baku-Tblisi-Ceyhan oil pipeline, which required considerable efforts by the United States and Turkey to make an initially contested idea a success story. The pipeline was completed in 2006 and stands as one of the best strategic projects that the United States and Turkey have successfully undertaken.

Similarly, U.S. and other allied aircraft based at a Turkish air base in Incirlik enforced the no-fly zone, protecting the Kurds of Iraq against the Saddam Hussein regime. The Iraqi Kurds, who owe their peace and prosperity in no little degree to Turkey's hosting of the coalition aircraft and its active role in quelling infighting among the Kurds in northern Iraq, nonetheless were first to show public ingratitude immediately before and after the war in 2003. That said, it might be argued that its role in protecting the Kurds until 2003 gave Turkey leverage in the subsequent developments in Iraq. Whether Turkey has been able to exploit this leverage in full is another point.

At the same time, by aligning its policies broadly with the United States, Turkey has been able to develop multiregional perspectives and some headroom to implement them. Since the 1930s, with notable exceptions, Turkey did not possess the intellectual, diplomatic, or economic interest to design and implement proactive regional policies. Several regional ventures such as the Central Treaty Organization or its precursor, the Baghdad Pact, were not Turkish ideas, and the fact that they were ultimately abortive did little to boost Turkish interest in regional efforts. To the contrary, the most popular and commercially most beneficial regional engagement occurred during the 1980–1988 Iran-Iraq war, where Turkey refused to take sides between the Saddam Hussein government and the Iranian revolutionaries. Turkey's so-called "active neutrality" policy avoided long-term acrimony, while significantly increasing trade revenues with both these countries.

The 1990s, on the other hand, saw the emergence of distinctively Turkish ideas for cooperation in the region. Indicative were the meetings begun in Istanbul in 1993 to promote economic cooperation among Black Sea countries. This process, which later was upgraded to a full-fledged international organization, the Black Sea Economic Cooperation Organization (BSECO), brought together not only Turkey and Russia—two centuries-old presumed adversaries—but also Armenia and Azerbaijan. In a hopeful olive-branch gesture, Turkey also invited Greece into this endeavor. Through a panoply of regional initiatives, Turkish diplomacy accumulated significant expertise in regional cooperation throughout the 1990s. Its efforts were not as effective in ameliorating the image of the Balkans or the Black Sea region, but regional countries were able to tag along with the pan-European blossoming of cooperation networks.[5]

Concomitantly, the Turkish intellectual scene started to produce regional thinking that rose above narrow nationalistic or paternalistic conceptions, although the debate involved just about every point of view. This new thinking, which has been taking shape since the 1990s, was supported by growing Turkish recognition of the need for Turkey to play a greater role in regional affairs and an effort to identify Turkey's potential assets beyond military power. One influential idea has been furnished by Ahmet Davutoğlu, who argued that Turkey is particularly well equipped to benefit from engagement in the surrounding geopolitical basins while contributing to regional relations through the country's rich history and geographic location.[6] Accordingly, Turkey's soft assets, including historical insight and cultural affinities, could be harnessed to policy instruments to yield a positive Turkish influence in the region. Thanks to these assets, Turkey has a "strategic depth" that is not being put to full use due to ideological and identity consciousness restraints. This idea managed to break through traditional analyses of geopolitics that are based on conventional attributes of power, which ultimately make limited policy sense for a midsize regional power like Turkey. The concept of "strategic depth" opened the intellectual door for a more thorough assessment and utilization of Turkey's nonmilitary assets in foreign policy.

Therefore, despite the remaining wariness among Turkish political, military, and intellectual elites, there is also an increased sensibility to follow active diplomacy to promote a benign regional framework that would not only better protect Turkish interests but also help alleviate regional problems, in most of which Turkey is not directly involved. In addition to security considerations, this new thinking is also supported and influenced by the explosion of economic and social links with neighboring countries, including at the grassroots level.

Consequently, although Turkey may vacillate between more introverted and extroverted positions in the period ahead, overall, Turkey's future regional policies are likely to be shaped by its broadening spectrum of civilian assets. Turkey can ill afford isolationist tendencies. It inhabits a neighborhood that it cannot ignore, no matter how much it may wish to.

Official Turkish discourse is replete with explicit pronouncements of the new regional emphasis. Prime Minister Erdoğan suggested that "Turkey does not confine itself in this respect in a strict sense to the framework of national interest alone, but rather pursues a pro-active foreign policy aimed at contributing to regional and global peace and security, and encourages as well as activates regional cooperation initiatives."[7] Similarly, Foreign Minister Abdullah Gül has argued that Turkey "must quickly overcome the psychology of confrontation based on the presumption that we are surrounded by enemies,

and we must rather adopt the psychology of a founding actor of an environment of cooperation and dialogue in our neighborhood."[8] As explained
above, these statements do not imply a radical break but a state policy in the
making, albeit with some trial and error, since the early 1990s.

Turkey's hesitating approach toward regional affairs has been incremen-
tally overtaken, owing to the call of its interests. Turkish policies contained
both military and nonmilitary diplomacy in the 1990s as Turkey emerged as
an active player in regional affairs. With the end of the Soviet Union, Turkey
discovered interests and affinities throughout Europe, Central Asia, and the
Middle East that had been effectively unaccounted for in mainstream Turkish foreign policy thinking. Indeed, as Ian Lesser observed, since the 1990s
Turkey has experienced a "sweeping enlargement of the country's external
horizons. The notion that Turkey's interests and potential influence stretch
from the Balkans to western China has proven quite realistic, even if some
of the early assumptions about Ankara's role in the newly independent Turkic republics of Central Asia proved somewhat overblown."[9]

In addition to the surge in political relations with the countries of Central
Asia as well as Azerbaijan and Georgia, there was an explosion of business
connections and investments. The vacillations and unfocused rush that
marked the early Turkish approach to these regions gradually settled into a
realistic policy that aimed to help consolidate the independence of these
countries as well as their integration into the international community. This
policy was accompanied by massive economic investment and sociocultural
exchanges. In the 2000s, Turkey has also begun to carefully assert the need
for democratization in the Turkic world.

Turkey's increased regional sensibilities particularly concerned the Middle
East, a constant source of insecurity for Turkey, and always perceived more in
terms of risks than opportunities. In the 1990s, a key foreign policy move was
the intensification of Turkish-Israeli defense and intelligence cooperation.[10]
As Sabri Sayari notes,

> The signing of a military training and education agreement in 1996 created a for-
> midable new alignment between the region's two militarily strongest states, which
> had important ramifications for regional balances of power. The Israeli-Turkish
> agreement was not conceived as a formal alliance and both countries repeatedly
> stressed that it was not directed against third parties. Nevertheless, one of Turkey's
> principal motives was to send a signal to Syria about the increased security risks
> of pursuing adversarial policies, especially its continued support for the PKK.[11]

Turkish-Israeli cooperation was developed adamantly under protests from
Arab neighbors, who had little to offer in its place and instead had been

unsympathetic and occasionally hostile toward Turkey's political and regional concerns. Over time, however, the initial adversity toward Turkish-Israeli military cooperation thinned in the Arab countries and came to be increasingly accepted.

At the same time, Turkish security policy in northern Iraq involved active engagement. This included cross-border military hot-pursuit operations to fight PKK terrorists who exploited the no-man's-land formed after Baghdad's defeat in the first Gulf War. In the process, the Turkish military has developed one of the best-trained and experienced low-intensity warfare capabilities in NATO.[12] The Turkish experience was particularly pertinent with regard to containing and combating terrorism in a democratic, pluralistic environment.[13]

Turkish foreign policy was equally active and should be credited for reconciling the violent competition and rivalry between the Patriotic Union of Kurdistan and the Kurdistan Democratic Party in northern Iraq. There were reports that since 1992, leaders of both groups were given Turkish diplomatic protection, which facilitated their interaction with the outside world.[14] Whether through the Ankara accords of 1996 or the 1998 Washington meeting, Turkey and the United States have actively promoted conciliation between these two feuding Kurdish groups. Accordingly, the statement issued at the 1998 Washington meeting underscored that the Patriotic Union of Kurdistan and the Kurdistan Democratic Party "recognize the irreplaceable role our separate consultations in Ankara and London played in making these talks a success."[15]

In 1996, Turkey and Greece went through a dangerous crisis over disputed territories in the Aegean Sea on top of other long-standing disagreements related, inter alia, to the delimitation of their respective territorial waters, airspace, and continental shelf and the demilitarization of specific Aegean islands. When Greece took the step of landing its military forces on one of the disputed twin Kardak/Imia islets, Turkey responded with a military operation of its own that effectively embarrassed the hard-liners in Greece. However, the crisis was defused without an actual clash. Following Turkey's reciprocal action, the two governments agreed to disentangle, the United States playing a key supportive role.

Another important event was the 1998 crisis with Syria, during which Turkey threatened to use force against Syria unless it stopped sheltering the PKK and expelled its leader, Abdullah Öcalan.[16] Syria complied with Turkish demands. The importance of this Turkish move can hardly be overstated.[17] The determined stance left no room for the continuation of the Syrian policy to support the PKK, which was exposed beyond doubt despite

Syria's assurances to the contrary. Syrian compliance brought about a watershed in bilateral relations between the two long-standing adversaries.

After being expelled from Syria, Öcalan set out on a long journey to a number of countries, including Italy and Russia. Turkey also issued a warning to Greece to stop supporting the PKK. When Turkey deployed full and determined diplomatic pressure with U.S. support, it became obvious that hostile policies toward Turkey could not be maintained with impunity. The fugitive terrorist leader, known in Turkey as the "baby killer," ended his run in Kenya, where he was captured exiting the Greek embassy and was brought back to Turkey by Turkish special forces. He was reportedly carrying a fake passport belonging to a Greek Cypriot journalist.[18]

This event proved fateful for Greek policies toward Turkey which, like the Syrian policies, were exposed as bankrupt. The resignation of three ministers from the cabinet[19] and the subsequent court cases heralded that a new Greek policy was in the making in place of hysterical animosity against Turkey.

In the wake of those successes of power politics, Turkey demonstrated maximum restraint and responsibility with regard to both Syria and Greece, both of which were caught red-handed in their dealings with the PKK terrorist organization. Turkey followed up with active diplomacy, which aimed to chart a new and benign course for bilateral, neighborly relations with both countries. When the two neighbors responded in kind, a new dawn broke in relations.[20] Particularly with Greece, people-to-people as well as business contacts intensified, helping to sustain a positive political *modus vivendi*. This helped calm occasionally irrational tempers that existed on both sides of the Aegean, while deferring the solution of more essential differences on a set of issues that had brought them to the brink of armed confrontation more than once over the past decades.

There seem to be sufficient incentives for both countries to maintain this *modus vivendi* and build a lasting peace. The Greek policy toward Turkey, engineered by Costas Simitis and George Papandreu, facilitated by Bülent Ecevit and Ismail Cem, and continued with subsequent Greek and Turkish governments, also recognizes that friendly relations achieve greater security and prosperity benefits for both sides. The economic relations and tourism exchanges have developed significantly since 1999, and this can help increase the willingness on both sides to sustain pacific approaches toward each other.

It is possible that the current exploratory talks between the Greek and Turkish Foreign Ministries, or potential future extensions of these talks, could ultimately yield results as confidence between the parties builds, a sense of interdependency takes root, and an empathy develops regarding the

other side's interests and viewpoints. Greece appears cognizant of the benefits of keeping Turkey on the EU track and would have little to gain by forcing Turkey's hand. But judging by its track record, one cannot rule out future
temptations to abuse the fact that Greece is a member of the EU while
Turkey is not.

Turkish regional activism has not been based solely on power politics. Instead, in the 1990s Turkey also emerged as a multilateral actor. It contributed
tangibly to multinational peace support operations in the Balkans and extended reconstruction help to the affected countries.[21] Turkey was the first
state to recognize the independence of all the former Soviet states. In Central Asia, Turkey has established the foundations for greater influence in the
region with relatively significant trade relations, energy projects, people-to-
people contacts, and a regular process of summits among Turkish-speaking
countries. Turkey was also actively engaged in the Arms Control and Regional Security group in the now defunct multilateral track of the Middle
East Peace Process.

At the same time, Turkey pioneered a number of regional cooperation endeavors that culminated in such hitherto unimaginable and novel successes
as the South East Europe Defense Ministerial process, the Multinational
Peace Force for South East Europe, the Black Sea Economic Cooperation Organization, and the BLACKSEAFOR, an on-call naval task force involving
all of Black Sea coastal states including Russia. Despite economic difficulties,
a devastating earthquake, a ring of hostile neighbors, and regional instabili-
ties and wars, Turkey was able to stick its neck out and get noticed as a significant player. The United States was already cognizant and fairly supportive of this role, and the EU, with whom Turkey had suspended political
dialogue by 1997 due to the EU's failure to recognize Turkey as a candidate,
followed suit just before the decade ended.

By the end of 1999, the EU Helsinki Summit had recognized Turkey as a
candidate destined to join the European Union on the same terms as other
candidates. In the same year, an influential study depicted Turkey as a "pivotal state" that has the potential to have a significant beneficial or harmful
effect on its region.[22] The concept of a pivotal state, as defined by Robert
Chase, Emily Hill, and Paul Kennedy and applied to the Turkish case by
Alan Makovsky, raised the specter that Turkey could exert good or bad influence on the region, depending on how Turkey itself develops domestically.
Subsequent debates argued in both directions. A negative interpretation was
suggested by Michael Robert Hickok, who observed that Turkey had the necessary attributes to become an independent player in regional affairs but
feared it becoming a potential regional hegemon, exerting influence in all its

neighboring regions.[23] Hickok went so far as to claim that "the growing un-predictability of Turkish security policy, coupled with Ankara's increased mil-itary strength relative to its neighbors, contributes to regional instability."[24]

This latter assertion was in stark contrast to the perceptions of the Turks, who rather saw their policy as one that effectively eliminated some of the sources of regional instability. Hickok was apparently concerned that while Turkey showed activism in regional affairs and engaged in a robust military modernization program, its democratic reforms were lagging and nationalism appeared to be on the rise in domestic politics. He also noted a disparity be-tween objectives and actual capabilities. However, the subsequent sweeping democratic reforms and continued military modernization have effectively nullified his argument.

By the 2000s, Turkey further intensified diplomatic efforts to address its regional security and stability concerns and went on to develop the seeds of multilateral and bilateral cooperation it had planted in the 1990s. In this context, together with now befriended Greece, Turkey has joined a four-party effort to advance the membership in NATO of Bulgaria and Romania, who have made this the primary objective of their foreign and security poli-cies. This process was greatly aided by the Turkish Parliament, which asked the Turkish government to support the Bulgarian and Romanian bids.

Turkish policy toward Iraq immediately before and since the 2003 war in-volved initiating a regional dimension including all neighbors of Iraq as well as Egypt. Bilateral relations with Syria, Iran, and Greece also continued to expand and improve. Turkey tried to strike a balance between acting as a good neighbor but nonetheless warning the Iranian and Syrian governments regarding their duties as responsible actors on the international scene. This was manifest in Turkey's clear messages to Iran that Ankara is opposed to Iran developing nuclear weapons. Emphasizing the diplomatic option, Turkey supported the efforts of the three European heavyweights, Britain, France, and Germany, to bring about a peaceful resolution to the international con-cerns about the Iranian nuclear program. Turkey also asked Syria to withdraw from Lebanon and cooperate fully in the UN-led investigation of the murder of the former Lebanese Prime Minister Hariri. The good relations with Israel were maintained and revitalized quickly after a brief period of coldness asso-ciated with public unease over the pre-disengagement security operations in the Gaza Strip. Following a visit by some Hamas leaders to Ankara in the wake of that party's election victory in early 2006, Turkey moved quickly to reaffirm its position to support the Palestinian president, Mahmoud Abbas, who visited Ankara in May 2006. Turkish president Ahmet Necdet Sezer and Prime Minister Olmert and Foreign Minister Livni of Israel also exchanged visits, underscoring the diplomatic traffic between two friendly countries. Although the plans to sell Turkish fresh water to Israel was cancelled by the latter due to commercial reasons, the two countries immediately embarked on exploring other new avenues of cooperation, particularly in providing natural gas through underwater pipelines from Turkey to Israel with extensions to Palestine, Jordan, and Lebanon.[25]

In Cyprus, Turkey's active diplomacy was credited for the emergence of a window of opportunity for a solution to this persistent problem based on the plan sponsored by UN Secretary General Kofi Annan. The hopes were shattered, however, by the Greek Cypriot referendum that flatly rejected the international plan in April 2004. The result of the Greek Cypriot vote was brought about under the negative influence of their president and the rather maladroit EU and U.S. policy to pressure the Turkish Cypriot side to accept the UN-brokered deal to resolve the Cyprus dispute while giving a free hand to the Greek Cypriot side of the island, even allowing them to join the EU after they rejected the UN plan.

Moving to the east, Turkey has consistently enjoyed warm relations with both Azerbaijan and Georgia. Relations with Azerbaijan are particularly warm, as described by the popular and shared motto "one nation, two states." Turkey has also lent solid and consistent support to Georgia's territorial integrity and resolution of its frozen conflicts. Black Sea and Caucasus countries that wanted to join NATO and the EU have enjoyed Turkey's support, as well as significant resources and opportunities for training and education, both bilaterally and under the Partnership for Peace (PfP) program. Turkey also advocated the inclusion of the Caucasus republics in the EU's European Neighborhood Policy when the initiative was first launched without their participation.

Although Turkey recognized Armenia's independence along with Azerbaijan's and Georgia's, Ankara continues not to establish formal diplomatic relations with Armenia. Nevertheless, Armenian diplomats regularly attend BSECO meetings in Istanbul and even maintain a resident representative there. While Turkey also keeps the border with Armenia closed, one can see many Turkish products in Yerevan, reportedly coming in through Georgia and Iran. There are bus and flight services between Turkey and Armenia, and significant numbers of Armenian laborers come to Turkey for employment. While relations between these two neighbors can change for the better in the time ahead, it will require Armenia to take steps toward recognizing Turkey's borders, ending the invasion of Azerbaijani territories and agreeing to set up a joint commission to research historical events, instead of actively seeking interventions by parliaments in third countries. Further democratization and positive encouragement by Armenian diasporas, particularly in the United States, France, and Russia, can contribute in this regard, although admittedly little is to be expected in the short term. Meanwhile, Turkey has also initiated meetings among Turkish, Azeri, and Armenian foreign ministers in a bid to build confidence. An informal dialogue was also launched between Ankara and Yerevan at expert level. These meetings and a joint commission of scholars proposed by Turkey to study historical events may present an opportunity to overcome this anachronistic problem between Turkey and Armenia.

In terms of regional policy, a subject of vital importance is Turkey's relationship with Russia. Since Czar Ivan III sent a diplomatic delegation to the Ottoman Empire in the 1490s, the Russians and the Turks have spent some twenty-three years in direct conflict and wars.[26] Unlike the borders with Iran, which have remained more or less the same since the 1639 Kasr-i Sirin Treaty, the Ottoman-Russian border was in flux, particularly during the Ottoman Empire's final century. Despite the nascent Soviet Russia's support for the Turkish War of Independence in the early 1920s, in the immediate wake of the Yalta Conference in 1945, Soviet Foreign Minister Vyacheslav Molotov laid claims on Turkish territory and demanded a base in the Turkish straits, a constant Russian obsession in the history of their relations. Soviet territorial and ideological expansionism was a factor that triggered Turkey's alliance with the United States, which continues to date.

After the collapse of the Soviet Union and the liberation of the Caucasian countries, the Russian Federation, for the first time in centuries, no longer had common borders with Turkey. In the post–Cold War era, the Russian Federation's initial reflexes continued to display suspicion and hostility toward Turkey, especially in view of Turkey's active engagement in Central Asia and the Caucasus and its staunch alliance with the United States. By 1996, the White Book of Russian Special Services, which might be regarded as a catalog of official security policy in Russia or at least an indication of the viewpoint of the security community in the country, presented Turkey as a "massive security challenge" that might move into the geostrategic niche in the Caucasus created by Russia's weakening state.[27] However, by the 2000s Russian perceptions of Turkey evolved "from a geopolitical challenger to a valuable partner."[28] In addition to Turkey's realism and restraint with regard to the Caucasus and Central Asia, sprawling economic relations have been playing an instrumental role in its dealings with Russia. In 2004, the trade volume between Turkey and Russia amounted to $11 billion, and it is expected to increase to $25 billion by 2007. The Russian Federation has risen to the rank of Turkey's second-largest trading partner after Germany. Turkey has also invested $1.5 billion in Russia, particularly, but not confined to, the construction sector. To complement the economic and commercial relations as well as people-to-people contacts, the two countries signed the "Joint Action Plan for Cooperation between Turkey and the Russian Federation in Eurasia" in 2001, thus launching a strategic dialogue on regional issues of mutual concern.

Since then, the two countries have defined their relationship as a multidimensional partnership, as suggested by the subtitle of the 2001 Joint Action Plan, "From Bilateral Cooperation towards Multidimensional Partnership." The premise of the Joint Action Plan was that fundamental changes in the world provided opportunities for developing fruitful bilateral and regional cooperation in the spirit of friendship and mutual trust. The document underlined that the two parties agreed to extend their good relations and political consultations in the field of economic cooperation to the Eurasian dimension. The plan also expressed the belief that their dialogue and cooperation in Eurasia would contribute to bringing about peaceful, just, and lasting political solutions to disputes in the region. Since then, regular high-level political dialogue has gained momentum alongside economic relations, including in the energy sector. Concomitantly, several Russian dignitaries have started to promote the idea of a Turkish-Russian common Eurasian identity and arguably managed to recruit some support from intellectual circles in Turkey, particularly in view of the discontent with European and more recently U.S. policies.

Therefore, Igor Torbakov argued that despite "longer-term competing agendas, Moscow is now more open to cooperation with Turkey in the Caucasus, and Turkey is becoming more adept at framing its involvement in the region in a way that does not offend other countries' sensibilities."[29] A more accurate explanation would include the fact that through deliberately targeted moves, Turkish diplomacy has increased Russian confidence enough to adopt a benign stance vis-à-vis Turkey, although its firm policies regarding the independence and territorial integrity of the ex-Soviet and ex–Warsaw Pact countries, NATO enlargement, and alliances with the United States and the EU remain. Carefully handling the relationship of the United States with Russia, despite occasional open criticisms targeted at Russian domestic policies, has also facilitated the development in Turkish-Russian relations.

As what goes on between Turkey and Russia has traditionally been important in setting the tone in the Black Sea basin, in the Caucasus, and more recently to some extent in Central Asia, Turkey's principled but friendly stance has contributed significantly to the regional climate. Any progress in the resolution of frozen conflicts or in addressing regional challenges is contingent on maintaining such a favorable environment. Fiona Hill has argued that "after centuries of imperial competition, frequent wars, and Cold War rivalry, a rapprochement and a pragmatic, stable economic and political partnership between Turkey and Russia in Eurasia would be tantamount to the reconciliation of France and Germany after the Second World War in Europe. It would change the nature of conflicts in the South Caucasus that have often been shaped by Russian and Turkish enmity. And it would open up prospects for economic development and integration in the Caucasus and elsewhere in Eurasia."[30] That appears to be a goal that both the EU and United States could and do support.

Countries that have been even less privileged in their twentieth-century relations with Russia continue to display deep distrust for the country. While Turkey sympathizes with their concerns and has actively promoted their membership in NATO in order to anchor them in this secure alliance, it nonetheless appears committed to a policy of engagement and cooperation in lieu of unfruitful confrontation with the vastly important Russia, which is now bracing for the post-Putin era.

Although Turkey and the Russian Federation are no longer neighbors, and that fact perhaps affords the Turks some luxury, the two countries are still neighbors over the expanse of the Black Sea. As Stephen Larrabee has noted, "One of the toughest issues facing Western policy makers in developing a Euro-Atlantic strategy towards the Black Sea region is how to deal with Russia."[31] The fact of the matter is that after a more or less static region during the Cold War, the Black Sea or perhaps more accurately the wider Black Sea region has been undergoing profound transformation. As Borys Tarasyuk has observed: "In a relatively short period of time the Black Sea area has evolved into a priority region for the world's leading powers and major international and regional structures. Enlargement by NATO and the European Union has turned the region into a zone of vital concern for the West."[32] In 1989 all littoral states except the NATO member Turkey were in the Warsaw Pact. By 2006, there are three littoral states in NATO, with the inclusion of Bulgaria and Romania; all countries of the region are members of the Euro-Atlantic Partnership Council; and two among them are linked to NATO through special arrangements, namely the NATO-Russia Council and the NATO-Ukraine Commission. The wider Black Sea region has become critical also for the EU, given that Bulgaria and Romania are slated to join by 2007 or 2008 and Turkey by 2015. The democratic wave surely has reached the wider Black Sea region, and this momentum has to be maintained and the goal of democratic peace for the region internationally supported.

This of course cannot be done in a single stroke; it requires a multidimensional effort. Different initiatives will need to be advanced in tandem.

Whether in terms of assuring the irreversibility of the progress toward democratic peace or consolidating security in the wider Black Sea region, there is a need to advance both regional and Euro-Atlantic and European cooperation.

The resolution of the hard security challenges, such as ethnic conflicts and territorial secessionism, as in South Ossetia, Abkhazia, Trans-Dniester, and Nagorno-Karabakh, require upgraded international engagement. However, the soft security agenda is broader. It is composed of both the potential spillover effects of these hard security challenges into soft security risks and other asymmetric threats and illicit activities. Whereas the Black Sea for now only witnesses isolated and sporadic activities of this kind, unless deterrent action is taken, they may increase and transform. In this regard, regional cooperation is crucial, and the fact that all maritime zones in the Black Sea are delineated either as territorial waters or as Exclusive Economic Zones only emphasizes this point.

As the country with the longest shores, possessing the straits that are the only entry point, and having the most maritime traffic in the Black Sea, Turkey has a major stake in the security and prosperity of the region. Against this background, Turkey has been playing a lead role in economic and political cooperation since the early 1990s and in regional security cooperation since the late 1990s. The two crown jewels of regional military cooperation have been the Balkan regional brigade (SEEBRIG) and the BLACK-SEAFOR. Following three years of negotiation launched in 1998, the BLACKSEAFOR was created in 2001 as an on-call naval task force comprising all littoral states. Since then, it has been activated several times. After the years of formation, since the Ankara meeting in January 2004, the objective is to render this force fully operational in combating asymmetrical threats such as terrorism and the proliferation of weapons of mass destruction. Already a joint "Maritime Risk Assessment in the Black Sea" paper agreed to in Kyiv in March 2005 provided a basis for the BLACKSEAFOR role. The tasks of denying potential terrorists the maritime area and disrupting illegal activity can be sufficiently fulfilled by that force, provided that the parties endow it with operational capability.

In the meantime, Turkey launched Operation Black Sea Harmony on March 1, 2004, to conduct maritime surveillance operations against suspect vessels mostly in the western Black Sea. The operation is closely linked with NATO's Operation Active Endeavor in the Mediterranean, thanks to the exchange of maritime security information and the shadowing and trailing of contacts of interest coming from the Mediterranean. While the operation has contributed to the security of all Black Sea traffic, for Turkey, Black Sea Harmony was only the precursor to a regional effort. Accordingly, Turkey has extended invitations to the littoral navies to join Black Sea Harmony. While Ukraine, followed by Russia, accepted as of 2005, the two new NATO allies, Romania and Bulgaria, as well as Georgia, were yet to follow suit as of mid-2006.

On the other hand, the Black Sea's major region-building enterprise since early 1990s has been the Black Sea Economic Cooperation Organization, although its full potential has yet to be fulfilled. The EU's contribution in this respect could be enormous, but it is consistently wanting. The United States, as an observer since 2005, could also provide a significant boost to this promising framework of regional cooperation.

A significant opportunity was missed in June 2003 when the Greek presidency decided not to allow the issue of institutional cooperation between the EU and BSECO to be brought to the table.[33] However, as Greece will be joined by Bulgaria and Romania, and eventually by Turkey in the Union, the EU will inevitably be a Black Sea power, with significant economic benefits to all sides. Overall, the strategy for the Black Sea must include support for the resolution of conflicts, democratization, economic integration, and regional cooperation building. Turkey's efforts to promote cooperation among littoral states should also be considered and supported in this vein.

Turkey forms the southern borders of the Black Sea region, and Central Asia is geographically farther away, but the distance is offset in a way by a common heritage in linguistic and ethnic roots. Separated by a Russian and Soviet curtain for centuries, Turkey rediscovered these kinsmen in the early 1990s. Thus, Turkey was first to recognize the newly independent Central Asian countries and to open embassies. In the ensuing reciprocal high-level contacts, some five hundred bilateral and multilateral agreements have been concluded with Turkmenistan, Uzbekistan, Kazakhstan, and Kyrgyzstan. By 2005, summits of Turkish-speaking states brought the leaders of Turkey, Turkmenistan, Uzbekistan, Kazakhstan, Kyrgyzstan, and Azerbaijan together in a multilateral format seven times. In their initial years after independence, Turkey has tried to facilitate their interaction with the rest of the world and vigorously advocated their membership in international organizations including the OSCE, the Economic Cooperation Organization (ECO) and the Euro-Atlantic Partnership Council (EAPC). Economic cooperation surged in the past decade, with more than one thousand Turkish firms investing approximately $3.5 billion in the region. The total trade volume of $565 million in 2001 increased to $1 billion in 2003. Relations were also intensive in the fields of education and culture. Turkey has extended more than ten thousand scholarships to students from these countries since 1992, in addition to technical assistance and training opportunities for public officials. Equipment, financial assistance, and military education necessary to increase their capacities to counter radical religious movements, terrorism, drugs, and weapons trafficking in the war against terrorism have been provided as well. Despite expectations from many quarters within and outside Turkey, the official policy toward the region has settled on a helpful, but not intrusive, pattern. While Turkey did mitigate criticisms against these countries for the slow pace of their political reforms, it nonetheless adopted a benignly active stance to encourage their further democratic evolution.

Zooming out in this increasingly important mid-Asian geography, Afghanistan also attracted significant Turkish involvement. Turkey assumed the command of the International Security Assistance Force (ISAF) in Afghanistan and extended reconstruction assistance. Turkey has commanded the NATO force in Afghanistan for two terms, the last one ending right before the parliamentary elections in Afghanistan on September 18, 2005. Following the liberation of Afghanistan from the Taliban by the United States, the reconstruction and nation-building effort has been a truly international endeavor. Several nations have made major contributions to the success of this enterprise. Turkey has been one of them. The relations between Turkey and Afghanistan date back to the early years of the Turkish Republic. The strategic genius of Atatürk had already identified Afghanistan in the late 1920s as a critical country in Eurasia. The ensuing cooperation included among others the training of the Afghan military. As a result, many military terms that are still in use in the country are Turkish. While this cooperation was interrupted during the Soviet and Taliban periods, after the fall of the Taliban regime, Turkey reemerged as a contributor to all Afghanistan. This included military, economic, and educational contributions, as well as concrete reconstruction and infrastructure assistance. On the multilateral front, former Turkish Foreign Minister Hikmet Çetin led NATO's political representation in Kabul until mid-2006. Turkey's experiences as part of NATO operations in the Balkans contributed to its success in ISAF. At the same time, as it was in the case of the Balkans, the cultural affinities and experience in civil-military cooperation helped form a bridge between the local population and the Turkish peacekeepers:

> Turkish soldiers took it as a duty to demonstrate to the Afghans that they are not occupying forces in the country. Accordingly, for instance, they chose to patrol on foot and not in cars, and when they patrolled, they never wore bulletproof jackets, even if it meant putting their lives on the line. For the locals, this meant respect. In return, local Afghans showed admiration for the Turkish troops and were willing to cooperate with them. In order to defuse the negative effects of the intimidation the Afghan people feel because of the economic, military, and manpower strength displayed by the international community, respect shown to the people is key to gaining their trust.[34]

Turkey should be expected to continue in the long-term mission in Afghanistan to rebuild this friendly and strategic nation. Already in 2006 Turkey moved to expand its contributions by establishing a Provisional Reconstruction Team in the Wardak province.

Turkey's regional involvements obviously include many other examples, as the country declared its foreign policy to be premised on multidimensional and multiregional engagement. Since 2004, diplomatic traffic involving Turkey underscored the broad-based recognition of its quantitatively and qualitatively significant foreign policy profile. In that year, Turkey hosted regional meetings bringing together the neighbors of Iraq; the foreign ministerial meeting of the OIC, at which Ekmeleddin İhsanoğlu, an eminent Turkish scholar, was elected to the post of secretary general; the NATO Istanbul Summit; the summit of the Turkish-speaking countries; the intellectuals' meeting of the EU and the OIC; expert-level preparatory meetings of the Democracy Assistance Dialogue (DAD) envisaged under the Broader Middle East and North Africa (BMENA) initiative; among others, not to mention the World Philosophy Congress, held for the first time in a secular Muslim nation. In addition, several important bilateral visits were hosted by Turkey, including the historical first visits of the Syrian and Russian presidents, the new Iraqi president, and the president of the European Commission, as well as numerous other leaders such as the Jordanian king, the British crown prince, and several other European leaders. President Bush also paid a milestone visit to Turkey in June 2004, delivering a speech in Istanbul beneath the Bogazici bridge connecting Europe with Asia. The visit of the Iranian president was postponed at the last minute by the Iranian side, due to problems stirred by the Iranian Parliament about Turkish investments in the country, which the Iranian leadership believed could overshadow the visit.

A similarly high regional profile continued in 2005. Turkish leaders have exchanged highly visible visits with neighboring countries in addition to traditional Western allies. In May 2005, the first elected Iraqi prime minister visited Turkey. The newly elected president of Ukraine, the leader of the Orange Revolution, also visited Ankara. The first visit by the Turkish prime minister to Israel and Palestine also occurred in 2005. At the same time, frequent exchanges of visits continued with the United States, including by Secretary Rice and National Security Advisor Stephen Hadley, as well as top military commanders.

In these and other visits and contacts, Turkey made an effort to bring in its own approach to regional issues, not contradicting Western policies, but reinforcing them with its own particular perspectives and interests. Therefore, when President Ahmet Necdet Sezer of Turkey visited Syria in April 2005, he did not fail to openly warn the Syrians that they needed to comply in full with UN Security Council Resolution 1546 demanding Syrian withdrawal from Lebanon after the former prime minister of Lebanon, Rafik Hariri, was brutally assassinated in Beirut.[35]

Turkey has shown an active commitment to engage directly with all parties in Iraq to support the political process. While warning Iraqi Kurds against separatism, Turkey quickly welcomed the selection of Jalal Talabani, leader of the Iraqi Patriotic Union of Kurdistan, as the interim president of Iraq in 2005. It also mobilized its efforts to convince Sunni Arabs to participate in the Iraqi elections, organizing extensive training opportunities for the Kurds, Sunnis, Shiites, and Turkmen in the democratic process and good governance. Altogether some 330 Iraqis representing eight political parties took part in these courses. By the end of 2005, Turkey had succeeded in bringing together U.S. officials led by the resourceful Ambassador Zalmay Khalilzad with several key Sunni leaders to discuss their participation in the election on December 15.[36] Turkey, whether through the Incirlik Air Base or via land transportation, remained the main supply route for the multinational force in Iraq and the Iraqi people. In this context, some 500,000 trucks went to Iraq through the Habur border gate in 2005 alone. While the Turks provided 270 megawatts of electricity to Iraq on average, efforts were already underway in 2006 to increase the supply to some 1,200 megawatts, namely one-fifth of Iraq's total electricity demand. Turks also showed interest in the Provisional Reconstruction Teams in Iraq. In the commercial field, Turkish companies exported no less than ten million tons of oil and oil derivatives to Iraq, and the overall exports reached two billion dollars in 2005. Come 2006, Turkey was cited by American officials as a model neighbor for its contribution to the reconstruction of Iraq and its role in political and economic developments.[37]

While Turkey immediately endorsed Iraq's first permanent government established in May 2006 under Prime Minister Maliki, it remained expressly critical of the PKK presence in northern Iraq and weighed in strongly in favor of Iraq's unity and integrity, warning against the negative ramifications for Iraq and the region of the Kurdish claims on Kirkuk and other localities in the country. In this context, Turkish officials criticized the massive population transfers by the Kurds into Kirkuk in order to change the ethnic composition of this key city ahead of the 2007 referendum.[38]

At the same time, Turkey has stepped up its reformist rhetoric and diplomatic efforts to promote an awareness in the surrounding countries of the need to take definitive steps toward democratization and economic liberalization. This was not only the case in the broader Middle East and in the OIC, but in the Caucasus and Central Asia as well. Thus, Turkey promptly called on Uzbekistan to effect democratic reforms following the 2005 riots that started in the city of Andijan, and it lobbied the Azerbaijani leadership to allow free and fair elections in 2005.

Turkish regional diplomatic engagement and pro-democracy and -reform efforts were supported by Turkish nongovernmental organizations, which have been developing networks with their fledgling counterparts in the neighborhood. On the intellectual field, Turkish engagement has also been growing, thanks to the many think tanks focusing on these regions. Many of them have begun to unlock the potential of Turkey's existing regional expertise. Several think tanks have recruited speakers of the various regional languages and dialects and experts who have maintained interest in the neighborhood. These NGOs have also cooperated with the governmental efforts in democratizing the surrounding regions. One such think tank, TESEV, has assumed a lead role in the Democracy Assistance Dialogue under the G-8's Broader Middle East Initiative. Several others organized meetings that addressed the democratization of the Middle East. The U.S. German Marshall Fund, an American think tank, has opened an office in Ankara in recognition of Turkey's regional role.

Of particular importance is the engagement of the Turkish business community in regional cooperation projects. Already active since the early 1990s in the Balkans, Russia, the Caucasus, and Central Asia, Turkish businesses have also started to show greater interest in regional projects in the Middle East. Among various examples, the trilateral Ankara Forum developed among Turkish, Israeli, and Palestinian businessmen is particularly worthy of note.

On April 27, 2005, the Union of the Chambers and Commodity Exchanges of Turkey (TOBB) organized a meeting in Ankara with Palestinian and Israeli business representatives. The Ankara Forum that came out of that meeting has established working groups to develop joint projects on tourism and the revitalization of the Erez Industrial Estate. These projects offer tremendous potential to create jobs and contribute to the resolution of the key problem of unemployment in Gaza. At the same time, they will contribute to Israel by assisting in the development of a viable economy just beyond its borders. It is important to note that this trilateral process of institutionalized business cooperation aims to reach beyond Palestine, Israel, and Turkey to the other countries of the region in due course. As Rıfat Hisarcıklıoğlu, the president of TOBB, has said in Washington, business people "cannot solve the main problems between countries but we can produce local solutions to all the main problems to a certain extent. Accordingly, we are moving forward with small but concrete steps and trying to activate a channel of communication and cooperation which will produce solutions."[39]

As important as this initiative is as a model of cooperation for the Middle East, the broader conceptual framework voiced by Hisarcıklıoğlu was no less significant as regards Turkey's regional engagement. Accordingly, the President of TOBB argued that:

> Turkey could play a vital role in integrating the region into the world economy. This could be done by integrating the regional economies to the Turkish economy. Hence regional integration is the keyword for the economic transformation of our region. At the same time, accelerating the regional integration of the Turkish economy will be extremely beneficial in the transformation of the regional economies. Turkey's importance as a regional state is based on the Turkish economy. The structural infrastructure of the Turkish economy and its level of development in the region should be seen as the most valuable strategic asset of our country in this era. From this perspective, it is vitally important for Turkey to complete its economic transformation in accordance with current competitive standards within the EU process. That is the meaning of EU membership for Turkey.[40]

The initiative thus involves Turkey, a major regional problem and its actors, contacts in the United States, and references to the EU. It is difficult not to see a model in this example. Turkey has furnished another model with behind-the-scenes diplomacy to facilitate the Pakistan-Israel meeting in 2005. President Musharraf of Pakistan and Prime Minister Sharon of Israel had asked for Turkey's assistance to open a channel of dialogue between their countries. The consequent historic meeting of the Pakistani and Israeli foreign ministers in Istanbul was held in September 2005 with the participation of Turkey's state minister, Mehmet Aydın. The Israeli minister announced that "it (was) no coincidence that this meeting took place here in Turkey, this great Muslim democracy, and Israel's long-standing friend."[41] In fact, Turkey has been a consistent friend of both Pakistan and Israel for decades. Such background mediation was also used for the meeting in Istanbul of the U.S. ambassador with the Sunni leaders, as mentioned above.

The EU and the United States have been mostly supportive of Turkey's regional efforts. Turkey's regional role has gradually been accepted as fact and even welcomed in Turkey's neighborhood as well. The evolution of Turkish security and foreign policy is closely monitored in its neighborhood and beyond. In the Middle East, Turkey's links with the West and even Israel, once a subject of acute criticism, are increasingly regarded as an asset more than a challenge to the neighboring countries and regions.

Turkey's membership in Western structures and particularly its membership in the EU would bring greater benefits to its neighborhood to the extent that the countries in the vicinity adopt similar postures and carry out reforms that align them more closely with the global system. That this appreciation is already taking root can be seen from the support for Turkey's EU membership being expressed by several of Turkey's neighboring countries. Thus, the Lebanese newspaper *Daily Star* underscored in an editorial that "Turkey, which has successfully implemented vast reforms, has encouraged other countries in the region to follow suit. Such initiatives are only a hint of the enhanced role that Turkey can play in the Muslim world with the added clout of EU membership. Ankara's ties with regional states make Turkey an ideal partner in shaping regional policy."[42]

The current debate abroad about Turkey is generally perceptive of the evolving Turkish stance on regional issues. The EU, a longtime backbencher in regional high politics, is growingly appreciative of Turkey's promise as a partner in addressing issues in Europe's neighbors, although it is nowhere close to unleashing the full potential of cooperation with Turkey in that regard. Since the 1990s, notable commentators such as Stephen Larrabee and Ian Lesser of the RAND Corporation were already pointing to increasing activism in Turkish foreign and security policy.[43] This calculated activism, which effectively alleviated some of the persistent problems haunting Turkey and indeed the region, has led to a relative betterment of the political and security climate in the surrounding regions, although significant perils and challenges still remain. It may be argued that Turkey is increasingly being recognized as a benevolent actor. Graham Fuller, for one, reasons that "this newer model is much better for Turkey, better for the region, and better for Europe and the world."[44] Currently, Turkey's regional postures are largely cited to its credit, as manifested in the EU Commission's acknowledging since 2004 that the efforts of Turkey to improve and deepen its relations with the neighboring countries are welcome.

Turkey faces the imperative to continue developing and pursuing an active foreign policy in its broad neighborhood. It has been careful in closely aligning its discourse and actions with its grand strategy of promoting a peaceful and stable environment conducive to its own development and security.

Centuries of interaction in this area of the world as a participant and as a witness have formed Turkey's understanding of regional dynamics. The Turks have this region in their cultural genes, and their sensitivities serve as the canary in a mine. In a way, Turks are like the audience in the television quiz show *Who Wants to Be a Millionaire?* When called upon in their collective but individually anonymous wisdom, they produce a breakthrough response. When Turkey argues, for instance, that Kurdish maximalism in northern Iraq and Kirkuk could explode whatever remains of Middle Eastern stability, one can heed it as a word of regional wisdom. Turks in their collective conscience contain the seeds of the mind-set of all the different peoples to which history and geography has exposed them, 360 degrees around their country. That is how cosmopolitan centers are formed and defined; and Turkey is the cosmopolitan hub of its neighborhood.

Turkey's neighborhood comprises a primary geopolitical focus, and managing the EU's proximity to it is a key challenge not only for the EU but also for the United States and definitely for Turkey. Regional policies provide another catalyst for Turkish cooperation with the EU and United States and their relevance for stability and progress in the surrounding regions, including the security of energy supplies.

The media is awash with issues that come under the rubric of this geopolitical challenge. These include the resolution of the Arab-Israeli conflict; the transformation of the broader Middle East; resolving the frozen conflicts in the southern Caucasus and also in southeastern Europe; anchoring Ukraine in Euro-Atlantic cooperation and institutions; promoting greater political, economic, and security cooperation with and democracy within the Russian Federation;[45] promoting stability and security in the Balkans and its integration into European structures; consolidating independence and democratization of Central Asian countries and promoting their good governance and economic development, as well as integration into the world; promoting stability in the Mediterranean and the Black Sea; achieving reconstruction of and stability in Iraq as well as Afghanistan; and avoiding a self-damaging nuclear weapons capability for Iran. All are issues that are common to the U.S., EU, and Turkish agendas, although different parties may attach different priorities to each.

More than once, the parties have come to favor different methods of addressing some of these issues, a fact that underlies some of the recent transatlantic disagreements and tensions. As a result, there may be a need to contemplate different relationships or a variable geometry of cooperation among the three in their different geographies, which complicates the task of coordination and consultation.

In fact, variable geometry is what defines Turkey's own neighborhood. I would argue that a defining observation about Turkey's "region" should be that there is no such unifying concept. No single appellation can cover all of Turkey's surrounding regions. Even the broad construct of "Eurasia" does not, since it appears not to include the Middle East.

Beyond the perhaps vain exercise of coining a title of convenience for Turkey's vicinity, the fact of the matter is that this neighborhood is marked not by a single or a couple of regions but instead by a number of geopolitical basins that are virtually unconnected to each other. The Black Sea, the Mediterranean, Central Asia, and the broader Middle East are in practical terms separate "regions" with markedly different characteristics and dynamics.

At the sociopolitical level, different qualities exist to the east and west of Turkey with little, if any, interaction among them. For instance, Iran and Bulgaria, both bordering Turkey, share nothing in social or political culture and define their political and security priorities in totally diverging terms. While the wave of pluralistic democracy has soared in Eastern Europe and has been engulfing the Black Sea basin, Central Asia has been lagging while undergoing state building, whereas the Middle East is only just beginning.

At the identity level, the countries in the Balkans, the Caucasus, Central Asia, and the Middle East do not share a common identity. There is no cultural construct that unites them. Even countries that are perceived by outsiders as belonging to a particular region may define themselves outside that region. To Slovenians and even Romanians, their respective countries do not belong to the Balkans, while others may have a different opinion. And although the Turkish idea of Black Sea economic cooperation has bridged the Caucasus and the Balkans and thus set out to create a "Black Sea" regional identity, this is a project under construction. There is no other such political innovation elsewhere, except for the Mediterranean under the Barcelona process. The EU Neighborhood Policy (ENP), although a good start, treats these regions only as the EU's "rimland" and envisages bilateral, not genuinely regionwide multilateral relationships.

At the institutional level, Central Asia and the Caucasus are tied up to the pan-European political and security network through their membership in the OSCE, NATO's PfP program, and the EAPC. A few hundred kilometers away, many experts and officials in the Middle East are known to quickly distance themselves from any reference to an expanded OSCE and PfP. Although since 1997 a number of Middle Eastern and North African countries have participated in NATO's Mediterranean Dialogue, this has only been a poor comparison to the prolific and successful defense and security cooperation mechanism under PfP and EAPC.[46]

Furthermore, the surrounding regions are also distinguished in terms of the development of intraregional cooperation links. The Caucasus and the Middle East are currently characterized by the absence of regionwide cooperative structures, while southeastern Europe has been establishing, with significant Turkish leadership, a joint peacekeeping force and a political-military mechanism to govern it since the 1990s.

Turkey's economic neighborhood also displays diversity and even disconnect. There are only a few countries in the Middle East that have adopted a free-market economic system, while Turkey's western neighbors have either joined the EU or are on the threshold of accession. Trade and other economic links are poor, and I do not know of anyone who has even bothered to quantify interregional investment levels and prospects. The fact that air flights among these regions are few should also be telling in terms of the level of business and social interaction.

While each region is a political construct of a mostly European imperial legacy, currently no political drive or aspiration for reconstitution exists on the part of the countries to the east, who continue to see themselves separate from those that lie beyond Turkey's western borders. This is a mutual feeling as well. The single exception could be Georgia and Azerbaijan's willingness to join NATO and the EU, and in their case, too, Europe does not encourage their bid.

There is no U.S., EU, or Turkish broad strategy that covers all of these regions in one stroke, notwithstanding the critical importance of all these regions for the United States, EU, and Turkey. The EU's ENP comes closest in extending a comprehensive reach, but not only does it exclude Central Asia, it only establishes bilateral links with the countries in EU's proximity and falls short of engendering intra- and interregional ties.[47]

In the long term and contingent upon the resolution of existing frozen and active conflicts, the progress of pacific relations, and advancement of democratic reforms, it will be necessary to bridge different regional dynamics and facilitate political, economic, and other interactions as well as common progressive agendas among the regions around Turkey. Therein may be a longer term task for Turkish diplomacy. Turkey is well enough equipped to assume a lead role in such a project, thanks to its extensive regional cooperation experience and various ties with all the players, including at the societal level. However, Turkey does not have the means or the taste to commit to this gigantic task alone, nor are the current circumstances in the region conducive as yet.

As one looks to the future, even the most optimistic viewpoints caution that Turkey's, and thus Europe's, broad neighborhood will remain volatile for a long time to come. Most of the countries in Turkey's neighborhood face difficulties in putting into effect the necessary urgent reforms that are needed to establish contemporary political and economic norms. Although several positive developments have been occurring in a number of places from Afghanistan to Ukraine, it may be too early to rule in favor of their irreversibility. The number of active and frozen conflicts in close proximity include the Arab-Israeli conflict, the Azerbaijani-Armenian dispute, the problems in Georgia and Iraq, and the Chechen conflict, among others. All of these have been costing their protagonists, the region, and Turkey dearly in economic, security, political, and social terms.

On the other hand, the percentage of Turkey's commercial relations with the neighboring countries is stuck at less than 20 percent, an anomaly, given that the country is situated at the crossroads of continents and is a neighbor or at close distance to 70 percent of the world's mineral energy resources. The potential should be enormous. Despite Turkish-led efforts to tap into this potential through cooperative arrangements such as the BSECO or the ECO, the quantifiable economic benefits have been rather disappointing, although political gains for regional relations have been significant. Channeling EU and U.S. investment into the BSECO's ready structures is the only effective and feasible project over the mid to longer term to achieve stability and cooperation and guarantee the progress of democracy as well as integration with the West.

Therefore, there are important interests as well as risks and opportunities in Turkey's close vicinity. The accumulating official Turkish discourse is explicit in recognizing that security, political stability, open-market economy, and transparency are essential to increasing commercial and economic relations, while most neighbors lag in putting these key concepts into practice. Turkey has no realistic choice but to engage more actively not only in the stabilization efforts in its periphery but also in the associated drive to promote political and economic reforms. Ankara's policy of active engagement may be supported, and sometimes complicated, by public opinion, as the Turkish people have a cultural affinity with the peoples of all the regions surrounding Turkey and an aversion to messy regional politics. Thus, with or without EU membership, Turkey should be expected to stay active in the region for the foreseeable future.

In the traditional risks versus opportunities dichotomy of security policy, the EU membership process will probably increase the likelihood of taking the opportunities view in Turkey and thus of seeking further synergies with the EU and the United States. As long as all parties involved continue to carefully distance regional policies from hegemonic inclinations and maintain focus on the need to seek peaceful evolution, stability, and broad-based cooperation, existing Turkish foreign and security policy instruments can engender synergies with both the EU and the United States. The Istanbul Cooperation Initiative tying the Arab Gulf countries to NATO is one example of such policy constructs.

This assumes that the EU and the United States will pursue congruent interests and policies vis-à-vis Turkey's region. In the expected scenario of steady progress toward eventual EU membership, one could forecast Turkey's actively seeking EU-U.S. convergence on regional issues. Concurrently, Turkey can be expected to try reconciling the concerns of the regional countries with those of the EU and United States in a bid to foster regional ownership, which had been essential for success in Central and Eastern Europe's integration into Euro-Atlantic structures. Obviously, this is much to reconcile and manage and at times perhaps unnecessarily complicated. The simplistic alternative is to hold unquestioningly to one particular policy line, whether American or European or region based or exclusively self-made. But in reality, political dynamism must be expected to mark Turkish foreign policies. Turkey will be Turkish, European, essentially pro-American, and unavoidably regional. The ensuing policy outcome could turn out to be very good or very bad, depending on how it is conceptualized in specific cases and how it is put into practice.

The necessity to reconcile different demands has been explicit in Turkish policy vis-à-vis the broader Middle East. Turkish officials have been active in both regional and Western forums in persistently delivering one set of complementary messages. To the regional audience, the emphasis is on encouraging reforms to protect the fundamental principles of human rights, the rule of law, transparency, accountability, pluralism, and gender equality. To the West, it is on noncoercion, local ownership, voluntary participation, and consistent peer pressure. The emphasis common to both is that democracy is not unique to a particular set of countries or a specific culture; it is universal.

The idea of a greater Middle East can be traced in a sense to Halford MacKinder's "inner or marginal crescent" and Nicholas Spykman's "rimland," the control of which they both deemed to be key strategic objectives although differing in specifics, including in the definition of the region.[48] Since then, concepts like the "arc of instability" or the "green belt" have been used extensively in various contexts. The term "greater Middle East" was already in use in the early 1990s. In this context, Ronald Asmus and Ken Pollack reinvented an older idea about emphasizing the area "from Northern Africa and Egypt and Israel at the eastern end of the Mediterranean and extend[ing] throughout the Persian Gulf to Afghanistan and Pakistan," or the so-called greater Middle East.[49] They argued that this region produces threats in the form of "foot soldiers for future terrorist attacks, the funding and financing for such attacks, the proliferation of weapons of mass destruction that can be used against us, the overflow of civil wars from one state to the next, and the refugee flows that all of these developments inevitably trigger."[50] They have advocated recasting the transatlantic relationship to meet these challenges through a Western strategy that addresses the root causes, not just the symptoms. In their words, "while continuing to wage the military war on terrorism, we must make an equally firm commitment to a political strategy that would help transform the Middle East itself. It would mean changing the nature of the anti-Western regimes from which our enemies draw sanctuary, support, and successors by seeking to create more participatory, inclusive, and accountable regimes that can live in peace with one another."[51] The initially confrontational tone of this discourse has undergone much refinement in the time since.

The so-called Broader Middle East Initiative was brought into officialdom foremost by the U.S. president's speech at the University of South Carolina in May 2003, followed by the speech at the National Endowment for Democracy in November of the same year announcing that "The United States has adopted a new policy, a forward strategy of freedom in the Middle East. This strategy requires the same persistence and energy and idealism we have shown before. And it will yield the same results. As in Europe, as in Asia, as in every region of the world, the advance of freedom."[52] The basic premise of this strategy is that "the expansion of political rights and political participation in the Muslim world is meant to combat the appeal of Islamist extremism."[53] Subsequently, the U.S. policy was fleshed out through various initiatives and major speeches. In addition, the proposal for a U.S.–Middle East free-trade area and various assistance programs under the umbrella of the Middle East Partnership Initiative hinted toward a comprehensive policy. A working paper reportedly prepared for the G-8 summit, which was published in al-Hayat newspaper on February 13, 2004, documented the "deficits" identified in the United Nations Development Programme's (UNDP) Arab Human Development Reports of 2002 and 2003 and thus focused on measures to promote democracy and good governance, a knowledge society, and economic opportunities. The working paper contained measures such as assistance in establishing or strengthening independent election commissions, intensifying contacts among parliamentarians, and—a critical element—direct funding of the NGOs in the region for the promotion of democracy. The Arab world saw the document as an external imposition that failed to take into consideration the differences among regional countries while not addressing the Arab-Israeli conflict. However, this reaction helped test the waters, and the final document adopted at the Sea Island G-8 Summit appeared to remedy these shortcomings to a large extent.

Several aspects of the new U.S. strategy had already been on the agenda of regional and extraregional actors for the last two decades. One of the earliest initiatives was the EU's Barcelona Process, or the Euro-Mediterranean Partnership of 1995, which aimed to address new security risks for the EU such as illegal immigration, drug trafficking, human smuggling, organized crime, and illicit trade. But problems in the Arab-Israeli peace process seemed to haunt the initiative throughout its existence. In a bid to raise the profile of the EU's engagement in the region both in the EU and in partner countries, 2005 was declared the Year of the Mediterranean. However, the level of turnout at the tenth anniversary summit in Barcelona in 2005 was disappointing, indicating a certain level of exhaustion. On the other hand, the EU's European Neighborhood Policy,[54] which was launched in the wake of the EU's latest enlargement in 2004 to supplement earlier initiatives, has set out a new framework based on a "privileged relationship" with countries on the EU's periphery, including southern Mediterranean countries, and offered positive incentives in return for progress toward implementation of political, economic, and institutional reforms. The ENP is based on contractual relationships with the EU tailored in line with the particular requirements of the partner countries. These include Country Reports drafted by the European Commission assessing political, economic, and social developments. These reports form the basis of Action Plans that govern implementation of expected reforms and European assistance to facilitate them. The implementation of these Action Plans in turn is monitored and results are fed back to the relationship between the EU and the individual country. As such, the ENP envisages a process of intensive relationship, which is what the EU does best. However, the jury is still out on the success of this initiative, especially as the EU will have to initiate and sustain democratization through benchmarking without membership prospects for these countries. The transformative power of the EU that has been working wonders on the countries that want to join the Union is yet to be tested in countries that do not have that prospect, at least in the foreseeable future. In addition to the EU, the OSCE and NATO had also launched Mediterranean initiatives in the 1990s, but their scope and prospects are more limited.

At any rate, Turkey was quick to respond in 2003 to the U.S. initiative to revive the democratization movement in the Middle East, with the Turkish foreign minister strongly urging "all the related parties to carefully examine this initiative and to candidly work on it."[55] Turkey had already been placing increasing emphasis on democratization in its foreign policy in tandem with the emphasis at home.[56] In fact, Turkey's emphasis on democratization and good governance in the Middle East precedes the Broader Middle East Initiative. The early signs of this idea can be found in Turkish officials' and intellectuals' reactions to the "clash of civilizations" argument. Turkish thinking appears to have developed from a position fervently opposed to the suggested inevitability of a clash of civilizations, particularly in the Muslim-Christian context, into one that advocates a proactive policy to overcome the challenges that the Muslim world faces.[57] The turning point toward a proactive policy came at the foreign ministers' meeting of the OIC in Tehran on May 28, 2003, where Foreign Minister Gül made a landmark declaration calling on the Muslim leaders to "first put our house in order."[58] Gül expanded on this idea in his subsequent speeches, including the one at the Economic Studies Foundation in Istanbul (İAV) and the World Economic Forum's Extraordinary Meeting in Jordan in June 2003.

Subsequently, Turkey's approach to the question of democratization and development in the Greater Middle East was confirmed by Prime Minister Recep Tayyip Erdoğan at a speech delivered at Harvard University.[59] The speech, which was published in several Arab media,[60] launched a frontal attack on so-called Middle East *exceptionalism*, which maintains that democracy is neither feasible nor desirable in that geography. Erdoğan thus appealed to the Muslim world and the countries of the Middle East to recognize that "Democracy is not particular to a specific group of societies. Democracy is universal and a modern day requirement."[61] The Turkish prime minister also pleaded the Western world to listen to the voices of the Muslim world with an open heart and support change by setting a good example. He asserted that the greatest strength of those societies that represent modern values is the attraction they create. Prime Minister Erdoğan reminded the Western world of its "particular responsibility to establish a more just global order and seek harmony among civilizations."[62]

Turkey has insisted at Western forums on such principles as regional ownership, no imposition, consistency, and gradualism. Similarly, a strong emphasis has been put on the need to address the Arab-Israeli conflict, nonetheless warning that this conflict should not be used as an excuse not to effect the necessary reforms. These points were consistently raised by Turkey in the leadup to the G-8 Summit at Sea Island, which culminated in the Partnership for Progress and a Common Future with the Region of the Broader Middle East and North Africa. At the G-8 Summit meeting at Sea Island, the Turkish prime minister announced Turkey's cosponsorship of one of the G-8's democratization projects, namely the Democracy Assistance Dialogue (DAD), which aims to facilitate an exchange of lessons learned from best practices and to promote dialogue among civil societies and governments. Since then Turkey has appointed a special coordinator for the broader Middle East, allied with Italy and Yemen to cosponsor the DAD, and organized civil society and governmental meetings in the context of the DAD. Indeed, of the various BMENA initiatives launched at Sea Island, the DAD has ranked as one of the most active. Turkey has also supported other BMENA activities, including the Fund and Foundation for the Future, both of which were initiated at the Forum for the Future meeting in Bahrain late in 2005. By 2006 the Democracy Assistance Dialogue (DAD), cosponsored by Turkey, was among the most active initiatives launched under the G-8 BMENA framework. Its particular success has been in attracting a significant level of engagement from the general public and the NGOs in the region.

The DAD's topical emphasis on the empowerment of women was particularly well conceived, touching upon a profoundly important aspect of democratization, one that could recruit almost unanimous moral support from within and outside the region. Turkey participated in all these initiatives not as a regional country but as a "democratic partner." This category involved countries that included Norway, Greece, and Spain. Spain and Turkey also cosponsored another initiative, this time reaching beyond the broader Middle East and aiming to enhance mutual understanding between Islamic and Western societies. Named the "Alliance of Civilizations," this initiative was launched by the UN secretary general in July 2005.[63]

The Broader Middle East Initiative was subject to much debate in the Turkish media and in academia. The overwhelming majority of views categorically rejected outside intervention in the region, with a clear reference to the Iraqi experience. However, a great majority also appeared to submit that change was necessary and democratization desired in the neighboring region. In addition, Turkey's potential role in the process was widely debated within Turkey.[64]

The transformation of the broader Middle East does not appear to be an idea that will wither away easily. The European Security Strategy and U.S. perceptions concur on the existence of a challenge emanating from this region. This challenge goes beyond the fight against terrorism and precedes 9/11, and it is not tied to the "clash of civilizations" hypothesis. Carl Bildt has reasoned that the Middle East constitutes a "failed region" that risks Balkanization and that over time also will risk the Balkanization of European societies. He argued: "Europe will have to welcome larger numbers of immigrants in the years to come for reasons that have to do with its own demography. But there is a serious risk that a series of explosions or implosions in the volatile region of the Greater Middle East will lead to pressures which might be too heavy, and which risks causing strife in our societies, also making the task of building understanding between different national and religious communities more complicated."[65]

The region is already on the path of reforms, as regional dynamics are set in motion and could be expected to increase in the time ahead. Despite the initial outcry, the reform discourse is no longer alien to regional governments. Elections and reformist discourses in several Arab countries in 2005 seemed to suggest that democratization was in full swing. The key to successful democratization in the region is to ensure that it is not imposed or seen to be so, although it can nevertheless be "encouraged" from outside. Elsewhere, in a study I coauthored with Mensur Akgun, Meliha Altunisik, and Ayse Kadioglu, we argued that while the democratization needs of every country in the region are different, the common object of any democratization project should be to opt for opening up the channels that would allow people to tailor the projects that are congenial in their particular contexts. To do this a balance or rather *a modus vivendi* should be maintained between institutionalization and participation. This balance has been struck in Western Europe by tradition. The experience of democratization, on the other hand, in Eastern and Central European countries in the 1990s were supported by international organizations like the EU, Council of Europe, OSCE and NATO. The creation and maintenance of this balance in the Middle East and North Africa is only possible with the support of a similar institutional international mechanism.[66]

It remains to be seen whether the G-8 DAD, the Foundation for the Future, as well as the EU's ENP, among many other initiatives, will sufficiently live up to this task.

At any rate, as the continued debate about the menacing possibility of "one person, one vote, one time" illustrates, democratization cannot be confined to a mere holding of free and fair elections. After all, establishment of constitutional liberties is fundamental to a liberal democracy. In cases where political participation via elections takes place prior to the establishment of such liberties, "illiberal democracy"[67] may well be the outcome. In the recent Iraqi examples, the strictly ethnic and sectarian voting has confirmed the thesis that voting alone does not engender pluralism nor indeed democracy as we know it.

Thus, the irreversibility of democratization must be an area of serious emphasis. The current manifestations of reform efforts in the region are not the first time that hopes have been raised. In the late 1980s and 1990s regional countries faced the need to adjust to the impact of the democratization wave emanating from Central and Eastern Europe. In that period, the effect of the transformations in Europe, the end of global bipolar confrontation, and the political fallout from the 1991 Gulf War stimulated reform in the Arab world. However, these earlier efforts were short-lived, and by the mid-1990s they were suspended and in most cases reversed. A strong and spawned-out emphasis by the outside world on democratic transformation must also not be taken for granted. Especially if the expected course is toward instability in friendly or critical countries, then the emphasis is likely to remain at the level of occasional discourse. This is as valid for Europe and Turkey as it is for the United States. On its part, Turkey appeared cognizant of this fact of life from the beginning, pushing vigorously for regionally owned and led reforms according to local conditions.

The bottom line is that whatever reason one may want to emphasize, international and great-power emphasis on this geographical region will continue until its countries learn to bring to bear their tremendous resource wealth on the modernization of their governance. Remaining outside the rules of the globalized world while possessing significant resources creates a security problem for this region, its countries, and peoples. The same can be said for those countries that do not possess this wealth but nonetheless inhabit a critical geography on the periphery of wealth, whether in Europe or in the greater Middle East. That is also the bottom line for Turkey's perception of this region. Until this region reconciles its problems and enters the zone of democratic peace, it will be a threat to itself and to its neighbors.

Turkey may at times be a hesitant player, but whether it likes it or not, it is already a key player. This is evident from the various statements of leaders in the Muslim world, including neighboring Syria and Iran, two countries with which Turkey has had complicated relationships. It should be noted that both Iran and Syria have expressed support for Turkey's membership bid to the EU, underscoring the importance of Europe coming to their doorstep.[68] Turkey's role is partly defined by the individual projects that it undertakes to support: the G-8, NATO, EU, U.S., OECD, OSCE, and other initiatives that touch on the broader Middle East.

Its role can also be seen in the possible improvements to the functioning of the OIC that a Turkish secretary general is trying to bring about—and it is hardly possible to overstate the importance of the ascendance to this position of a person from a democratic and secular nation. Secretary General İhsanoğlu is the first person to be elected to this position by the member countries through voting, a sign of change within this conservative organization. It is also an indication that Turkey's democratic and secular regime and its Western vocation no longer obviate important roles for Turkey in the region and within the Muslim world.

Nonetheless, the greatest impact that Turkey will likely have on the reform agenda in the region will come about by being itself: a democratic, secular, social state observing the rule of law. It is inconceivable that neighboring peoples and regimes will not follow and scrutinize closely Turkey's own reforms on the road to EU membership. The influence that Turkey carries in the region as an inspiration for reforms is increasing. As Graham Fuller observes, "Today's Turkey, based on the remarkable realities of its evolution during recent years, is in fact now becoming a genuine model that finally offers a degree of genuine appeal to the region."[69]

At the same time, however, the Turkish public will surely become increasingly aware of the invaluable experience the country has been acquiring in the course of the EU membership process and will be increasingly willing and able to share it with others in the neighborhood. As public interest in the promotion of democratization, the rule of law, and associated reforms in the broad neighborhood develop over time, Turkey will become ever more capable of articulating its contributions in that regard. The business community will also sooner or later step in more prominently as it realizes that reforms in the rule of law, transparency, accountability, and democratization actually help increase security for investments and commerce. The numerous studies they have commissioned for reforms in Turkey in the past will eventually form a basis for similar contributions from others in the neighborhood. All segments of the Turkish population will eventually benefit from the positive evolution in the neighborhood and thus will be increasingly committed to assisting it. The EU accession process will force Turkey to make critical upgrades in its governance, and the lessons learned will not only inspire reformers in the neighborhood but will also rally their interest in studying and adapting with the help of the Turks the Turkish experience to their own specific cases. Turkey will also further develop its civil society interfaces with Europe and thus help foster greater interaction between Europe and the broader Middle East in this regard, too. Turkey will be a major beneficiary of the positive evolution of its broad neighborhood into democratic regimes, open societies, and market economies. In this scenario, Turkish foreign and security policy will be able to concentrate on building webs of regional economic, cultural, and political cooperation. At some stage, a soft security framework could also be introduced. The numerous initiatives that Turkey has led in the immediate post–Cold War environment in the Balkans and Black Sea could be thus carried, in cooperation with the United States and the EU, into the broader Middle East in the future.

The challenge, however, will be in managing the short term. Until the region is stabilized on the foundations of democratic peace, stability itself will continue to be a major concern. Whatever the idealistic visions promise for the region over the long term, geopolitics and an environment of progressive stability must be maintained. Great visions can falter if the impending issues are not properly handled—particularly two issues, namely, developments related to Iran's nuclear program and Iraq's future as a territorially united state. These pose the greatest unknown variables concerning the evolution of the regional environment and thus the future course of Turkish foreign and security policy. Both issues merit separate examination, but the scenarios involving an Iran with nuclear weapons and a disintegrated Iraq are alike in that they seem capable of imposing unforeseen pressures on the definition and redefinition of the regional security environment and future Turkish policies. The two issues are also fundamentally different in so many respects. Iran's program elicits a near international concern, and international bodies including the UN Security Council are already much involved in the developments. Iraq, however, is yet to grasp the full attention and emphasis of the international community. The future of Iraq thus continues to create major concern in Turkey. In Iraq, as in Iran's nuclear program, Turkey's interests are in congruence with the interests of the EU, the United States, and the neighborhood. However, it is not yet evident that the EU in particular has become apprised of the implications of further chaos in Iraq. Iraq's failure to remain a united country would not be a problem for Turkey alone. Nonetheless, it would be a problem for Turkey, with ramifications on the evolution of Turkish foreign and security policy, its Europeanization, desecuritization, and continued Westernization in the time ahead, not to mention the health of Turkey's partnership with the United States and the EU.

These two examples, albeit very important, are not the only regional issues that challenge Turkey in the days to come. But whatever the regional scenario, the extent to which the EU and the United States respond to Turkish concerns and recruit its participation from the early stages onward will probably be key to winning Turkey's allegiance. The greater such solidarity, the more Turkish authorities will be able to justify and support multilateral remedies. Less solidarity or perceptions to that effect will force the Turkish public and government into a tendency to dissent. Greater comity with Turkey will ease Turkey's anxieties and facilitate its continued Western policy orientation and Europeanization.

There are admittedly a lot of unknowns on these points. Will the EU allow room for Turkish involvement in its own decision shaping, or rather choose to pressure Turkey to acquiesce in its own policies? Will the Turkish-U.S. alliance be robust enough to realize similar Turkish bona fide input into U.S. policy choices? Will the United States and/or EU explore or ignore potential Turkish contributions? Will the EU, or parts of the EU membership, and the United States manage to agree on a joint analysis and course of action or instead succumb to divergence of views and pull Turkey in different directions? Will this joint EU-U.S. policy be in Turkey's interest? Will Turkey itself be able to elaborate its own positive contributions to the debate and policy beyond drawing imaginary defensive red lines? Such questions have not often been asked at the outset of the transatlantic alliance. It could be more or less taken for granted that Turkey is a part of that alliance.

The Europeanization and Westernization of Turkey's foreign and security policy can no longer be dissociated from the imperative to engage constructively in the surrounding regions. They are becoming part and parcel of the same complex equation. Furthermore, Europeanization and Westernization may no longer be the same thing. But both will be inextricably related to the way the EU or the United States treat Turkey in the next decade, how they treat each other, and ultimately how effective the eventual formula will be for promoting positive change in the region without causing further turmoil.

Notes

1. Ibrahim al-Marashi, "Middle Eastern Perceptions of US-Turkey Relations after the 2003 Iraq War," *Turkish Policy Quarterly* 4, no. 1 (Spring 2005): 136.

2. See Shireen Hunter, "Bridge or Frontier? Turkey's Post–Cold War Geopolitical Posture," *International Spectator* 34, no. 1 (January/March 1999): 63–78. See also Mustafa Aydın, "Securitization of History and Geography: Understanding of Security in Turkey," *Journal of Southeast Europe and Black Sea Studies* 3, no. 2 (May 2003): 163–84.

3. Bill Park, "Strategic Location, Political Dislocation: Turkey, United States and Northern Iraq," *Middle East Review of International Affairs* 7, no. 2, (June 2003), 12.

4. Raymond Banner, "Greek Lawyer Pleased to Defend Bosnian Serb," *New York Times*, August 4, 1996.

5. See: Ünal Çeviköz, "European Integration and New Regional Cooperation Initiatives," *NATO Review* 40, no. 3 (June 1992).

6. Ahmet Davutoğlu, "Stratejik Derinlik: Türkiye'nin Uluslararası Konumu" [Strategic Depth: Turkey's International Position], *Küre Yayınları*, September 2002.

7. Recep Tayyip Erdoğan, "Turkish Foreign Policy in the 21st Century" (Address to the Council on Foreign Relations, January 26, 2004).

8. Abdullah Gül, Address to the Turkish Grand National Assembly, December 22, 2003.

9. Ian O. Lesser, "Turkey in a Changing Security Environment," *Journal of International Affairs* 54, no. 1 (Fall 2000): 184.

10. Çevik Bir and Martin Sherman, "Formula for Stability: Turkey plus Israel," *Middle East Quarterly* 9, no. 4 (Fall 2002): 23–32; Mustafa Kibaroğlu, "Turkey and Israel Strategize," *Middle East Quarterly* 9, no. 1 (Winter 2002): 61–65; Ofra Bengio and Gencer Özcan, "Changing Relations: Turkish-Israeli-Arab Triangle" *Perceptions* 5, no. 1 (March–May 2000): 134–46.

11. Sabri Sayari, "Turkish Foreign Policy in the Post–Cold War Era: The Challenges of Multi-Regionalism," *Journal of International Affairs* 54, no. 1 (Fall 2000): 172.

12. Ümit Özdağ and Ersel Aydınlı, "Winning a Low Intensity Conflict: Drawing Lessons from the Turkish Case," *Review of International Affairs* (London) 2, no. 3 (Spring 2003): 101–21.

13. The Turkish experience in this regard even precedes the fight against PKK. See İhsan Bal and Sedat Laçiner, "The Challenge of Revolutionary Terrorism to Turkish Democracy, 1960–80," *Terrorism and Political Violence* 13, no. 4 (Winter 2001): 90–115.

14. Uğur Ergan, "Barzani'ye Kirmizi Pasaport darbesi," *Hurriyet*, August 12, 2002.

15. Final Statement of the Leaders' Meeting, September 17, 1998, Washington, DC. The statement was signed by Jalal Talabani of the PUK and Masoud Barzani of the KDP and was witnessed by David Welch of the United States. Full text: www.meij.or.jp/text/minorities/ik19980917.htm.

16. Mahmut Balı Aykan, "The Turkish-Syrian Crisis of October 1998: A Turkish View," *Middle East Policy* 6, no. 4 (June 1999): 174–91.

17. Ely Karmon, "A Solution to Syrian Terrorism," *Middle East Quarterly* 6, no. 2 (June 1999): 23–32.

18. Murat Yetkin, *Kürt Kapanı: İam'dan İmralı'ya Öcalan* [Kurdish Trap: Öcalan from Damascus to Imrali] (İstanbul: Remzi Kitabevi, 2004). Also: Amberin Zaman, "Turkey Warns Greece in Kurdish Rebel Case," *Washington Post*, February 23, 1999.

19. BBC News, "Greek Ministers Resign over Ocalan," February 18, 1999.

20. For an assessment of Turkish-Greek relations see Melek M. Fırat, "Soğuk Savaş Sonrası Yunanistan Dış Politikasının Yeniden Biçimleniş Süreci" [The Process of Reshaping of the Post–Cold War Greek Foreign Policy] in *Türkiye'nin Komşuları* [Turkey's Neighbors], ed. Mustafa Türkeş and İlhan Uzgel (Ankara: İmge, 2002).

21. See: Aaban Ealia, "Turkey's Balkan Policy in the Early 1990s," *Turkish Studies* 2 no. 1 (Spring 2001): 135–46.

22. Alan Makovsky, "Turkey" in *The Pivotal States: A New Framework for U.S. Policy in the Developing World*, ed. Robert Chase, Emily Hill, and Paul Kennedy (New York: W.W. Norton & Company, 1999).

23. Michael Robert Hickok, "Hegemon Rising: The Gap Between Turkish Strategy and Military Modernization," *Parameters* 30, no. 2 (Summer 2000): www.carlisle.army.mil/usawc/Parameters/00summer/hickok.htm.

24. Hickok, "Hegemon Rising."

25. United Press International, "Turkey, Israel Plan Undersea Oil Pipeline," April 30, 2006.

26. Aleksandr Vasinski, "Moskova ile Türkiye arasındaki Köprü" [The Bridge Between Moscow and Turkey], *Izvestia*, August 25, 1997. Turkish translation at www.byegm.gov.tr.

27. Pavel Baev, "Russia Refocuses Its Policies in the Southern Caucasus" (Harvard University Caspian Studies Program, Working Paper Series, no. 1, July 2001), 13.

28. Baev, "Russia Refocuses Its Policies," 8.

29. Igor Torbakov, "Turkish Foreign Policy in the Post-Soviet Space," *Eurasia Insight*, December 23, 2002, www.eurasianet.org/departments/insight/ articles/ eav122302.shtml.

30. Fiona Hill, "Seismic Shifts in Eurasia: The Changing Relationship between Turkey and Russia and Its Implications for the South Caucasus," *Journal of Southeast Europe and Black Sea Studies* 3, no. 3 (September 2003): 55.

31. F. Stephen Larrabee, "The Russian Factor in Western Strategy toward the Black Sea Region," in *A New Euro-Atlantic Strategy for the Black Sea Region*, ed. Ronald D. Asmus, Konstantin Dimitrov, and Joerg Forbrig (Bratislava, Slovakia: GMF, 2004).

32. Borys Tarasyuk, "A Ukrainian View of a New Euro-Atlantic Strategy in the Black Sea," in *A New Euro-Atlantic Strategy for the Black Sea Region.*

33. Mustafa Aydın, "Europe's Next Shore: The Black Sea Region after EU Enlargement" (EU-ISS Occasional Paper 53, June 2004). This paper also provides an extensive survey of Black Sea regional cooperation and the potential role of the EU.

34. Ethem Erdağı, "The ISAF Mission and Turkey's Role in Rebuilding the Afghan State" (Washington Institute, Policy Watch no. 1052, November 18, 2005). Also, Hilmi Akın Zorlu, "Turkey Has Been Successful as the Leader of the International Force in Afghanistan (Washington Institute, Policy Watch no. 687, November 27, 2002).

35. "The Visit of the President Ahmet Necdet Sezer to Syria," *Newspot* 3 (March–April 2005), www.byegm.gov.tr/YAYINLARIMIZ/newspot/2005/mar-apr/n3.htm.

36. "Irak için Istanbul Operasyonu" [The Istanbul Operation for Iraq], *Hürriyet*, December 5, 2005.

37. "US Iraq Coordinator Jeffrey: We Discussed the PKK Threat with Iraqi Kurdish Leaders," *The Journal of Turkish Weekly*, May 24, 2006.

38. The Washington Institute for Near East Policy, "Turkey: Between the West and the Middle East," Policy Watch, no. 1074: Special Forum Report Featuring Yigit Alpogan, January 31, 2006.

39. Rıfat Hisarcıklıoğlu, Remarks at the CSIS-TOBB U.S.-Turkish Contact Group, Washington, DC, September 12, 2005.

40. Hisarcıklıoğlu, Remarks.

41. Herb Keinon, "Pakistan: Ralliers Protest Israel Ties," *Jerusalem Post*, September 1, 2005.

42. Editorial, "Starting Turkey's Talks on Time Will Enhance Europe's Role in the Region," *Daily Star*, September 21, 2005.

43. Stephen F. Larrabee and Ian O. Lesser, *Turkish Foreign Policy in an Age of Uncertainty*, MR-1612-CMEPP (Santa Monica, CA: RAND, 2003).

44. Graham Fuller, "Turkey's Strategic Model: Myths and Realities," *Washington Quarterly* 27, no. 3, (2004).

45. For an analysis of Turkish-Russian relations, see: Duygu Sezer Bazoglu, "Turkish-Russian Relations: The Challenges of Reconciling Geopolitical Competition with Economic Partnership," *Turkish Studies* 1, no. 1 (Spring 2000): 59–82. See also Hill, "Seismic Shifts in Eurasia."

46. See: Burak Akçapar, "Partnership for Peace as an Instrument of Continuity and Change in the Euro-Atlantic Region," in *A History of NATO: The First Fifty Years of NATO*, ed. Gustav Schmidt (London and New York: Palgrave, 2001).

47. For a comprehensive discussion of the ENP, see: Andreas Marchetti, *The European Neighborhood Policy: Foreign Policy at the EU's Periphery* (Bonn: University of Bonn Center for European Integration Studies, 2006).

48. See: Halford J. Mackinder, *Democratic Ideals and Reality: A Study in the Politics of Reconstruction* (New York: H. Holt and Company, 1942); and Nicholas J. Spykman, *The Geography of the Peace* (New York: Harcourt, Brace and Company, 1944).

49. Ronald D. Asmus and Kenneth M. Pollack, "The New Transatlantic Project," *Policy Review* no. 115 (October/November 2002): www.policyreview.org/OCT02/asmus.html. See also Ronald D. Asmus, "Rebuilding the Atlantic Alliance," *Foreign Affairs* 82, no. 5 (September/October 2003): 20–31.

50. Asmus and Pollack, "The New Transatlantic Project."

51. Asmus and Pollack, "The New Transatlantic Project."

52. George W. Bush, Speech at the 20th Anniversary of the National Endowment for Democracy, United States Chamber of Commerce, Washington, DC, November 6, 2003.

53. Tamara Cofman Wittes, "The New U.S. Proposal for a Greater Middle East Initiative: An Evaluation," The Brookings Institution, Middle East Memo no. 2, May 10, 2004.

54. http://europa.eu.int/comm/world/enp/index_en.htm.

55. Abdullah Gül, Address to the Bourgas Free University, text available at www.mfa.gov.tr/groupa/ai/middleeast.gul.htm.

56. Kemal Kirişçi, "Between Europe and the Middle East: The Transformation of Turkish Policy," *MERIA* 8, no. 1 (March, 2004): 48.

57. Burak Akçapar, Mensur Akgün, Meliha Altunışık, Ayşe Kadıoğlu, "The Debate on Democratization in the Broader Middle East and North Africa: A Civic Assessment from Turkey" (Istanbul Paper no. 3, TESEV/GMF, June 2004).

58. "Türkiye'den Sürpriz Çağrı" [Surprising Call from Turkey], *Radikal*, May 29, 2003.

59. Recep Tayyip Erdoğan, "Democracy in the Middle East, Pluralism in Europe: A Turkish View" (Speech at Harvard University, January 30, 2004). Full text at: www.turkishweekly.net.

60. For instance: *Bahreyn Tribune*, February 18, 2004; *Sudan Vision*, February 24, 2004.

61. Erdoğan, "Democracy in the Middle East." See also Alwin Powell, "Erdogan Calls for Cooperation: Turkish Prime Minister Touts Middle Eastern Democratic Process," *Harvard University Gazette*, February 5, 2004.

62. Erdoğan, "Democracy in the Middle East."

63. See the UN Press Release number SG/SM/10004, dated July 14, 2005.

64. Akçapar et al., "The Debate on Democratization."

65. Carl Bildt, "Europe and the Greater Middle East" (Speech at the Istanbul Policy Center, Sabanci University, January 28, 2003).

66. Akçapar et al., "The Debate on Democratization," 16.

67. Fareed Zakaria, *The Future of Freedom: Illiberal Democracy at Home and Abroad* (New York and London: W.W. Norton & Company, 2003).

68. For instance, see the interview given by President Beshar El-Assad of Syria to the Turkish press where he said: "When Turkey joins the EU, Syria will border Europe. This is very important." Mehmet Ali Birand, "Irak'ta Kürt Devleti Benim de Kırmızı Çizgim" [A Kurdish State in Iraq is also my redline], *Hürriyet*, January 1, 2004.

69. Fuller, "Turkey's Strategic Model," 51.

CHAPTER FIVE

Of Europe and America

Two contemporary European philosophers, Jürgen Habermas and the late Jacques Derrida, seemed to agree on very little throughout their long careers. Since the 1980s the debate between the German and the Frenchman had turned increasingly acrimonious. Derrida once bitterly complained that "those who have accused me . . . have visibly and carefully avoided reading me," with reference to Habermas.[1] The event that triggered the rapprochement between them was the 9/11 terror attacks against the United States. In response, the two philosophers wore their public intellectual hats and furnished their separate interpretations in Giovanna Borradori's *Philosophy in a Time of Terror*.[2] In this scintillating read, the two philosophers built on their respective thinking. Habermas attributed the outbreak of terror mainly to a failure of communications, as would be expected from the very person credited for the development of the concept and theory of communicative reason or communicative rationality. Derrida, on the other hand, noted among other things the failure to replace the outmoded Christian notion of toleration, which is in fact only charity, with a concept of world hospitality.

Borradori's interviews did not involve a direct collaboration between Habermas and Derrida. Yet her effort marked the beginning of a political comity. While their followers were holding their breath, the two philosophers could not find the time to revisit their previous philosophical quarrels and disagreements. Derrida died shortly after. However, they did spark a fascinating philosophical debate among European thinkers on an issue that had already been overpopulated, namely the U.S.-European relations and the future of the EU's common foreign and security policy.

Thus, on May 31, 2003, in an effort organized and coordinated by Habermas and Derrida, leading dailies in Germany, France, Italy, Spain, and Switzerland published articles authored by several of Europe's prominent intellectuals on the state of European-American relations. Consequently, numerous others joined the debate from both sides of the Atlantic.[3] The May 31 salvo was inspired by the protest marches on February 15, 2003, in various cities in western Europe against the impending U.S. invasion of Iraq. For Habermas, these public demonstrations, the largest since WWII, were a sign of the birth of a distinct "European," as opposed to a "national," public sphere.

Certain binding characteristics, in Habermas's view, distinguished Europeans from Americans. The Europeans were bound by "secularism in politics, broad popular agreement on calming the maelstrom of capitalism's creative destruction; an appreciation of the paradoxes and pitfalls of technological progress; an ethic of solidarity over the prerogatives of individualism; familiarity with the potential brutality of state power (and hence the abandonment of death penalty); recognition of the limits to the rights of state sovereignty; and a more self-critical attitude with regard to weaker outsiders that flowed from the experiences of decolonization."[4] The Americans, on the other hand, were characteristically "less secular, more violent and bellicose, and cultivating a more unforgiving variant of capitalism."[5]

Habermas, then called for the urgent development of a European counterweight to American power. He borrowed a term coined in 1994 by the Christian Democratic politicians Wolfgang Schäuble and Karl Lamers, to propose a Core Europe (kerneuropa), composed of Germany, France, Benelux, and Italy, to take the lead. In other words, all those who supported the Americans in the war on Iraq (except Italy) would be excluded from this core. Spain, Poland, Hungary, the Czech Republic, Denmark, Portugal, and the United Kingdom, which signed the "Letter of the Eight" to support the United States, were all out of Core Europe, not to mention the ten signatories of the Vilnius Letter.[6]

Every other participant in the Habermas debate had their respective viewpoints, yet most seemed to agree on the rejection of the war in Iraq and the call for a strong Europe. Not all of them argued in favor of a counterweight to the United States, with influential thinkers such as Timothy Garton Ash among others disagreeing on that point. Umberto Eco suggested that "with the US shifting its attention to the Middle East and the immense universe of the Pacific, Europe might not count anymore." Therefore, he argued, "in order to survive, so to speak, Europe is condemned to find common strategies for foreign policy and defense. Otherwise it will become, no offence to anyone, Guatemala."[7]

Long before the intra-European debate about U.S.-European relations was rekindled by Habermas and Derrida, the transatlantic debate had already engulfed the U.S. side. The American thinkers were known to have produced an extensive critical literature on European contributions to transatlantic security, arguing for many decades in favor of greater burden sharing. The consistent failure of the Europeans to step up their defense spending and political support of Washington's policies had created disappointment and bitter criticism in the United States. In fact, Robert Kagan questioned whether the EU and the United States shared the same values or even belonged to the same world. According to Kagan, the United States and the EU were as different from each other as the figurative natives of Venus and Mars.[8] How much power each side held and the varying historical experience, particularly with regard to the use of force, determined their foreign and security policies and views.

It is almost impossible to do full justice to the rich transatlantic debate. Obviously, when Europe and the United States debate a common issue, tremendous intellectual energy is unleashed. The truth is that the transatlantic debate has already become like aerobic exercise: it is repetitive, but ultimately healthy. Transatlantic relations have been debated to exhaustion for decades, with each official disagreement feeding additional fuel back into intellectual discussions. As David P. Calleo reminds us, "The same basic issues run through five decades of discourse about Western interdependence. Is the transatlantic relationship properly balanced? Are the West European allies treated as genuine partners? Do they carry their proper share? Do European and American basic interests diverge? Who, in fact, is exploiting whom?"[9]

In this broad debate, differences as well as commonalities have been studied in excruciating depth and breadth. Some have underscored common democratic values, others diverging power and strategic culture. There was even the argument that unless something is done about it, "the coming clash of civilizations will be not be between the West and the rest but within a West divided against itself."[10] Others observed the inextricable interdependence of transatlantic economies, pointing out that there is more European investment in Texas than U.S. investment in Japan, and that European firms owned $3.3 trillion worth of U.S. assets.[11] If globalization is a fact of the international system or, as Thomas Friedman argues, the international system itself,[12] then this is nowhere as prevalent as in the transatlantic relationship. Both the United States and Europe are not only the leading drivers of globalization, but they are also bound and hemmed in by it.

Still, the EU and the United States may have different views on how the current era of globalization influences their policy options. Thus, the rift over Iraq was portrayed as a debate about world visions. For the then French foreign minister Dominique de Villepin, the struggle was less about Iraq than it was between "two visions of the world," while his German counterpart, Joschka Fischer, was asking forcefully, "What kind of world order do we want?"[13] Ultimately France and Germany did not join the United States in the 2003 war and remained critical. The Americans were resentful of the moral high road suggested by those Europeans. Robert Kagan recalled that these countries' attitudes differed between Kosovo and Iraq.[14] Robert Jervis also questioned passionately whether Europeans were "really so averse to force, so wedded to law":

> When facing terrorism, Germany and other European countries have not hesitated to employ unrestrained state power the likes of which U.S. Attorney General John Ashcroft would envy, and their current treatment of minorities, especially Muslims, hardly seems liberal. The French disregarded legal rulings against their ban of British beef; they also continue to intervene in Africa and to join other European states in flouting international laws requiring them to allow the import of genetically modified foods. Most European nations also favored the war in Kosovo. Finally, had Europeans suffered a direct attack like that of September 11, it's unlikely that they would have maintained their aversion to the use of force.[15]

It does give a certain perspective, and a tentative comfort, to recall that the U.S.-EU relationship has weathered many storms before. The sheer weight of the common interest and agenda almost always helps to focus minds to find a reasonable way out of any impasse. However, the fact that there have been many previous instances of discord within the transatlantic alliance or that there is a commonality of democratic values and economic interdependence does not mean that the differences are not real. The management of transatlantic affairs is not a transient task, but one that is a permanent requirement that requires constant attention and delicate care.

The heat in transatlantic and intra-European disagreements over Iraq has given way already in 2004 to reconciliation, although not full cooperation. Starting with UN Security Council Resolution 1546 on Iraq in 2004, the G-8 Summit at Sea Island, and the NATO Istanbul Summit, fences have been mended. The trip to Europe by President George W. Bush after his second inauguration in early 2005, preceded by the tour of Secretary of State Condoleezza Rice, have engendered a new spirit of conciliation and a search for common ground, although apparently not so much as to improve anti-U.S. sentiment in European public opinion.[16] Hopes engendered by Chancellor Gerhard Schröder's visit to the United States in 2005 to repair relations between the two critical transatlantic actors increased with the elections that brought Angela Merkel to power. Chancellor Merkel, on her part, made it clear that improving relations with the United States would be a priority for her government, although she too did not endorse changing course in German policy with regard to Iraq.

Europeans and Americans have much in common, but one hesitates to conclude in full confidence that the transatlantic debate is over for good. Despite renewed and energetic efforts and initial successes by the second Bush administration and European counterparts to restore the glory of the transatlantic relations, many transatlantic thinkers forecast more bumps ahead, sooner or later.

It is important to note, however, what the coming transatlantic crises will not entail. The worst such recent crisis was over the Iraq war in 2003, and judging from the noise and passion on both sides of the Atlantic, one would have thought that the transatlantic partnership was being pulled to pieces. In fact, all that happened was that several European countries did not join the coalition forces and criticized the U.S. administration for starting the war. Some EU countries did join the United States in Iraq. There was no EU condemnation of the U.S. invasion. No EU country tried to convene, for instance, the UN General Assembly against the United States. Certainly no one contemplated aiding the Iraqi dictator. Thus, when speaking about a transatlantic rift, one must remember to put things in perspective.

At the same time, the extant transatlantic structures do not always forge a reliable basis for effective multilateralism that produces tangible cooperation. The management of transatlantic relations has been traditionally entrusted to a large extent to NATO. The North Atlantic Council, NATO's highest decision-making body, and its various subcommittees functioned throughout the Cold War not only to formulate NATO policies, but also to serve as a forum to discuss and iron out transatlantic differences. That said, NATO was never the sole forum to serve these purposes. At the very least, bilateral diplomacy and back-room bargaining always complemented NATO's plenary forums. As the EU accelerated along its path to foster political and military structures and functions, U.S.-EU summitry has been launched to shore up or perhaps patch up the North Atlantic Council. Obviously, neither forum could contain, let alone prevent, the rift that emerged in the runup to the 2003 war in Iraq. It may even be argued that the distaste in the United States for a "war by committee"—drawing on a particular interpretation of the experience with NATO operations in the Balkans—might have shortened fuses in Washington. The responsibility for the failure to manage differences between the two shores of the Atlantic was put in a sense on NATO. By February 2005, a point was reached where then German Chancellor Schröder argued that "NATO was no longer the primary venue where transatlantic partners discuss and coordinate strategies."[17]

These may be the days that Ivo Daalder refers to as the end of Atlanticism.[18] American and European foreign policies no longer center around the transatlantic alliance to the same extent they did in the past. Even diplomatic traffic is declining across the Atlantic in comparison with intensive contacts within Europe. This can be seen in the tectonic shifts in the wake of the Cold War and the progress of European integration. The removal of the monolithic Soviet threat, and basically almost everything that has happened in Europe since the Berlin wall came down, have culminated in the demand for greater autonomy in European thinking.

As such, the type of Atlanticist relationship perceived by Justin Vaisse, in which "Washington decides unilaterally, and European allies are expected to conform without having a say, sometimes without proper information and discussion" cannot hold.[19] It would be unfair to claim that the United States does not understand that times have changed. However, the Americans argue, the United States will act, if necessary alone, to address perceived security challenges, and Europe, to be treated equally, must make the necessary investment in capabilities and find the resolve to act, not just consult.

Institutional developments within the European Union, which arguably reflect elite political aspirations, are not extrinsic to the debate about transatlantic relations and NATO. All things considered, the possibility of an EU defense capability that is increasingly autonomous from NATO, coupled with an increasingly assertive EU foreign and security policy, cannot be discarded in the long run despite the setbacks registered by the French and Dutch *no* votes to the proposed EU constitution. The question may well be when, rather than if. But the date may well be distant, developing in incoherent steps rather than in grand leaps.

Currently an economic superpower and providing an alternative economic attraction thanks to the Euro, the EU is in the process of maturing its political institutions and common worldview. And as Mark Leonard explains, it is already exerting immense influence in its neighborhood through the enlargement process. Europe's irreversible transformative power vis-à-vis the countries that want to join the Union is complemented by the proliferation of the European obsession with the rule of law and multilateralism on the global stage, producing such outcomes as the Kyoto Treaty or the International Criminal Court.[20] The prospects of the EU's Constitutional Treaty may have been put in doubt after the French and Dutch voters in May 2005 poured cold water over this document, which was the product of aspirations to forge a tighter political union out of the EU. The reasons for this crisis were diverse but had much to do with the perceived ultraliberal orientation of the Constitutional Treaty at a time when stagnating EU economies and high unemployment were creating reaction from the European masses. The Dutch rejectionists also were questioning the virtues of the Euro.[21] Although the constitution did include a provision that obligated the EU to take into account the guarantee of adequate social protection, and the Charter of Fundamental Rights as part and parcel of the constitution did strengthen social protectionism in Europe, this was all fine print for the campaigners.[22] A superficial debate produced a profound shock after the decades of hard work in Europe.

As EU leaders and bureaucracies scramble to find a way out of the impasse created by the rejection of the constitution in two founding member states, for the time being the view, ironically defended foremost by France, to promote further federalism within the EU may have suffered a setback. With the current constitutional draft or a version of it, or even in the absence of it, the EU can be expected to overcome the current crisis and move on.

In fact, the history of the EU is replete with serious crises that were ultimately resolved and that made the Union stronger. On August 30, 1954, France vetoed the European Defense Union, which retarded the development of a common foreign and security policy until the 1990s. On January 14, 1963, General De Gaulle started the vetoes of the United Kingdom's membership to the European Communities, resolved a decade later with its accession. The so-called "empty chair" crisis that started on July 1, 1965, due to the Common Agricultural Policy, resulted in no less than a seven-month refusal of France to attend meetings. When Prime Minister Margaret Thatcher asked for a decrease in British contributions to the common European budget, a five-year crisis ensued, which was resolved in the UK's favor. In a June 1992 referendum, the Danes turned down the Maastricht Treaty only to accept it in May 1993 after obtaining a number of concessions. On September 17, 1992, Italy and the United Kingdom suspended their membership in the European Monetary Union. In March 1999, members of the Commission of the European Communities resigned due to allegations of corruption. The Nice Treaty of December 2000 was a product of four days and four nights of final negotiations that only delivered a more restricted and convoluted compromise text. The Irish first rejected the Nice Treaty in a referendum held in June 2001 and endorsed it in 2002 when they obtained concessions. The Swedes voted no to the Euro in 2003. The current draft constitution itself first seemed to hit the rocks on December 13, 2003, and could only be agreed at the diplomatic level in June 2004. Crises have been part of how the EU has functioned and progressed since its inception.

This may be precisely how political-economic unions mature. In Mark Leonard's words, "The European project has taken Samuel Beckett's injunction to heart: If at first you don't succeed, 'Fail, fail again, fail better.'"[23] This line of thinking is indeed what Jean Monnet, the key founding figure of the

European integration project, anticipated long ago when he said: *L'Europe* *"se fera dans les crises et elle sera la somme des solutions apportées à ces crises"* (Europe will be made in the crises and it will be the sum of the solutions brought to these crises).[24]

Irrespective of the fate of the current constitutional draft, most if not all of the provisions related to foreign and security policy can be expected to survive the current storm in one way or another, and sooner or later. While one can debate which of the constitution's innovations will survive in the end, it is best not to throw away the house copy of the draft constitution at this stage. In that spirit, an analysis of the constitution may still be in order, despite the French and Dutch referenda.

Antonio Missiroli indicates that the EU constitution's foreign policy and common defense articles provide an "enabling" text. Accordingly, "the treaties approved since the Maastricht Treaty (in 1992) have been mostly about constraining the general scope and function of the Union's foreign, security and defense policies. With the constitution, such constraints are either scrapped or the conditions for doing away with them in the future are set."[25] The EU Constitutional Treaty signed by the EU member and candidate countries' leaders in Rome on November 30, 2004, stipulated a single legal personality for the Union. As far as foreign and security policy is concerned, two innovations were particularly noteworthy. One was the idea of designating a Union foreign minister who was to be tasked with the development and representation of the Union's common foreign and security policy.

The other significant novelty was the so-called common defense and solidarity clauses. Thus, the Constitutional Treaty states that "the common security and defense policy shall include the progressive framing of a common Union defense policy. This will lead to a common defense, when the European Council, acting unanimously, so decides. It shall in that case recommend to the Member States the adoption of such a decision in accordance with their respective constitutional requirements."[26] More explicitly, the constitution states that "if a Member State is the victim of armed aggression on its territory, the other Member States shall have towards it an obligation of aid and assistance by all the means in their power, in accordance with Article 51 of the United Nations Charter."[27] As regards the solidarity clause, the EU and its member states are bound to "actively and unreservedly support the Union's common foreign and security policy in a spirit of loyalty and mutual solidarity and shall comply with the Union's action in this area. They shall refrain from action contrary to the Union's interests or likely to impair its effectiveness."[28] The member states would also be expected to contribute civilian and military assets to support the EU's CFSP positions.

Clearly, these stipulations mark important steps toward the attainment of a more articulate foreign, security, and defense profile for the EU. Their importance should neither be understated nor exaggerated. Even if the EU manages in the end to push these provisions through national approval procedures in some form, it remains to be seen how much the ink on paper will actually translate into tangible policies and actions. Missiroli argues that "both clauses, however, bestow legitimacy on any future development in this domain, as did NATO's Article 5 when it was first approved in 1949. The article, under which an attack against one or more of the Alliance's members is considered an attack against them all, only became operational some time after the political commitment was subscribed to and was only invoked 52 years later, in the wake of the 9/11 terror attacks in the US."[29] While that example is true at face value, it may also lead one to wrong conclusions about the EU. The now defunct Western European Union also contained a strongly worded collective defense clause, which endowed that organization with no additional clout.

The draft EU constitution did not envision the EU as a potential rival for the United States, nor did it aim to do away with NATO. To the contrary, the draft constitution explicitly stated that commitments and cooperation in CFSP shall be consistent with commitments under the North Atlantic Treaty Organization, which, for those states that are members of it, remains the foundation of their collective defense and the forum for its implementation. In retrospect, if there is any point in having a collective defense commitment for the Europeans, it would make sense only in NATO and not in the EU.

To the extent that the aspirations reflected in the draft constitution can be realized, the Union will have the machinery to become a stronger foreign and security actor in the world. In this context, the constitution should be read in conjunction with the European Security Strategy (ESS), which sets out the foreign and security policy vision for the Union. Irrespective of the fate of the Constitutional Treaty, the ESS is still in force.

Thus, following the damaging intra-EU and transatlantic disagreements, the ESS adopted in December 2003 can be considered an effort by the EU to learn from previous mistakes. The ESS, based on the draft entitled "A Secure Europe in a Better World" prepared by the EU foreign policy chief Javier Solana, details the EU countries' shared perception of the international security environment, the security objectives of the EU, and how the EU intends to achieve these objectives.[30] The ESS constitutes a necessary step to make the EU a more effective actor on global security issues. The tasking to draft this strategy resulted from the acknowledgment that "the absence of a shared threat assessment was a key factor behind the sharp divisions in the EU".[31]

Concerning the threats, while the ESS lists global warming, energy security, and various regional crises as threats to European security, it underscores the proliferation of weapons of mass destruction, international terrorism, and failing state systems and organized crime as three key strategic threats. It also recognizes relationships that could exist among the three, stating that taking these different elements together, Europe could be confronted with a very radical threat. The ESS makes a point of noting that none of the threats was purely military, and each of them required a mixture of instruments.

The EU list contains significant semantic overlaps with the U.S. National Security Strategy (NSS) of March 16, 2006.[32] On one level, the two documents agree that failing states, terrorism, and proliferation of weapons of mass destruction pose the greatest threat. The NSS like its EU counterpart also devotes consideration to twenty-first-century global challenges such as the spread of AIDS, the threat of pandemic flu, and impending man-made as well as natural and environmental disasters.

At another level, with the changes in the NSS from 2002 to 2006, the two documents were also more compatible in terms of the objectives of security policy. Thus, the ESS wants to address the main threats, foster security in the EU's neighborhood, and build an international order based on effective multilateralism. In turn, the U.S. National Security Strategy aims to promote freedom, justice, and human dignity by ending tyranny, promoting effective democracies, and extending prosperity through free and fair trade and wise development policies. The NSS also sets out the target of leading an expanding community of democracies.

There is a discernible interaction in the development of the U.S. and EU security strategies. The 2002 NSS[33] had laid out a very controversial doctrine of preemptive strike, popularly dubbed the Bush Doctrine, which became even more controversial after the Iraq experience. It also talked about "a distinctly American internationalism that reflects the union of our values and our national interests." The European Security Strategy drafted a year later in a way responded to the 2002 NSS. Although the document never mentioned the NSS, several European commentators alluded to a distinctively European approach to security in a bid to distance themselves from the United States. While threat perceptions were more or less similar on both sides of the Atlantic, the European security document emphasized the principle of effective multilateralism by underlining that international cooperation is a necessity. It underscored that the EU needs to pursue its objectives both through multilateral cooperation in international organizations and through partnerships with other key actors. The subsequent 2006 NSS was arguably influenced not solely by the power dynamics in Washington but also by the European approach to security that appeared to be more palatable to the global audience than the 2002 U.S. strategy. Thus, although the 2006 NSS reaffirmed the possibility to use force preemptively, President Bush in his introduction recalled that "Many of the problems we face—from the threat of pandemic disease, to proliferation of weapons of mass destruction, to terrorism, to human trafficking, to natural disasters—reach across borders"; and he stated, "Effective multinational efforts are essential to solve these problems. Yet history has shown that only when we do our part will others do theirs. America must continue to lead." Albeit tempered by the emphasis on American leadership, the reference to effective multinational efforts, reminiscent of the European emphasis on effective multilateralism marked a change in discourse from the 2002 document.

The ESS and the U.S. National Security Strategy contain important overlaps, which however should not be mistaken for complete harmony, say several commentators. Felix Berenskoetter, for one, noted that between the two strategy documents there were significant differences in terms of the realms of responsibility, threat perception, tasks and strategies, and external partners.[34] Comparing the 2002 NSS and the ESS, he referred particularly to a "mind gap" between the U.S. agenda, which was guided by utopian thinking, and a European strategy that appeared more disposed toward realism. However, as most generalizations go, this is not as clear-cut as it may first seem. The ESS, while acknowledging the possibility to use force, nonetheless tries to restrict it to the domain of conflict prevention in an idealistic fashion. The EU's emphasis on civilian tools and international legal means is closer to the idealistic worldview than to the realist one. The greater headroom envisaged under the NSS for the use of military force, unilaterally or as part of coalitions of the willing, on its part is hardly idealistic.

The defining difference exists more in the realm of democracy promotion or in other words, in the perceived remedy for global disorder. ESS emphasizes democracy in Europe, while the U.S. envisages a forceful campaign to spread democracy and liberal ideology. As Berenskoetter observed, "Declaring it possible to overcome 'Hobbesian' anarchy among great powers and to strive towards a liberal world order goes against the grain of all 'realist' thinking and, ironically, locates the dream of a Kantian paradise in the prose of the NSS. Compared with these transformative ambitions, the ESS's overarching concerns of maintaining regional stability and a multilateral order cannot be labelled 'utopian.'"[35]

Obviously the U.S.-EU gap has narrowed at the level of official discourse with the 2006 NSS, which stated that the American "national security strategy is idealistic about goals, and realistic about means."[36] That said, a certain mind gap does remain between a global superpower with unique means to project military might around the world and an emergent superpower whose strengths lie preeminently in political and economic might. It also flows from the geographical restraint mostly in and around Europe that is implied by the ESS compared to the genuinely global reach of the U.S. National Security Strategy.

The ESS was welcomed in the United States as having successfully laid the grounds for the revitalization of transatlantic cooperation by pinning down the commonalities as well as the differences in American and EU strategic thinking. It was suggested that rather than creating a schism between them, the ESS brings the EU and United States closer. Yet the two strategies, while compatible, are also fairly distinct, reflecting the respective priorities, strategic culture, and the structure of power of the two sides. The way these documents are interpreted in practice with regard to specific policy challenges will in fact define the relationship.

There are sufficient elements of convergence in the U.S. and EU strategy documents to allow cooperation rather than causing inevitable conflict. On the other hand, the preferred policy approach to address threats may be different. This could also be seen as a positive influence on the health of the transatlantic relationship, however. The hard and soft approaches, if successfully blended, can provide a potent formula for increased security for all. Therefore, unless one is committed to a particular political viewpoint, it is easy to hold off on passing judgment about the future of transatlantic security and defense cooperation and alliance.

The EU's actual defense assets and capabilities are not extrinsic to this debate. The EU is proceeding in an often faltering though continual manner toward a duplicative defense arrangement that is increasingly independent of NATO and the United States. Unmistakably, there has long been a French requisition for autonomy from the United States in defense matters. The so-called "Atlanticist" versus "Gaullist" debate is not new. Philippe Roger convinces one that particularly in France anti-Americanism is seemingly not tentative.[37] Ignacio Ramonet, the editor of the influential *Le Monde Diplomatique*,[38] seems to embed this anti-Americanism in an unforgiving critique of neoliberal globalization. And he is joined by numerous other intellectuals.

Particularly in the late 1980s and early 1990s there were advocates within the French defense establishment for genuine autonomy for Europe in the field of security and even defense. In the debate concerning NATO's future following the dissolution of the USSR, France was the main advocate of a more autonomous European defense system. As Jolyon Howorth reports, "France has consistently argued that there is an alternative to a hegemonic

NATO, and has regularly proposed 'alternative' scenarios."[39] Yet it is also true that there was at least a period in the 1990s when the France came close to a deal that would have brought it back onto NATO's military side after it departed in 1966, expelling NATO headquarters from its initial site in Paris to Brussels. That deal could have "reharmonised the Atlantic and European projects," laments Ronald Asmus, wondering "how much of the subsequent European Security and Defense Policy (ESDP) debate and the difficulties between the EU and NATO might have been muted if this deal had been consummated."[40]

In the post–Cold War period, the European defense architecture went through a dramatic overhaul. On the transatlantic front, NATO has adopted a new and openly published strategy and engaged in internal as well as external adaptation. Starting in 1994, the concept of a European Security and Defense Initiative has firmly taken its place in almost every relevant NATO document. The ESDI offered a technical-military arrangement that would allow the Western European Union (WEU) to use NATO assets and capabilities. In the bigger picture the ESDI meant that NATO had acknowledged a greater security role for the EU.

In this connection, numerous steps were taken to enhance European roles, including support to the WEU to serve as the institutional basis of the ESDI, creating the Combined Joint Task Force (CJTF) concept through which NATO assets would be made available to the WEU. NATO staffs were also given the task of providing support by reviewing WEU contingency plans.

The high point for the ESDI was the 1996 Berlin agreement, which was "predicated on a two-way deal involving a U.S. commitment to support a meaningful European military capacity (through CJTFs and other means) and a French commitment to move toward full integration of a restructured Alliance."[41] The Berlin agreement accorded NATO the right of first refusal as well as the promise of improved European capabilities in return for the right to use NATO assets needed for operations conducted by the WEU.

The immediate problems in the implementation of the ESDI in the Balkans made a dramatic impact on developments with regard to the EU's defense policies. Particularly, although the United Kingdom vetoed a proposed merger of the WEU and EU in 1997, by the end of 1998 it was ready to advocate an "autonomous" political and military capacity for the EU. The December 1998 French-British accord reached in the scenic French city of St. Malo produced a watershed in EU defense: In Jolyon Howorth's words, "Implicit in the St-Malo process is the gradual emergence of an autonomous EU capacity—both institutional (decision-making) and military (force structures)—which was always likely to grow into something which the Alliance in general and the United States in particular would look upon with feelings ranging from suspicion to alarm."[42]

The meeting in St. Malo effectively launched the European Security and Defense Policy or ESDP, culminating in a series of steps that detailed the institutionalization of the EU defense efforts. One of the most significant such elaborations was furnished in the Treaty of Nice, which was signed in February 2001 to amend previous EU treaty-law.

The Nice Treaty defined among other things the scope of the EU's autonomous capacity to launch and conduct EU-led military operations, where NATO as a whole would not be engaged, and allowed for the establishment of permanent political and military structures. The treaty also provided for the inclusion in the EU of several functions of the WEU. The headline goal and military capabilities goals, previously established in Helsinki, were also elaborated at Nice.

On the other hand, the genuine contribution of the Nice Treaty to European and indeed potentially global security came in the field of nonmilitary crisis management, a valuable European niche whose importance has been vindicated in the post-9/11 world. The treaty devoted a section to strengthening the civilian capabilities needed in crisis management tasks, such as policing, the rule of law, civilian administration, and civilian protection, while underscoring the importance of promoting synergy between civilian and military instruments. This emphasis has been confirmed by postconflict reconstruction missions from the Balkans to Afghanistan that have required a combination of military and civilian capabilities. The importance of this European strong suit was underscored in a study lead by Michele Flournoy and Julianne Smith, who suggested that NATO and the EU should consider an agreement to provide NATO access to EU civilian and constabulary capabilities for crisis-management operations. Just as the so-called "Berlin Plus" arrangement provides the EU with NATO's common assets and capabilities for military operations, the study concluded that a "Berlin Plus in reverse" arrangement should allow NATO recourse to the EU's assets in civilian crisis management.[43]

While the EU was effectively copying itself over the WEU and absorbing all its functions except collective defense, and adding on top of it civilian crisis-management capabilities, the Nice Treaty contained a major flaw in terms of respecting the interests of non-EU associate members, most notably Turkey. Turkey's long-standing rights in European defense arrangements seemed to evaporate. Of the non-EU NATO allies, the strongest reaction came from Turkey, which was farthest back in line to EU membership and which had made important contributions to Europe's defense for half a century. The EU seemed to sidestep Turkey in the area of security and defense, Turkey's strongest and EU's weakest suit. In retrospect, this aspect of the Nice Treaty, as well as the discussions that preceded and followed it, looks as surreal now as it did then. Needless to say, it did not survive.

Turkey's omission was not explained properly, save by the argument that decision making is a privilege only of the EU members. While decision making in the WEU, too, was confined to members, the daily arrangements achieved through time and experience in the WEU had come to reflect a more pragmatic view and more effective participation in decision shaping by the associates. In the words of Ömür Orhun:

> The EU cannot solve this problem through rhetorical claims of institutional prerogatives or autonomous decision-making rights. In fact, nobody denies the EU's, or for that matter, NATO's decision making autonomy. The crux of the matter is to try to find sui generis solutions to a sui generis situation. For that, we do not need to look beyond the realm of European security, since such a sui generis solution—a workable and satisfactory model—has already been found in the Western European Union. Here it is advisable to remember that although the Modified Brussels Treaty does not legally or institutionally foresee an associate membership status, such a status was "invented" through a political decision in 1992, since a necessity was felt in that respect.[44]

As the EU was aspiring to a more serious role than the WEU, these arrangements at least had to be maintained or, more appropriately, advanced. In the absence of such a positive attitude, the Nice Treaty's disregard for Turkey brought strong Turkish resistance in NATO to the EU's recourse to NATO's assets and capabilities. Amounting to a diplomatic filibuster, this resistance retarded the ESDP and embarrassed its key proponents. The acrimony ended only by an agreement on passable working corrections to the Nice Treaty, with the promise of progress in Turkey's membership process.[45] Consequently, after the 2002 NATO Prague and EU Copenhagen summit meetings, NATO and the EU launched a strategic partnership, for the moment putting aside the row over implementation of the so-called Berlin-Plus in NATO.

However, this did not mean the end of the transatlantic debacle. In fact, things got much worse. There was a vociferous exchange of heavy rhetoric on both sides of the Atlantic and within Europe regarding Iraq. In addition, amid much controversy, only a year after the launch of the NATO-EU strategic partnership, the European Council created an autonomous EU operational planning facility. Operational planning is a key capability that NATO has both for itself and if need be for the EU as well. Therefore, the EU planning cell was incontrovertibly duplicative. The proponents of the cell argue that the EU is a distinct "organization" and should not need to rely on NATO's capabilities. They also state that if the EU is to become a military actor, then it should have a functioning autonomous planning capability. These arguments throw gasoline on fire, kindling concerns about imminent European decoupling and the consequent demise of NATO.

The planning cell might be considered to have put brakes on an earlier initiative by France, Germany, Belgium, and Luxembourg in the mini-summit in April 2003. This meeting of the "chocolate makers," as the United States chose to pejoratively label them, proposed a mutual defense clause and the creation of a collective EU operational planning unit not attached to the existing EU Military Staff but instead located in the Brussels suburb of Tervuren. This implied a core European defense grouping distinct from the EU's collective endeavors.[46]

The December 2003 deal engineered by a concerned United Kingdom has managed to turn around, for now, this separate grouping and avoid a standing permanent headquarters for the planning cell. There were also complex liaison arrangements with NATO. But no matter how much the immediate impact of the autonomous EU planning capability is minimized for the moment, as French commentators have asserted, "The worm is in the fruit and it will grow."[47] If that is not a hollow statement, then controversy within the EU will continue and the idea of European autonomous arrangements will progress. In fact, the EU constitution has codified the so-called structured cooperation among willing EU members. Accordingly, a group of states can, under the constitution's "permanent structured cooperation" scheme, make their own arrangements and take action in defense policy. With or without the EU constitution, coalitions of the willing and variable geometries remain popular not only in Washington but also in the European capitals. While these endow commendable flexibility to the EU and in fact are essential for the short-term viability of the Union, it should also be a concern that they do not evolve into a new "kerneuropa," or a Union within the Union. Already, whether in Habermas's advocacy of a core Europe or in ideas recalling a multispeed Europe in defense matters, a risk of the disintegration of European defense arrangements is suggested. Yet it may also be more likely that the specter of "falling behind" in Europe might serve as an inducement for thinking more "European." Arguably, what led the British to sign up on the St. Malo deal was just such a consideration. Others in the time ahead may not be immune either.

If therefore the trend before the 2003 Iraq war continues, then the old questions about duplication, decoupling, and their likely impact on NATO will still be with us. In that regard, one needs to revisit the question of whether ESDP duplication/decoupling could mean that NATO's lifelines will be drained of the European assets and capabilities that are distinctly useful. As regards the duplication of assets, Kori Schake did not agree that this is necessarily bad for NATO:

> Both Europe and the United States could benefit from the constructive duplication of military assets that already exist within NATO. European governments assume that when the EU performs military missions it will usually need to borrow or rent "NATO" assets, most of which are really owned by the US. However, those assets which the EU is most likely to need are also in short supply in US forces.
>
> The high tempo of operations in the past ten years has worn out US equipment at a much faster pace than expected, prompting a crisis in the funding of new weapons systems. Europe could win much greater American support for the ESDP if it developed its own capabilities in areas that reduced the burden on over-extended US forces. . . .
>
> So the Europeans should allocate some of their scarce resources to the duplication of capabilities that both enhance EU autonomy and reduce their dependency on over-stretched US forces.[48]

Hypothetically speaking, while full duplication of military assets would mean greater interoperability within the alliance, given the level and trends of defense expenditures, this is not achievable. Therefore, it is probably correct to say, as the former chairman of NATO's Military Committee General Klaus Naumann did, that "throughout this coming decade, Europe will not be capable of performing major military operations at the high-intensity level beyond a rather narrowly defined European area of interest."[49]

However, despite many commentators to the contrary, it is hard to accept at face value that a military capacity that is significantly short of that of the United States is necessarily too short. As James Steinberg indicates, European military weakness is seriously overstated. The recent interventions of British forces in Sierra Leone and French forces in the Ivory Coast are but two examples indicating that "most military operations do not require 'high end' forces at all."[50]

A recent study by the Centre for European Reform in the United Kingdom observes that America's defense policy remains the benchmark for nearly all discussions on European defense, and this creates a harmful sense of impotence and resignation among European defense officials. The study recommends therefore that Europe develop its own "way of war" that would encourage European armies to prepare for more demanding missions than they have performed thus far.[51] This distinct "way of war" would define a European approach to using armed forces, one that recognizes budgetary realities, takes lessons from recent experiences, and capitalizes on Europe's relative strengths. Accordingly, although they would not copy U.S. armed forces in every way, Europe's armies should try to complement them. The study also proposes that Britain and France take the lead, a different "core group" than what Habermas had in mind, but an equally debatable point.

Obviously, key to this endeavor is ensuring complementarity with U.S. forces. As Klaus Naumann has warned, unless the recently formed EU Battle Groups are endowed with capabilities that ensure information dominance, strategic mobility, precision engagement, and sustainability outside of Europe, interoperability with U.S. forces will be increasingly at risk.[52] The wider the gap in such capabilities, the more likely it is that military doctrine and planning could also diverge.

The question, then, is how to manage the differences and indeed to mold them into a positive mixture. If Europe had capabilities absolutely identical to the United States, this would not be better for U.S., European, transatlantic, or global security. A weakness in American strategy is to rely too heavily on the use of punitive military power. If Europe copied American capabilities, the shortfalls in American capabilities to sustain post-conflict stabilization and reconstruction operations would then become common shortfalls of the transatlantic alliance. The experience in Iraq undoubtedly shows that the highest-end military technology, while essential in many combat operational missions, may not suffice to reach the political objectives of a military campaign. The Europeans claim to have relative strengths in the tasks of maintaining postcombat law and order and building state machinery, complementing the U.S. high-end power. It is owing to European contributions that NATO has been credited with particular aptitude in such missions ever since the 1997 crisis in Albania.[53] It remains to be seen whether lessons learned from Iraq will produce a U.S. leap in post-conflict stabilization and nation-building capabilities. But even if it does, given the longevity required for such operations, European capabilities will still be acutely needed.

For Europe and the transatlantic alliance, building interoperability among the armed forces and broader security sector forces, including the police, border control, and customs, is probably as important as maintaining expeditionary high-end interoperability between Europe and the United States. European civilian and U.S. military crisis-management capabilities are complementary, and with a fair degree of healthy duplication of assets, the combination of comparative advantages promises a win-win deal.

However, the issue is not only the duplication of assets but also of planning and command arrangements, as well as the decoupling of European defense arrangements from NATO. There the answer is admittedly fuzzier. Kori Schake submits that some of the concerns in this context are valid. But as explained above, most EU nations view—and are expected to continue to view for a long time—the United States and NATO as essential to their security, and they will not be willing to cause the demise of the transatlantic alliance. Therefore, for their sake and everyone else's, the gradual decoupling that is underway should be checked constantly in order to ensure that future steps are taken not based on whims and fantasies but rather on mature discussion, need, and value added.

All this debate is conducted against the question of whether NATO is a victim of its own success and is left without a mission following the end of the Cold War and the elimination of a direct military threat, as well as the apparent success of the military part of the stabilization efforts in the Balkans. It is true that NATO's relevance is questioned and hotly debated, but that debate has been a constant recurrence for NATO for decades, and in reality, the alliance has almost never been this busy. As NATO's website portrays, the greatest and most visible change in NATO is that its activities since the end of the Cold War are in ending conflict, restoring peace, and building stability in crisis regions. Indeed, the alliance has led three complex peace-support operations—in Afghanistan, Bosnia-Herzegovina, Kosovo, and Macedonia, while supporting another one in Dahir, Sudan. The alliance has also stepped in to take part in the fight against terrorism. In Operation Active Endeavor, NATO ships have been patrolling the eastern Mediterranean, monitoring shipping to detect and deter terrorist activity since October 2001 as part of its response to the 9/11 terrorist attacks.

Lord Robertson noted that "when the British Guardian newspaper, not one of the Alliance's most enthusiastic advocates, runs an article under the by-line 'Peace, Love and NATO' next to a cartoon of John Lennon wearing glasses emblazoned with the NATO star, you know that some things are going well."[54] While such optimism can be attributed to his then professional duty as NATO's secretary general, the truth cannot be too far off the mark. This is most evident from the hectic work schedule at NATO headquarters on a variety of tracks—consultations; defense and operational planning; setting standards; managing ongoing operations; developing NATO's own capabilities; running its relationships with Russia, Ukraine, the PfP, EAPC, and the Mediterranean Dialogue and Istanbul Cooperation Initiative countries; and even enhancing civil emergency cooperation and other areas of alliance activity. It is even making a humble contribution to the training of the Iraqi security forces, although there it is certainly punching very much below its weight. NATO is not conducting all these activities with unanimously enthusiastic and generous input from its members. Yet it is nonetheless there, managing to do all of the above. One can argue that in most of these missions it is fulfilling a rather limited role. That is a relative argument. The basic point remains that NATO is far from idle and obviously still in some demand.

There is widespread recognition that NATO must be able to take roles outside Europe. By the end of the Cold War, the dictum, coined wisely by U.S. Senator Richard Lugar, was "out of area or out of business."[55] Since then, NATO indeed went out of area and not out of business. Now, the same dictum reads "further out of area or out of business." Formally, since 2000, NATO nations have tasked their alliance to confront threats to their security from wherever they may come: "To carry out the full range of its missions, NATO must be able to field forces that can move quickly to wherever they are needed, sustain operations over distance and time, and achieve their objectives."[56] The NATO Istanbul Summit made that tasking operational, thanks to decisions pertaining to NATO roles in Afghanistan and Iraq. Graduates from NATO's training courses in Iraq have reportedly begun to run a Lessons Learned Centre, which aims to increase the efficiency of the Iraqi Armed Forces.[57] NATO has also expanded the geographical focus of its bilateral security cooperation efforts, building on the PfP and the Mediterranean Dialogue, to the broader Middle East region through the Istanbul Cooperation Initiative, which four of the six members of the Gulf Cooperation Council joined as of early 2006.[58] Also in the context of NATO's wider geographical engagement, one could mention its role to help the African Union (AU) expand its peacekeeping mission in Darfur by airlifting additional AU peacekeepers into the region and assisting with their training.

NATO, as both its critics and supporters rush to point out, is Europe's link with the United States. The United States should continue to reassure the NATO allies that the phrase "missions define the coalitions" does not mean that there is no overarching comity with the NATO allies. For the Europeans to have faith in NATO being the primary forum to develop common responses to common threats, risks, and challenges, the United States should pronounce and demonstrate this unequivocally. As Ronald Asmus notes, "The vision of the EU as a counterweight is only likely to become reality if the US pursues policies that make this a self-fulfilling prophecy."[59] His argument chimes with Nicole Gnesotto's observation that "while the Europeans find it fairly easy to agree on a more or less common view of the world, they are divided on the Union's role in managing the world's crises. Since that role is broadly a function of the type of relationship that each member country wants to build with America, bilateral or within NATO, the Europeans have never managed to agree on the actual purpose of their diplomatic and military cooperation."[60] They also are not expected to agree on the fundamental raison d'être of their security and defense policy anytime soon unless they are forced to by the turn of events.

There is intellectual support particularly in Western Europe for the EU to build up its foreign and security policy in order to balance out the U.S. power. The Habermas-Derrida initiative marks this support. For those seeking European autonomy, the first line is "Less America in Europe, more ESDP" as the defining formula in post-9/11 Europe.[61] However, this point is destined to face strong disagreement within Europe, particularly if it is to mean "no America in Europe."

As the debate continued, the Atlanticist camp found a new lease on life on May 1, 2004, with the admission of ten new members to the EU. Karsten Voight, a former German Foreign Ministry coordinator for German-American relations, stated that the entry of the essentially pro-American countries of Central and Eastern Europe into the EU signifies the end of any attempts within the EU to define itself and its evolving foreign and security policy in opposition to the United States. In his words, "You can no longer muster a majority for that."[62] He added that "these countries continue to see the United States, rather than any European neighbor or the EU itself, as the principal guarantor of their young democracies, and the essential political reference point in creating a future that is secure and prosperous."[63] Philip Gordon also suggested that Europeans, and particularly those in the so-called "Old Europe," should have learned that "the result of efforts to oppose the United States on international strategic issues—especially when the United States has a plausible case for action—is not a unified EU standing up to America, but a divided EU that has little effect."[64]

That is true today. Nonetheless, looking to the future, Charles Kupchan speculated that "the new Union members are admittedly less enthusiastic than older ones about Europe's emergence as a counterweight to the US. But as the continent's security order inevitably becomes more European and less Atlantic, central Europeans will realize that it is in their interests to throw their weight behind a stronger EU."[65] This projection sounds plausible. Yet it is still premised on the expectation that a strong EU will necessarily be in opposition to the United States, or a counterweight.

It is not necessary to presume that backing the goal of strengthening the EU as a foreign and security policy actor should inevitably mean supporting the emergence of an adversary to the United States. Suggesting an inverse relationship or a zero-sum game between U.S. and EU power can be grossly misleading. A stronger EU could just as well produce a more effective partner or complement to the United States. It may even be useful that the allies advise each other when obvious mistakes are likely to be committed. Similarly, greater EU capability in defense and security matters is not the end of EU-U.S. cooperation and U.S. influence in Europe. Ronald Asmus notes that the United States needs the EU to sustain peace and stability in Europe, to help anchor to the West the young and still fragile democracies on the continent's periphery, and to meet the new challenges of the twenty-first century. Then "the task facing American diplomacy is how to assist those in the EU who want to build a political unified Union that is a strategic partner of the United States."[66]

There is already useful transatlantic cooperation centered in Europe's neighborhood, namely the Balkans, Russia, Ukraine, Belarus, Moldova, the Caucasus, and the broader Middle East including the Mediterranean, as well as Central Asia, albeit in different degrees and scales. The effort by Germany, Britain, and France, as the EU-3, to ensure that Iran does not develop nuclear weapons is a case in point. Since October 2003, the EU-3 have engaged Iran in negotiations, asking Iran to relinquish its uranium-enrichment program, which can be adapted for military purposes. This initiative has been endorsed by the United States, which has no diplomatic relations with Iran. Subsequently, Britain and France joined the United States in tightening the restraints around Iran at the UN Security Council, joined by Germany outside the Council. The Europeans also joined the Americans in cutting off direct aid to the Palestinian Administration government after it came under the rule of the Hamas party in 2006. Similarly, the United States benefited from European support in isolating Syria following the brutal assassination of the former Lebanese prime minister Rafik Hariri.

Regardless of all the disagreements and the exaggerated characterizations of rifts, to the Turkish eye there is more that binds the two shores of the Atlantic than separates them. The geopolitical epicenter of the world is already shifting away from Europe. While the United States and the EU may argue about their respective strategic cultures and capabilities, they may sooner rather than later be confronted with the reality that the geopolitical focus of the future will shift farther East. That is a new universe for the United States and even more for the EU. They will then rediscover that the players in that region are powerful in economic and increasingly in military terms, only to be matched by their growing political power. For the counterweight role, whether in political, economic, or perhaps other terms, there are potentially stronger candidates outside the transatlantic community. A Europe that is wary of Turkey's size will watch in awe countries that are over a hundred million—even a billion—people strong. The United States and Europe, appearing helpless to resolve the Balkan or Caucasus disputes, will be called on to mitigate rivalries among fellow great powers in the grand Asian continent. The United States will probably continue to be the superpower, but there will be other powerful participants in global life. Then, multilateralism will present itself, not as a policy alternative but instead as an inescapable exigency in most cases. The example of North Korea is already providing sufficient clues for the limits of unilateral coercive actions, even for the United States, in the brave new world. Already, Asmus notes, "the ability to influence Russia, for example, is directly affected by the degree of U.S.–EU cohesion. When it comes to the grand task of managing the rise of China as a global economic and military player, Washington and Brussels are clearly in a better position to influence Chinese behavior if they have a common approach."[67]

The current or future leaders in Europe may or may not be friendlier toward the United States. Yet obviously, this cannot be the sole or even the primary yardstick for assessing Europe. Europe, too, can make geopolitical mistakes, and in such a case, it is debatable whether it would be better for the United States to coauthor or to steer clear of such blunders. At any rate, the need is there to reemphasize transatlantic relations and remedy their shortcomings. This should go hand in hand with a new perspective for NATO. In the evolving new transatlantic bargain, parties should be allowed to pursue common interests through their respective capabilities, instruments, and methods, but keep a constant eye on how to bridge them and make them mutually reinforcing. On any set of issues, either extant or future, NATO ought to act as the primary joint instrument of first use and first refusal, even if that requires updates to NATO.

It must also be a priority of the transatlantic leaders to spend maximum efforts to recover part of NATO's political consultation and coordination function across the Atlantic. Although NATO cannot be laden with the expectation to house all transatlantic cooperation, it is infinitely more meaningful and effective than ad hoc EU-U.S. summits. Ad hoc summitry and bilateral dealings cannot measure up to the task, and constant interaction will be needed even if that requires further reforms in NATO's "governance." Institutional interaction and regular negotiation helps iron out differences in the short term and promotes common analysis and action in the longer run. Within the EU, a joint culture of cooperation will be forged among Europeans old and new as time goes by. Europeans will converge increasingly more among themselves than with others outside the Union, due to the disproportionately advanced and comprehensive intra-European network. The contacts, interaction, and interdependence among the Europeans have already grown to unparalleled intensity and will continue to grow. Several who seem to be outside this "core" will be increasingly pulled in. All the while, the United States will remain the key, but nonetheless largely external, actor. It will connect through NATO.

The institutions are important both in terms of reflecting the underlying political consensus and in carrying this bargain forward. A vibrant NATO will erase a great deal of the concerns about transatlantic fissure, pinning down basic transatlantic cooperation. A robust EU common foreign and security policy will take European integration forward. An effective partnership between NATO and the EU will be a reassurance that the transatlantic community holds together.

Turkey is part and parcel of the transatlantic bargain, although it fares miserably in terms of intellectual representation in the debate. All aspects of transatlantic relations and institutional developments directly influence the country. The same also goes naturally for the EU's institutional steps in the area of common foreign and security policy. The point about remaining outside of the intra-European network, if at all a concern for the United States, is most certainly an issue for Turkey, particularly if its negotiation process fails in producing accession. Turkey has consistently been not only a significant muscle for NATO, but also one of its most prominent supporters. By the same token, as Turkey has made or offered undeniable contributions to the EU's fledgling military and civilian crisis-management capabilities, it has also supported the objective of a stronger EU political role in international affairs. Most important, Turkey has regarded pro-EU, pro-U.S. and pro-NATO policies ultimately as mutually reinforcing, or at the least not contradictory.

For the Turks, the bitter disagreements between their European and U.S. allies have been disturbing. It is customary for Turkish officials to caution that the widening political gap between Europe and the United States makes things more difficult for Turkey. Turkey wants its allies to agree in the end, as was the case more often than not in the good old days. That said, certain of their agreements excluded Turkey. The EU inherited a Cyprus problem apparently as part of such an agreement.[68] Therefore, the concern for Turkey is not only that the EU and the United States agree, but that this agreement take Turkey and its interests on board.

Turkey will be as interested as anyone else in how the United States manages its dominant military power and its relations with Europe and the world. As Turkey's links with the neighborhood intensify, it will be increasingly interested also in the tenor and content of relations between the United States and the regional countries, the Muslim or the Turkic worlds. At any rate, its vital relations with the superpower ally will exert essential influence on the evolution of Turkish foreign and security policy on the road to EU membership. Turkey's primary foreign policy goal may be to join the European

Union, but its primary diplomatic focus will have to remain with the United States. Those who think that this must be a problem for Turkey's EU prospects should take another look at how similar this situation is for any other country in the EU or indeed around the world.

Notes

1. Jacques Derrida, "Is There a Philosophical Language?" in *Points . . . Interviews, 1974–1994*, ed. Elisabeth Weber (Stanford, CA: Stanford University Press, 1995), 218.

2. Giovanna Borradori, Jürgen Habermas, Jacques Derrida, *Philosophy in a Time of Terror: Dialogues with Jürgen Habermas and Jacques Derrida* (Chicago: University of Chicago Press, 2003).

3. Daniel Levy, Max Pensky, and John Torpey, eds., *Old Europe, New Europe, Core Europe: Transatlantic Relations after the Iraq War* (London and New York: Verso: 2005). This volume provides a comprehensive account of the debate organized by Habermas and Derrida, which involved important intellectual figures such as Umberto Eco, Adolf Muschq, Gianni Vattimo, Susan Sontag, Timothy Garton Ash, Richard Rorty, and Iris Marion Young, among others.

4. Levy, Pensky, and Torpey eds., *Old Europe, New Europe, Core Europe*, xv–xvi.

5. Levy, Pensky, and Torpey eds., *Old Europe, New Europe, Core Europe*, xvi.

6. The so-called Letter of the Eight, expressing support for the impending U.S. invasion of Iraq, was signed by the prime ministers and presidents of five EU members and three candidate Central European countries on January 30, 2005, and was published in the *Wall Street Journal*. It was followed on February 6 by the Vilnius Letter, which offered an even more outspoken declaration of support for the U.S. position. The signatories to the Vilnius Letter included Estonia, Latvia, Lithuania, Slovakia, Slovenia, Croatia, Albania, Macedonia, Bulgaria, and Romania.

7. Umberto Eco, "An Uncertain Europe between Rebirth and Decline," in *Old Europe, New Europe, Core Europe*, ed. Levy et al., 20.

8. Robert Kagan, *Of Paradise and Power: America and Europe in the New World Order* (New York: Vintage, 2004).

9. David P. Calleo, "Transatlantic Folly: NATO vs. the EU," *World Policy Journal* 20, no. 3 (Fall 2003): 17.

10. Charles Kupchan, "The End of the West," *Atlantic Monthly*, November 2002.

11. Joseph P. Quinlan, *Drifting Apart or Growing Together? The Primacy of the Transatlantic Economy* (Washington, DC: Center for Transatlantic Relations, 2003).

12. Thomas Friedman, *The Lexus and the Olive Tree* (New York: Farrar, Straus & Giroux, 2000).

13. Joschka Fischer, "America Had No Verdun," *Der Spiegel*, March 24, 2003.

14. Robert Kagan, "America's Crisis of Legitimacy," *Foreign Affairs* 83, no. 2 (March/April 2004).

15. Robert Jervis, "The Compulsive Empire," *Foreign Policy* no. 137, (July–August 2003).

16. The German Marshall Fund of the United States, "Transatlantic Trends 2005." The full study can be found at www.transatlantictrends.org.

17. Gerhard Schröder, speech given at the 41st Munich Security Conference, December 2, 2005, text available at www.securityconference.de.

18. Ivo H. Daalder, "The End of Atlanticism," *Survival* 45, no. 2 (Summer 2003).

19. Justin Vaisse, "From Transatlanticism to Post-Atlanticism," *In the National Interest* 2, no. 27, July 9, 2003. www.inthenationalinterest.com

20. Mark Leonard, *Why Europe Will Run the 21st Century* (New York: Public Affairs, 2005).

21. "Charlemagne: Another Fine Mess," *Economist*, May 28, 2005.

22. "Charlemagne," *Economist*.

23. Mark Leonard, "Europe Will Survive a French Non," *Foreign Policy* no. 141, April 20, 2005. www.cer.org.uk/articles/leonard_foreignpolicy_20april05.html.

24. Quoted in France 3, "Dossiers: L'Europe au fil des crises," http://referendum-constitution-europeenne.france3.fr/dossiers/10967808-fr.php.

25. Antonio Missiroli, "The Constitutional Treaty: 'Enabling Text' for Foreign Policy and Defence," *European Voice*, October 21–27, 2004.

26. Constitutional Treaty, Article I-12, paragraph 4, under the section Categories of Competence. For the full text of the Constitution, see: http://europa.eu.int/constitution/index_en.htm.

27. This would be without "prejudice (to) the specific character of the security and defense policy of certain Member States," a reference concerning mainly the neutral members of the EU.

28. Constitutional Treaty Part I, Article 15.

29. Missiroli, "The Constitutional Treaty."

30. See: Peter Van Ham, "Europe Gets Real: The New Security Strategy Shows the EU's Geopolitical Maturity," *AICGS Advisor*, January 9, 2004. Also: Borut Grgic, "European Security: A Strategy with No Muscle," *International Herald Tribune*, December 13, 2003. The text of "A Secure Europe in a Better World" can be found at http://ue.eu.int/uedocs/cmsUpload/78367.pdf.

31. International Institute for Strategic Studies, "The European Security Strategy," *Strategic Comments* 9, no. 9 (November 2003).

32. The NSS serves as a non–legally binding guidance document required by the Congress under the 1986 Goldwater-Nichols Act. The text of the U.S. National Security Strategy dated March 16, 2006, can be found at www.whitehouse.gov/nsc/nss/2006/nss2006.pdf.

33. The text of the U.S. National Security Strategy dated September 17, 2002, can be found at www.whitehouse.gov/nsc/nss.html.

34. Felix Sebastian Berenskoetter, "Mapping the Mind Gap: A Comparison of U.S. and EU Security Strategies," *Security Dialogue* 36, no. 1 (March 2005): 71–92.

35. Berenskoetter, "Mapping the Mind Gap," 88.

36. U.S. National Security Strategy (March 2006), 49.

37. See Philippe Roger, *L'ennemi americain: Genealogie de l'antiamericanisme français*, (Paris: Seuil, 2002).

38. Ignacio Ramonet, *Wars of the 21st Century: New Threats, New Fears* (Melbourne and New York: Ocean Press, 2004).

39. Jolyon Howorth, "European Integration and Defence: The Ultimate Challenge?" (Chaillot Paper 43, Institute for Security Studies of WEU, Paris, November 2000), 14.

40. Ronald D. Asmus, "Rethinking the EU: Why Washington Needs to Support European Integration," *Survival* 47, no. 3 (2005): 95. See also Ronald D. Asmus, *Opening NATO's Door: How the Alliance Remade Itself for a New Era* (New York: Columbia University Press, 2002).

41. Howorth, "European Integration," 24.

42. Howorth, "European Integration," 26.

43. Michele Flournoy, et al., *European Defense Integration: Bridging the Gap between Strategy and Capabilities* (Washington, DC: CSIS, October 2005). See also Helga Haftendorn, "Ein Koloß auf tönernen Füßen," *Internationale Politik* 60, no. 4 (April 2005): 80–85.

44. Ömür Orhun, "European Security and Defence Identity—Common European Security and Defence Policy: A Turkish Perspective," *Perceptions* 5, no. 3 (September–November 2000). www.sam.gov.tr/.

45. The document is Annex II of the 2002 Copenhagen Summit Presidency Conclusions, found at: www.europa.eu.int/abc/doc/off/bull/en/ 200210/i1015.htm# anch0034.

46. International Institute for Strategic Studies, "EU Operational Planning," *Strategic Comments* 9, no. 10 (December 2003).

47. International Institute for Strategic Studies, "EU Operational Planning."

48. Kori Schake, "EU Should Duplicate NATO Assets," *CER Bulletin*, no. 18, June–July 2001.

49. Klaus Naumann, "What European Defence Capability Requires," *World Security Network Newsletter*, March 21, 2005.

50. James B. Steinberg, "An Elective Partnership: Salvaging Transatlantic Relations," *Survival* 45, no. 2 (Summer 2003): 128.

51. Steven Everts, Lawrence Freedman, Charles Grant, François Heisbourg, Daniel Keohane, and Michael O'Hanlon, *A European Way of War* (London: Centre for European Reform, 2004).

52. Naumann, "What European Defence Capability Requires."

53. For a detailed discussion of the topic, see Burak Akçapar, "Partnership for Peace's Influence as an Instrument of Continuity and Change in the Euro-Atlantic Region" in *A History of NATO: The First Fifty Years*, volume 1, ed. Gustav Schmidt (New York: Palgrave, 2001).

54. Lord George Robertson, "Toward a New Transatlantic Consensus" (speech at the Munich Conference on Security Policy, August 2, 2003).

55. Senator Richard Lugar, "NATO: Out of Area or Out of Business" (remarks delivered to the Open Forum of the U.S. State Department, August 2, 1993, Washington, DC).

56. Communiqué of the 2002 Reykjavik meeting of the NATO Foreign Ministers, paragraph 5.

57. NATO Update, "NATO Trainees Lead New Iraqi Center," November 30, 2005.

58. These include Bahrain, Qatar, Kuwait, and the United Arab Emirates. The remaining two are Saudi Arabia and Oman, who reportedly also showed interest, although not joining as of beginning 2006.

59. Asmus, "Rethinking the EU," 101.

60. Nicole Gnesotto, Editorial, *ISS Newsletter*, October 2003.

61. Nicole Gnesotto, "ESDP: A European View," Paper for the IISS/CEPS European Security Forum, Brussels, July 8, 2001.

62. Karsten Voight quoted in John Vinocur, "The Big Winner in the EU Expansion: Washington," *International Herald Tribune*, December 9, 2002.

63. Voight, quoted in Vinocur, "The Big Winner."

64. Philip H. Gordon, "One Year On: Lessons from Iraq" (Chaillot Paper 68, *One Year On: Lessons From Iraq*, (Paris: EU-ISS, 2004), 166.

65. Charles A. Kupchan, "Resent, Resist, Compete," *World Today* 60, no. 7 (July 2004). See also Charles A. Kupchan, *The End of the American Era: U.S. Foreign Policy and the Geopolitics of the Twenty-First Century* (New York: Alfred Knopf, 2002).

66. Asmus, "Rethinking the EU,"101.

67. Asmus, "Rethinking the EU," 99.

68. This agreement was divulged by Richard Holbrooke in his comments at the Turgut Özal Memorial Lecture, the Washington Institute for Near East Policy, in November 2003: "The long-standing plan, which I have been closely associated with, was a three-pronged approach: first, to get the EU to invite Cyprus to join the EU; second, to use this to push the two Cypriot communities into a productive negotiation that would produce the long-sought bi-zonal, bi-communal federation; and third, to open accession talks for Turkey to join the EU." Obviously, Greek Cypriots joined the EU, rejected the federation, and within the EU continued their recalcitrance against the Turkish Cypriot State and Turkey, this time as a full-fledged, veto-yielding member.

CHAPTER SIX

America as Partner

The United States and Turkey are two longstanding allies and partners with a long list of positive items of strategic cooperation and a short list of sensitivities. This time-honored relationship has withstood a number of strains in the last half century. Turkish public opinion has been critical of the United States on Iraq, as it was on Vietnam. The United States also disappointed the Turks in the Johnson Letter of June 5, 1964, which warned Turkey that it would not side with its ally if the Soviet Union intervened against Turkey due to Cyprus. And the United States criticized Turkey in the aftermath of the 1974 Turkish intervention in Cyprus, following a coup orchestrated by the military junta then ruling Greece. Other crises involved the Kennedy administration's bargaining with the Soviet Union over the missiles deployed in Turkey and, more recently, the 2003 Turkish Parliament's decision not to allow U.S. forces to invade Iraq from Turkish territory. These and several other crises engendered feelings of dismay on one side or the other.

Despite occasional problems and fragilities, the relationship has consistently culminated in upgraded partnerships. As a result, both sides have been standing to benefit immensely from their cooperation and friendship over a half century. In addition to much publicized lows, there have been infinitely more highs than can be counted in one stroke. While public polls in Turkey currently point to a new low in public perception, the same public cheered the U.S. president when he visited earthquake-stricken Turkey only a few years before Iraq. They applauded again when the U.S. president reaffirmed U.S. support for Turkey's EU membership after Iraq. The same public continues to

enjoy American movies and music and sends their children in large numbers
to American colleges when given the opportunity.

Although Turkish-American relations do not benefit from a powerful infrastructure of people-to-people affinities or expansive domestic political or
economic constituencies, cooperation remains the course for the two countries. This is in no small degree due to the fact that both countries are part
of the global democratic network, and in almost every issue of common concern, the benefits of cooperation far outweigh non-cooperation. The challenge, however, is to adjust and renew the fundamental tenets of the partnership in times of galloping change in the regional and global scene.

While Turkey's location and the facilities it provided to U.S. power projection capabilities has been a linchpin of the relationship for decades, Turkey
now has the potential to draw on more diversified assets to reinforce joint capabilities and pursue shared objectives. This is a nascent aspect that will need
first to be fully identified and understood and then woven into the fabric of the
partnership. It is time for some serious policy planning and public relations.

By the summer of 2006 there was ample reason to believe that both the
challenge and the need for creative thinking were fully grasped by both
countries. A case in point was the document entitled "Shared Vision and
Structured Dialogue to Advance the Turkish-American Strategic Partnership" announced by Foreign Minister Abdullah Gül and Secretary of State
Condoleezza Rice in Washington on July 5, 2006.[1] The document has established a concrete mechanism building on existing channels of dialogue and
supplementing them with additional forums. A particular innovation of the
document was the emphasis placed on broadening the dialogue beyond civilian and military officials to business groups, media, civil society, scientists
and engineers, academicians, think tanks, and students, as well as legislators.
To the extent that it will be implemented, the document therefore marked
an investment in the next generation of Americans and Turks as part of this
broad-based dialogue.

As a fundamental tenet of the bilateral relations, the document noted that
Turkey and the United States share the same set of contemporary values and
ideals in their regional and global objectives, which are defined by promotion of peace, stability, and prosperity. As such, the document appeared to indicate a point of departure for the respective foreign policy objectives of the
two countries. Furthermore, both the content and the breadth of issues listed
in "Shared Vision" demonstrated the importance of the common agenda of
the United States and Turkey. The document stated:

> Turkey and the United States pledge themselves to work together on all issues
> of common concern, including promoting peace and stability in the broader

Middle East through democracy; supporting international efforts towards a permanent settlement of the Arab-Israeli conflict, including international efforts to resolve the Israeli-Palestinian conflict on the basis of a two-state solution; fostering stability, democracy and prosperity in a unified Iraq; supporting diplomatic efforts on Iran's nuclear program, including the recent P5+1 initiative; contributing to stability, democracy and prosperity in the Black Sea region, the Caucasus, Central Asia and Afghanistan; supporting the achievement of a just and lasting, comprehensive and mutually-acceptable settlement of the Cyprus question under the auspices of the UN and in this context ending the isolation of the Turkish Cypriots; enhancing energy security through diversification of routes and sources, including from the Caspian basin; strengthening transatlantic relations and the transformation of NATO; countering terrorism, including the fight against the PKK and its affiliates; preventing WMD proliferation; combating illegal trafficking of persons, drugs and weapons; increasing understanding, respect and tolerance between and among religions and cultures; and promoting together effective multilateral action to find solutions to international challenges and crises of common concern.[2]

The document also contained unequivocally strong support for Turkey's accession to the EU and the accession process now underway.

No matter how one looks at this document—the first that the United States has signed with any country—it stands as an acknowledgment that Turkey is a valuable player and partner in a host of issues that top international agendas. Although the "Shared Vision" announcement did not introduce any new issues into the existing list of the bilateral agenda, it is likely to serve as a reference for further efforts to address common concerns. As such, the document entailed a leap in Turkish-American relations following the 1999 landmark when the two countries started to characterize their relationship as a strategic partnership. However, the full-blown impact of the document is contingent upon its successful implementation, which in turn necessitates a broad appreciation of Turkey's new strengths as well as its long-standing qualities.

Turkey's new capabilities are a derivative of its positive regional engagement and global message. Turkey is everything that the United States could want in this volatile neighborhood. Obviously, Turkey's relations with the countries in its broad neighborhood have been increasingly complex. The country's leaders and diplomats have been exerting maximum efforts to transform old foes into friends, with the business community in a supporting role. Many intellectuals cannot help wonder if this emphasis on the neighborhood means that Turkey is drifting away from Europe and America, especially in the wake of the Turkish Parliament's decision not to allow the invasion of Iraq from Turkish territory despite the country's strong antipathy toward the tyrannical Saddam Hussein regime. It is argued that now that the United States no longer confidently relies on Turkey as a military launching ground for operations in the Middle East, and given that Turkey's accession to the EU is not to be taken for granted, Turkey may be veering away from its traditional Western orientation, with consequences also for Turkish-U.S. relations.

The question was first coined by Thomas Friedman in late 1990s in another context,[3] but the theme of "who lost Turkey?" has become fashionable of late. Various experts commenting on the Turkish-American partnership in the wake of the 2003 invasion of Iraq note degradation in Turkish-U.S. relations indicate that the two traditional allies no longer share a common threat, underscore the critically negative role that the U.S.-led invasion of Iraq played in the strategic partnership between Ankara and Washington, and draw attention to the repeated public opinion surveys in Turkey that display distrust for presumed American intentions in Turkey's neighborhood. Thus, Ian Lesser notes: "For decades, the relationship between Ankara and Washington has been described as 'strategic'—sustained and supportive of the most important international objectives of both sides. Today, the strategic quality of the relationship can no longer be taken for granted as a result of divergent perceptions of the Iraq war, and more significantly, new international priorities on both sides. As a result, a bilateral relationship of great geopolitical significance, but one that has operated without fundamental reassessment since the early years of the Cold War, is now in question."[4]

Ian Lesser also notes that although Turkish-U.S. relations have been seen through the prism of geopolitics, the key questions are not whether Turkey is a bridge or a barrier, a flank or a front, and thus not geographic. Phil Gordon and Ömer Taşpınar do, however, come back to the importance of geopolitics, writing that "a quick look at the map clearly illustrates the geostrategic stakes involved in keeping Turkey on a European track. It is not only the most advanced democracy in the Islamic world, but it also shares its southern borders with Syria, Iraq, and Iran. In the Caucasus, Turkey borders Azerbaijan, Georgia, and Armenia and thereby serves as an energy corridor through which the vast oil and gas reserves of Central Asia and the Caspian Sea pass to the West."[5] The truth is probably that both points are correct and it is geopolitics but also much more.

Beyond the point about whether to frame Turkish-American relations in a geopolitical context or which metaphors to use to define the relationship and Turkey's role, the fact of the matter remains that it seems no serious thinker would suggest that the relationship between the United States and Turkey is unimportant. The Council on Foreign Relations report authored by

Steven Cook and Elisabeth Sherwood-Randall in June 2006 has made specifically this point, underscoring that at a time of emerging schism between the West and the Islamic world, America's relationship with Turkey—a Western-oriented, democratizing Muslim country—is in fact more important than ever.[6] Hence, argued Philip Gordon and Ömer Taşpınar of the Brookings Institution: "Ultimately, a stable, Western-oriented, liberal Turkey on a clear path toward EU membership would serve as a growing market for Western goods, a much needed contributor to European labor forces, a democratic example for the rest of the Muslim world, a stabilizing influence on Iraq, a valuable actor in Afghanistan (where Turkey has already led the International Security and Assistance Force twice), and a critical ally for the United States in the war on terrorism. A resentful, unstable, nationalist Turkey would be the opposite in every case."[7]

Nor is there a belief that the perceived damage is too big to repair. To the contrary, there is an awareness that steps need to be taken to put things back on track. Thus, most experts appear united in calling for a serious strategic dialogue. Lesser argues that while a new and more predictable strategic relationship is possible, it will have to involve "new approaches, a wider range of participants and issues for engagement, and not least, more modest expectations on all sides. It will also require an end to the idea of cooperation based largely on Turkey's location—the real estate perspective—and the development of an approach based on forward planning and concerted policies."[8] Lesser caps his argument by referring to Ankara's new favorable standing in its vicinity and posing the critical question that is perhaps key to the future of the Turkish-American strategic partnership: Can Turkey's new regional activism support Western objectives? The answer is a resounding yes, but obviously only if Turkey can identify with the West and if the Western interests are reconciled with Turkey's own interests.

As repeated public opinion polls in Turkey have demonstrated, there is a residual wariness among Turks regarding U.S. policies, and it is aggravated by Turkey's close proximity to Iraq. But this cautionary Turkish viewpoint cannot be regarded as permanent, self-perpetuating, or isolated. How Turkish public opinion will evolve in the time ahead will likely be determined by developments on two tracks. First, and most important, how the United States approaches Turkish interests will be crucial. Second, how the United States acts on the international stage will likely provide a multiplying effect on Turkish public opinion.

Starting from the latter, how the United States is perceived in the world will be influenced to a large extent by how the United States defines its own role and place in the world. This is important in part because of Turkish society's openness, which allows easy access to all sorts of views from around the world, not only from U.S. sources. Turkish public opinion is thus influenced by how the world sees the United States. It is also equally important because how the United States sees itself and its role in Turkey's region and the world has a direct bearing on Turkish interests. The question about the U.S. self-image and its global image is of course subject to lively debate, foremost within the United States.

It is understandable for a country that possesses such unsurpassed power to ponder what it can do and what it wants to do with its might. Asking "What is the central purpose of America's unprecedented global power?" Zbigniew Brzezinski points out that the United States risks falling into a situation where it will be "perceived as self-absorbed and the anti-American ideologues will gain international credence by labeling the United States a self-appointed vigilante."[9] He cautions that a trend has already started where global sympathy with 9/11 "has given way to widespread suspicion of the true motivations of the exercise of American power."[10] He adds that solitary national security being a "chimera," the "quest for security must include efforts to garner international support."[11]

Joseph Nye, on his part, complains that the United States has been losing its soft power in the world and argues that "in the global information age, the attractiveness of the United States will be crucial to our ability to achieve the outcomes we want."[12] He proceeds to make the case against a habit of ad hoc coalitions: "Rather than having to put together pickup coalitions of the willing for each new game, we will benefit if we are able to attract others into institutional alliances and eschew weakening those we have already created."[13] He cites a study by Arquilla and Ronfeld that argued that power will come not only from strong defenses but from strong sharing.

Brzezinski cautions that the world could plunge into either global chaos or global community, depending on what choice the United States makes between global domination, which could hasten violent turmoil, or global leadership to address the underlying causes of global strife. Choosing the latter calls for "the mobilization of worldwide support on a scale that dwarfs even the alliance that defeated the totalitarianism of the twentieth century."[14]

Just as the idea of global hegemony or "empire" promises no good for the United States and the world, the same is true also for a voluntary or involuntary U.S. absence from endeavors to create a better and more secure world. Gautam Adhikari points out that it would be hard to resolve a major world crisis without the active help of the United States. As such, "America continues to occupy the world's leadership position. But it's a board chairman's job, requiring persuasion, the creation of consensus and discreet flexing of power, as well as popular acceptance. Its tasks cannot be performed by a lone maverick. If the United States wants to reassert itself as a widely accepted, and respected, leader of the democratic world, it will have to carry the world with it."[15]

In the second term of the Bush presidency, the secretary of state has declared that the time for diplomacy is now. Both President George W. Bush and Secretary Rice appear to have made the choice for effective multilateralism in a number of outstanding policy issues, whether with regard to Iran, Syria, or North Korea. The world will hold its breath and follow the developments.

The rest of the world and particularly the transatlantic community have a huge stake in assisting the United States to make the right choice. Nowhere is this more significant than in the fight against terrorism. If 9/11 has played any role in prompting this discussion, then another such attack would surely cloud all visions, and even cause a heavy toll on individual liberties throughout the West. If chaos, erosion of the international legal system, and a slide toward less liberal democracies are to be avoided and the fundamental human right to life and dignity is to be honored, there is no substitute for transatlantic and indeed global solidarity in combating terrorism.

There is near unanimous agreement with the assertion that the fight against terrorism cannot be won without complete international solidarity. There is no such unanimity when it comes to putting it into practice. Despite positive developments in the UN in regard to formulating the international legal basis for a comprehensive fight against terrorism, not all countries display sensitivity that is commensurate with the task at hand. Turkey has learned this all too painfully in its experience with the PKK and other terrorism. Anyone who believes that the fight against terrorism, which cannot be associated exclusively with any religion, culture, or geography, is somebody else's issue has yet to be enlightened.

But the issue appears indeed much broader than counterterrorism. In almost all of the key regional and global issues, the EU, Turkey, and indeed the world will need the United States to defend the international rule of law. The benefits of an international community of higher moral standards far outweigh that of any hegemonic or imperial one-night stand. If missions randomly define the coalitions, reluctance and resignation and even suspicion will set in on the part of U.S. allies and friends.

Given that in the Hobbesian world that hosts most of these threats the United States is the only effective global actor, neither Turkey's security interests nor those of the extant EU can be pursued without cooperation with the United States. In turn, it must be equally obvious to the United States that in the age of globalization its unique power—which no state contests—does not and will not allow it to achieve security without the cooperation of others. In most instances, the EU and Turkey are the most likely allies of the United States, assuming, of course, that the United States agrees to listen, share and coalesce, and maintain high moral standards.

On its part, a Turkey whose views and interests are heeded by the United States will be a more willing partner and ally. This implies the need for the United States to forge a genuine dialogue, with a fair share of advice from Turkey. Admittedly, there is an immense imbalance in power between the two allies. Furthermore, the United States, as the predominant global power, must not be averse to submitting its national policies to a "review" by others, as consultation and due respect may in the end win over the allegiance of its friends.

Nonetheless, the need to engage in timely, detailed consultations and develop on both sides a reflex of coordination is evidenced by the fact that at times, following its own path toward common objectives promises to be Turkey's best contribution. In other words, a Turkey that is better attuned to its neighborhood is a more capable and useful ally than a Turkey that is compelled to agree with every U.S. policy. As Uğur Ziyal stated, "Turkey would be able to contribute more to the causes of stability, peace, democracy, free trade and modernity if it can successfully blend its regional, local colors with those of its Western vocation and membership."[16] In interstate relations, such latitudes can be achieved only if supported by a high degree of confidence and an expansive basis of bilateral relationship.

Therefore, as Turkey and the United States consolidate mutual faith and confidence, they must also give greater attention and emphasis to broadening the pillars of cooperation, including in the hitherto lagging fields of economic and commercial relations.[17] Indeed, one of the major weaknesses of the Turkish-U.S. partnership has consistently been a dearth of the kind of economic and commercial bonds that exist between Western Europe and the United States. Oddly enough, the half-century-old alliance has also not been translated into a vibrant intellectual interaction between the two nations, particularly the Turkish viewpoint being most often absent from the U.S. intellectual scene.

Instead, the partnership was built within the purview of security and foreign policy elites, and it remained under the negative influence of anachronistic ethnic Armenian and Greek lobbies in Congress, which demonstrated zero regard for the strong mutual interests inherent in U.S.-Turkish relations. The public relations efforts in both countries were dismal in their reach and impact. Hence, when the dominant policy and intellectual elites did not agree in their outlook, the overall climate of relations suffered.

Come 2003, Turkish-U.S. relations entered a phase marked by fragility following the Turkish Parliament's decision not to grant U.S. demands related to the impending war in Iraq. The war was deeply unpopular through-out Turkey. Particularly in the lead-up to the war, many American intellec-tuals appeared unwilling or unable to appreciate the undercurrents that have engendered such a monolithically negative stance, encompassing both the left and right of the Turkish political spectrum. The government, which had tried to justify authorizing the United States to open the northern front in realpolitik terms, failed to convince the increasingly assertive and engaged public and media, as well as Turkish legislators.

Undoubtedly, one important factor in the Turkish mind was and remains weariness with the PKK terrorism issue. The war came only four years after the capture of PKK head Abdullah Öcalan, which was widely perceived in Turkey to resolve the problem. The war threatened to reignite the issue—and it did. The fact that northern Iraq had been a staging ground for incursions into Turkey by PKK terrorists since the end of the first Gulf War in 1991 only compounded Turkish concerns about another war in Iraq. Northern Iraq continues to be the base for some five thousand armed terrorists in Kurdish-controlled northern Iraq, and the fact that the PKK resumed incursions into Turkey on June 1, 2004, greatly aggravates Turkish sensitivities. Turkey has adamantly called on the United States and the Iraqi government to take ac-tion against PKK terrorists in Iraq. The PKK presence in Iraq continues to be a black spot on the war against terrorism and also casts a dark shadow over Turkish-U.S. relations and the public perception of the United States in Turkey.

Another factor in Turks' negative attitude toward the war was fatigue with the never-ending Iraqi conundrums. The Turkish people have been suffering from events in this troubled neighbor for decades. Since the 1980s Iraq has been continually at war with itself and with the outside world. First it was the Iran-Iraq war, during which Turkey successfully maintained active neutrality vis-à-vis both countries. Then, it was the Iraqi invasion of Kuwait in August 1990, followed by the Gulf War, which drew Iraq out of Kuwait but retained Saddam Hussein's leadership. Turkey emerged as one of the primary losers from this war despite its support from the outset in the U.S.-led international effort. The economic fallout from the loss of Iraq as a trading partner was gi-gantic. And the power vacuum created in the north of Iraq allowed the PKK to base itself in that region. The background to Turkey's sensitivity about Iraq was explained by Ian Lesser in 2000:

> The Gulf War experience left an uncomfortable legacy in Ankara. . . . Many Turks worried that Operation Provide Comfort, an American-led effort that between 1991 and 1996 aimed to safeguard the Kurdish areas of northern Iraq, would encourage Kurdish separatism within Turkey. Many well-informed,

Western-oriented Turkish observers remain convinced that the West actually sought (and seeks) the establishment of a "Kurdistan" carved, in part, from Turkish territory—a perception that might seem incredible from the perspective of other NATO members. Nevertheless, Ankara provided crucial support to the operation. Many in Turkey have interpreted their country's role in the Gulf War and subsequent experiences as a series of compromises on Turkish interests and sovereignty.[18]

While that was written way before the 2003 war against Iraq, the perceptions lingered and heavily influenced the parliamentary debate regarding the U.S. request to use Turkish territory to invade Iraq. Although the United States was explicit in committing to Iraq's territorial integrity, the Turkish public and elites remained unconvinced due to the consistent hostile messages from the Iraqi Kurdish leaders against Turkey. Quoting from Soner Çağaptay, "Turkey is ill at ease with the emergence of a Kurdish proto-state in Iraq, which will likely only strengthen should the rest of Iraq deteriorate into chaos. As Turkey is faced with an autonomous Kurdish state on its borders, many among Turkey's security-military elite question whether it was the U.S. strategy since the start to establish such a state."[19] Çağaptay also argues that "many Turkish officials fear that Kurdish separatists in Turkey will abuse Iraqi federalism to their advantage."[20]

At the same time, this is only part of the problem. Kurdish separatism in Iraq would be a recipe for disaster, not only for Iraq but also for the region. In such a scenario, with Iraq pulled into an all-out civil war, the whole region would be destabilized. Turkish interest in avoiding such an abyss is paramount, reflecting the stakes of the Iraqis, the neighbors, and the international community writ large, including the United States in no lesser degree. It would be delusional but also equally unfair to expect Turkey to remain indifferent to chaos in Iraq.

In this respect, the question of Kirkuk is a ticking time bomb for Iraq and the region. This oil-rich city, whose oil wealth is second only to Rumailah in the south, is a multiethnic microcosm of Iraq, and indeed of the Middle East. Different ethnic and religious groups in Iraq lay claim to this city. However, the Kurds seem to have exploited the current situation and strengthened their hold on the city, against the protests of the Turkmens and Sunni Arabs in particular. While it is true that the "Arabization" policy of Saddam Hussein had previously changed the demography of the city through forced expulsions of the Kurds and the Turkmens, the mass population movement into the city and its environs went far beyond those expelled. Neutral observers have long been calling attention to the Kirkuk problem, emphasizing "a broadly acceptable solution to the question of Kirkuk, whose unresolved status may ignite a war between Arabs and Kurds."[21] As the International Crisis Group notes, despite the reassurances of the Kurdish leaders, "other Iraqis accuse the Kurds of being motivated precisely by the desire to grab Kirkuk's significant oil resources as a stepping-stone toward secession."[22] Keeping Kirkuk under a special status, as is the case in Baghdad, would go a long way in avoiding a dangerous precipice.

Kirkuk, of course, also lies at the heart of a bigger question in Iraq and the region, namely the future of the Kurdish region in the north of Iraq and the unity and integrity of Iraq in the postinvasion era. In 2004 there was a feeling that a "profound shift" had occurred in Kurdish strategy, as the International Crisis Group reported, amounting to a historic compromise of "accepting an autonomous region as the maximum objective of the Kurdish national movement."[23] The International Crisis Group also reported "a willingness, expressed in interviews with ICG, to abandon the exclusive claim to Kirkuk in favour of a sharing arrangement under which the city and governorate would receive a special status."[24]

However, even then the same ICG was expressing regret that "Kurdish leaders have yet to announce their decision or start preparing the Kurdish people for this profound and seemingly genuine strategic shift. Indeed, there is a growing discrepancy between what the Kurds want, what they say they want and what non-Kurds suspect they want."[25] The subsequent events have demonstrated the same maximalist if not secessionist tendency of the Kurdish leaders. Indeed, already the Kurdish claims have gone beyond Kirkuk to Mosul and other areas in the north. Thus, a leading Kurdish figure, Nechirvan Barzani, has "raised the stakes by saying that Kirkuk and other disputed northern areas should be ceded to Kurdish control in exchange for their backing the new national government."[26]

The Kurdish secessionist or at least expansionist discourse has already proved contagious in Iraq. As the ICG reports, "In apparent response to Kurdish demands for broad powers for their region, some Shiite negotiators introduced the notion that other regions could be established as well with no limit on the number of governorates that could join, leaving open the possibility of a 'super' region of nine predominantly Shiite governorates."[27]

The incorporation of Kirkuk and other areas into a Kurdish region with pent up expectations of secession will be a recipe for disaster for all of Iraq and its neighbors. Kurdish secession will likely drag the United States into guaranteeing the security, economy, and commerce of such a landlocked state for an indefinite period against a consternated and further alienated region. Every state in the Middle East, including Israel, would then have to take a side on this issue. The United States, the EU, and the international community, including Turkey, have thus declared their policies to keep Iraq unified.

The United States and Turkey have been warning the Kurdish leaders to refrain from provocative statements, maximalist territorial and political demands, militaristic swagger about the Kurdish militia, and mass population transplantations. But, indeed, Kurdish brazenness has come about partly because the United States, with almost every other trusted ally before 2003 now marginalized in the politics of Iraq, appears to be more attentive to the Iraqi Kurds. In the meantime, the Turks continue to brace for the worst case but wish the Kurds of Iraq would take Amir Taheri's words to heart: "At the start of the 21st century, the Kurds cannot pursue their legitimate aspirations through the prism of 19th-century romantic nationalism, which has mothered so many wars and tragedies all over the world."[28]

Turks, Americans, and Europeans are united in not wishing the Kurds to suffer again the atrocities in Iraq's painful history. Turkey has contributed almost as much as anyone else to the well-being of the Kurdish north. The economic vitality of the Kurdish region owes much to Turkish commerce and investments. The alternative to Kurdish separatism is not the renewal of the scourge of Halabja. It is rather a peaceful and prosperous coexistence in Iraq and a peaceful and protective neighbor across the border in modern, democratic, secular, Western, and European Turkey.

In the immediate aftermath of the U.S.-led invasion of Iraq, the disappointingly unresponsive attitudes of the Coalition Provisional Authority in Iraq toward Turkish concerns, and the perceived preferred status accorded to the Iraqi Kurds over Turkey were gross failures of political appreciation and tact that further exacerbated the broad disillusionment in Turkey with the United States.

Perhaps the nadir in Turkish-U.S. relations was reached on July 4, 2003, when U.S. forces arrested and hooded an accredited Turkish special-operations unit in northern Iraq. Soner Çağaptay observes that for most Turks this was a "deliberate provocation and a clear sign that Washington favored Iraqi Kurds over a North Atlantic Treaty Organization (NATO) ally."[29] That incident created a deep wound in Turkish-American relations and contributed in no little degree to the critical perceptions of the United States among the Turkish public.

However, starting in 2004, Turkish and U.S. authorities have managed to see eye to eye with regard to Iraq, except on the pressing issue of taking action against the PKK in Iraq. Although the United States, which recognizes the PKK as a terrorist organization, was itself uneasy with their presence and seemingly aware of the poisonous effect they create on overall Turkish-U.S.

relations, it has claimed to be unable to commit forces to eradicate them while the insurgency was exacting heavy losses in Iraq. Obviously, the United States received no help from the Iraqi Kurds in that regard either.

Turkey's support of the political process and economic reconstruction in Iraq has been unequivocal. Turkey has been the best neighbor that Iraq could have. Thanks to the expansive web of contacts with almost all parties in Iraq, Turkey was able to provide training in democratic practices to the Shiite and Sunni Arabs, Kurds, and Turkmens of Iraq. It has urged a unity government and supported wholeheartedly the unity, integrity, democracy, and prosperity of its neighbor. Turkey remains to date a helpful player in Iraq in economic and political terms.

Turkey's support of the United States with regard to Iraq has not been negligible either. This includes the opening of Turkish airspace to U.S. aircraft during the war and allowing coalition forces to use Turkish airports, harbors, and military bases to support Iraq's reconstruction according to U.N. Security Council Resolutions. The noncombat logistical needs of the coalition forces have continued to flow through Turkey, despite the killing of some one hundred Turkish truck drivers by the insurgents.

Since 2003, despite lingering fragilities in Turkish-U.S. relations, there have been significant attempts to revive the old positive spirit of the Turkish-U.S. partnership. These involved top leaders in the administrations of both countries, including mutual visits at the highest levels. Prime Minister Erdoğan and Foreign Minister Gül visited Washington in 2004 and 2005, and President Bush went to Turkey in 2004. Dr. Rice included Turkey in her first tour of Europe and the Middle East early in 2005 and again in 2006. Trilateral commissions were set up among Turkey, Iraq, and the United States to address the hard issues such as the security of the truck drivers and the removal of the PKK terror organization from northern Iraq, although the latter did not seem to produce concrete results. Turkey also offered to send troops to Iraq to help stabilize the country, and the offer was withdrawn only after the United States decided against it due in large part to the resistance of the Iraqi Kurds. In hindsight, one cannot help thinking that a Turkish contribution to the security environment might have been significant.

Cooperation on the broader slate of U.S.-Turkish partnership also continued unabated, including the success in Afghanistan, as Turkey assumed the command of the ISAF in 2002 and again in 2005. Turkey warned Syria to pull its troops from Lebanon in accordance with the UNSC resolutions, expressed serious concern over the Iranian nuclear program, and engaged with the Iranian leadership to urge them toward satisfying the demands of the international community. Turkey also joined with the United States to call for restraint and democratic reforms in Uzbekistan and endorsed the U.S. bid to be an observer in the Black Sea Economic Cooperation Organization. Turkey similarly continued to support democratic reforms in the broader Middle East, including as a cosponsor of the Democracy Assistance Dialogue.

There has been success, therefore, in the clear and forthright efforts on both sides to put things back on track. Turkish-U.S. relations entered 2006 with positive expectations. The bilateral agenda is full of existing and potential areas of cooperation between two long-standing allies. These include the fight against terrorism, implementation of G-8 and other initiatives regarding the broader Middle East, resolution of the Arab-Israeli conflict, the situation in Iraq, Afghanistan, and the revamping of the transatlantic bonds, just to name a very few.

At the same time, the traditional defense-military pillar of the Turkish-U.S. partnership must also be bolstered. Turkey's adoption of the Revolution in Military Affairs can be a case in point. Promoting Turkey's defense-industry infrastructure with greater transfer of technology and joint research and development, as well as establishing Turkey as a Western military training center, would be as beneficial for the United States as it would be for Turkey.

However, in addition to defense and security issues, not forgetting cooperation in the defense industry, one could argue that for the positive agenda to trickle down to the respective publics, the economic, commercial, and indeed intellectual interaction between the two allies must be given new levels of emphasis. Politicians and intellectual circles on both sides face a major responsibility in that regard, and there may be a need to think creatively.

Obviously, the official circles cannot be exempt from the responsibility to think progressively in order to bring Turkish-U.S. partnership to new heights. As explained earlier in this study, even in the case of Europeanization, where integration produces a strong push for policy convergence and transfer on national foreign and security policies, interaction is a two-way street. Member states transfer policy while receiving. The end product may turn out to be a different policy prescription than what would have ensued if only national decision making were invoked. And, at any rate, the collective principles and values are reflected in the final policy. A comparable interaction would be beneficial in the EU-U.S.-Turkey context. That requires vision, hard work, persistence, open-mindedness, and indeed humility on both sides. Judging by the diplomatic traffic and cooperation on the ground, the ingredients appear to be in place for yet another revamped strategic partnership.

The EU and Turkey's preferred soft approach, Turkey's regional sensibilities, know-how, and defense assets, if need be, together with U.S. power, including soft power, promise a formidable mix. This can only be engendered if the United States, the EU, and Turkey bring in their respective contributions and consult each other with the aim of learning and adjusting to foster a collective strategy. The future of Turkish foreign and security policy will be influenced not only by the domestic or EU dynamics, but also by how much such positive interaction with the United States and transatlantic allies can be realized.

Turkey has a strong interest in promoting such a transatlantic consultative and cooperative reflex, partly because Turkey's EU membership process would benefit. The support of the United States for Turkey's membership to the EU continues to be valuable even if it is not welcome in some EU countries. As a result, the United States has been increasingly subtle in the way it supports Turkey. While its political advice is useful, and arguably necessary given the circumstances, it is certainly not enough to culminate in Turkey's accession into the EU. The United States can best promote Turkey's bid by investing in Turkey. That investment, in turn, would greatly benefit the Turkish-U.S. strategic partnership as well.

One way to achieve that is by actively promoting and helping to put to use Turkey's assets in foreign and security policy. If the major case for Turkish membership to the EU is political, geopolitical, and economic, then the United States can support the Turkish bid by deliberately helping to increase the stock value of Turkey's assets. U.S. support for Turkey's assumption of critical diplomatic and other roles in specific regional and global issues could go a long way in this regard. A potential role in the resolution of the Arab-Israeli conflict is only one example where Turkey's assets could be of use. Whether in the western Balkans, the Caucasus, Central Asia, or the Middle East, Turkey must be allowed to define its own involvement in consultation and coordination with Washington and be supported by the superpower to engage effectively.

Similarly in the course of the difficult negotiations with the EU, the United States can also lend concrete support by helping Turkey counter the Greek Cypriots' exploitation of Turkey's membership desire for their narrow purposes.

Finally, the United States can make greater contributions to Turkey's economy. While U.S. support at the IMF and the World Bank during the past economic crises in Turkey has been substantial, creative thinking to promote greater U.S. investment flow toward Turkey makes mutual strategic and economic sense. An effective support the United States can give to Turkey's EU membership is a massive investment in the Turkish economy and in its visible diplomatic engagement in the resolution of regional problems, while cooperating with Turkey to shield against regional threats and challenges.

Of course, in so doing the United States and Turkey must have faith in each other. On this score, regional politics is particularly pertinent. Turkey must not be expected to withdraw from its efforts to forge better relations with the neighboring countries. Turkey is a country that has consistently suffered due to its rough neighborhood, and improvements in relations with neighbors are much needed. The breathing space to forge ahead in Turkey's political, economic, social, and security development can only be brought about in a cooperative international environment. U.S. support in this regard is critical and should not be contingent on Turkey's cutting back on its momentous enterprise of encircling the country with stable, friendly, and progressive neighbors, which is also very much in the U.S. interest. The United States, with its important interests in this neighborhood, ought to be the first country to see the benefits of the Turkish approach to regional politics, upgraded as necessary with greater U.S. and EU support.

In the final analysis, only a country with Turkey's attributes can be the bedrock of stability needed in the region. For anyone to warm up to that function, it has to have first a democratic and secular regime; a peaceful disposition; and significant political, economic, and military clout. Add on top of it a robust and engaged foreign policy and a determined effort to promote peaceful evolution in the neighborhood, and one has defined Turkey, a key ally of the United States and a negotiating candidate to the European Union.

Notes

1. For the text of the document, see www.state.gov/r/pa/prs/ps/2006/68574.htm.

2. www.state.gov/r/pa/prs/ps/2006/68574.htm

3. Thomas Friedman, "Who Lost Turkey?" *The New York Times*, August 21, 1996.

4. Ian O. Lesser, "Turkey and the United States: From Geopolitics to Concerted Strategy," Sakip Sabanci International Research Award, 2006, www.brookings.edu/comm/events/20060523sabanci_2.pdf.

5. Philip Gordon and Ömer Taşpınar, "Turkey on the Brink," *Washington Quarterly* 29, no. 3 (Summer 2006): 67.

6. Steven A. Cook and Elisabeth D. Sherwood-Randall, *Generating Momentum for a New Era in U.S.-Turkish Relations* (Council Special Report No. 15), June 21, 2006.

7. Gordon and Taşpınar, "Turkey on the Brink," 67.

8. Lesser, "Turkey and the United States."

9. Zbigniew Brzezinski, *The Choice: Global Domination or Global Leadership* (New York: Basic Books, 2004), 215.

10. Brzezinski, *The Choice*, 214.

11. Brzezinski, *The Choice*, 214.

12. Joseph S. Nye Jr., *Soft Power: The Means to Succeed in World Politics* (New York: Public Affairs, 2004), 133.

13. Nye, *Soft Power*, 133.

14. Brzezinski, *The Choice*, 37–38.

15. Gautam Adhikari, "The End of the Unipolar Myth," *International Herald Tribune*, September 27, 2004.

16. Uğur Ziyal, "Perspectives in Turkish Foreign Policy: Looking Forward after Iraq" (speech delivered at the American Enterprise Institute, June 2003), www.aei.org/news/newsID.17731,filter./news_detail.asp.

17. For a discussion, see: Burcu Bostanoğlu, "Global Security Calculus: Forcing the Turkish-American Strategic Alliance to New Orientations," *Milletlerarası Münasebetler Türk Yıllığı* [Turkish Yearbook of International Relations] 31, no. 2 (2000): 227–32.

18. Ian O. Lesser, "Turkey in a Changing Security Environment," *Journal of International Affairs* 54, no. 1 (Fall 2000).

19. Soner Çağaptay, "Where Goes the U.S.-Turkish Relationship?" *Middle East Quarterly* 11, no. 4 (Fall 2004). www.meforum.org/article/657.

20. Çağaptay, "Where Goes the U.S.-Turkish Relationship?"

21. International Crisis Group, "Unmaking Iraq: A Constitutional Process Gone Awry," (Middle East Briefing No. 19, Amman/Brussels, September 26, 2005), 12.

22. International Crisis Group, "Unmaking Iraq," 7 (n. 40).

23. International Crisis Group, "Iraq's Kurds: Toward an Historic Compromise?" (ICG Middle East Report No. 26, Amman/Brussels, April 8, 2004): i.

24. International Crisis Group, "Iraq's Kurds," i.

25. International Crisis Group, "Iraq's Kurds," i.

26. Rory Carroll, "Bomber in Uniform Kills 12 Iraqi police," *Guardian*, February 25, 2006.

27. International Crisis Group, "Unmaking Iraq," 8.

28. Amir Taheri, "The Wrong Way for Kurds," *New York Post*, June 25, 2004.

29. Çağaptay, "Where Goes the U.S.-Turkish Relationship?"

CHAPTER SEVEN

Negotiating Accession

Turkey's importance to the United States and in no lesser degree to the European Union, and vice versa, is not contested. Yet the debate about Turkey's eventual membership to the EU is far from over. That said, the bottom line is that Turkey has started accession negotiations with the European Union toward the shared objective of full membership and nothing less. The discussions about whether Turkey will or should join are secondary to the actual process of negotiations that is currently unfolding. Even the influential opponents of Turkey's accession, such as Wolfgang Schäuble of the governing Christian Democratic Union party in Germany, appear to be saying that at the end of the negotiations "it will emerge whether those who are, like me, against Turkey's full membership are right or not."[1] The mood is probably similar on all sides, including in Turkey. Whether in favor or against Turkish membership, all parties are bracing for the negotiations.

The accession negotiations involve an intricate process. In a way, this process reflects a neatly organized logical progression from the task to the outcome. Technically, the outcome is not automatic membership but rather the so-called Accession Treaty that includes all that has been agreed to between the candidate and the existing members during the negotiations. The actual membership is achieved only once the Accession Treaty is ratified in each of the extant EU member states and also endorsed by the European Parliament. Already, France and Austria have hinted at a national referendum on Turkey's accession. Obviously, even after the governments agree on the terms of Turkey's membership, the parliaments take a vote. That in itself will be a gargantuan step, especially if the current absence of popular support in much of the EU for the entire enlargement enterprise survives until that date. Even the latest round of accessions that brought in ten countries in May 2004 came under criticism. In fact, Turkey's own standing is damaged by the broader public discontent with the latest round of enlargement that increased the EU's population by seventy-five million. As difficult as winning over public opinion will be, the EU and Turkey will engage in an intensive political and societal dialogue to prepare this outcome. The Negotiating Framework for Turkey, the basic document that sets out the modalities and parameters of the accession talks, stipulates that the negotiations can only be concluded after the establishment of the financial framework for the period from 2014.[2]

In the meantime, the object of the negotiations is to make certain that Turkey assumes the obligations of EU membership. This is achieved foremost by adopting and implementing some one hundred thousand pages of EU legislation organized under thirty-five policy areas, or "chapters" in EU-speak, under the watchful eye of the European Commission and the EU member states. Accordingly, Turkey will have to transpose all applicable EU legislation pertaining to the following policy chapters:

> Free movement of goods; Freedom of movement of workers; Right of establishment and freedom to provide services; Free movement of capital; Public procurement; Company law; Intellectual property law; Competition policy; Financial services; Information society and media; Agriculture and rural development; Food safety, veterinary and phytosanitary policy; Fisheries; Transport policy; Energy; Taxation; Economic and monetary policy; Statistics; Social policy and employment (including anti-discrimination and equal opportunities for women and men); Enterprise and industrial policy; Trans-European networks; Regional policy and co-ordination of structural instruments; Judiciary and fundamental rights; Justice, freedom and security; Science and research; Education and culture; Environment; Consumer and health protection; Customs union; External relations; Foreign, security and defense policy; Financial control; Financial and budgetary provisions; Institutions; Other issues.[3]

This long list may seem like the curriculum of a law school, and it is no doubt a tall order. The strong emphasis on the EU's community law or the *acquis communitaire* is unquestionably justified. The EU, after all, is a structure ultimately built on this body of laws and their primacy over national laws. As an independent legal order, the *acquis communitaire* takes precedence over national legal instruments. The acquis is composed of three layers of rules. The first layer stems from the treaties establishing the European Communities, including their subsequent revisions. These include the treaties of Rome, Maastricht, Amsterdam, and Nice. This primary legislation is agreed to by direct negotiation among EU member states and then ratified by the national parliaments. This, in fact, concurs with the conventional form of producing international law. The secondary legislation flows from these treaties and includes: (1) *Regulations* that are directly applicable and binding in all EU member states without the need for any national implementing legislation; (2) *Directives* that are binding in terms of the objectives that the member states must fulfill, albeit through their own ways and means; (3) *Decisions* that are specifically addressed to members states, enterprises, or individuals, and binding directly on the addressed party without national implementing legislation; and (4) *Recommendations* and *opinions* that are nonbinding. The final layer of the *acquis communitaire* pertains to case law comprising judgments of the European Court of Justice and the European Court of First Instance.

Specifically, the Negotiating Framework for Turkey lists the following items of the constantly evolving EU acquis, which Turkey will have to apply as they stand at the time of accession, both in terms of legislative alignment and timely and effective implementation:

- The content, principles, and political objectives of the treaties on which the Union is founded;
- Legislation and decisions adopted pursuant to the treaties, and the case law of the Court of Justice;
- Other acts, legally binding or not, adopted within the Union framework, such as interinstitutional agreements, resolutions, statements, recommendations, guidelines;
- Joint actions, common positions, declarations, conclusions, and other acts within the framework of the common foreign and security policy;
- Joint actions, joint positions, conventions signed, resolutions, statements, and other acts agreed within the framework of justice and home affairs;
- International agreements concluded by the communities, the communities jointly with their member states, the Union, and those concluded by the member states among themselves with regard to Union activities.

Turkey will have to digest and incorporate EU laws into its national legal order and implement them. The first step in the negotiation process, therefore, is geared to understanding what exactly EU law involves, prospecting to what extent Turkey already conforms to this law, and establishing what more needs to be done. This is achieved by what is called an "analytical examination" or "screening" exercise for each chapter, where the Commission would first explain the EU acquis to Turkey, and then it would be Turkey's turn to explain its legislation to the Commission. Screening helps assess Turkey's state of preparation for opening negotiations in specific areas. The exercise also helps identify preliminary indications of the issues that will most likely come up in the negotiations. The Commission would then recommend the opening of specific negotiations individually for any given chapter once it concludes that there exists sufficient compliance with the EU rules and regulations pertaining to that policy area. The first policy chapters that were thus screened and recommended for negotiation were "science and research" and "education and culture." In the former, the negotiations were already completed in a single intergovernmental session in June 2006.

All EU members need to endorse the opening of negotiations on each of the thirty-five chapters and agree on the benchmarks for the provisional closure, and sometimes opening, of each chapter. Accordingly, each EU member country shall have the power of veto on the opening and closing of the membership negotiations. The Greek Cypriots already wielded unsuccessfully the threat of veto for the first chapter that was negotiated.

In the course of the negotiation period, Turkey will progressively adopt the EU acquis while managing the likely resistance from various interest groups touched by the changing rules of doing business in Turkey. While Turkey will provide reports to the EU on its progress in the alignment with and implementation of the acquis, the Commission will also monitor Turkey's progress in all areas, making use of various methods and instruments, including on-site expert reviews.

The purpose of the negotiations is to determine the terms under which Turkey will adopt, implement, and enforce the acquis. As in previous accession negotiations, Turkey will be able to ask for transitional arrangements to phase in its compliance with specific legislation by a date agreed on during the negotiations. Therefore, much of the negotiations will revolve around requests from Turkey for transitional measures. These transitional arrangements that Turkey will require to smooth out the adoption of the EU rule book will be advocated by Turkish negotiators. They will be met by their EU counterparts, who will aim to guard against amendments to the existing rules or policies of the Union that disrupt their proper functioning or lead to significant distortions of competition. On the EU part, negotiators will be asking for long transitional periods, derogations, specific arrangements, or permanent safeguard clauses in areas such as freedom of movement of persons, structural policies, or agriculture. In their turn, the Turks will employ their negotiation assets to deny such permanent special arrangements demanded by the EU, arguing against a second-class membership.

The issue of "permanent safeguards" is a particular novelty for Turkey's case. The Negotiating Framework for Turkey states that "long transitional periods, derogations, specific arrangements or permanent safeguard clauses, i.e. clauses which are permanently available as a basis for safeguard measures, may be considered. The Commission will include these, as appropriate, in its proposals in areas such as freedom of movement of persons, structural policies or agriculture."[4] Fadi Hakura notes that the framework document emphasizes the "perpetual availability instead of enforcement" of the safeguard measures; and that "this subtle difference implies that these strictures will not be applicable unless invoked by a member state."[5] The member states may nonetheless be tempted to invoke safeguard clauses. As Katinka Barysch underscored, this may happen for instance to stop Turkish workers from taking employment in other EU countries or to bar Turkey from enjoying full access to the EU's lucrative farming and regional subsidies.[6] After all, even the current members are fiercely feuding over these subsidies, which together form a respectable portion of the EU's budget. Hakura rightly argues that whether EU members will end up insisting on such measures will depend on the prevailing circumstances. These may be too hard to foresee today. The logical step would be to leave the chapters on free movement of persons, agriculture, and structural policies toward the end of the negotiations. There is already an intra-EU dynamic toward making fundamental reforms to the EU's agricultural and structural policies, which in turn may "reduce budgetary outlays by the time of Turkey's accession, thus reducing the probability of long term restrictions."[7] That said, however, Barysch shows empathy by stating that "the Turks are right to say that such special rules would amount to double standards and cowardice: rather than giving its budget a much-needed overhaul, the EU could simply bar Turkey from taking part in its main spending policies. And rather than reforming their labour markets to make them more flexible, EU countries could keep the doors closed to low-cost workers."[8]

The Negotiating Framework, while stipulating a minimum period for negotiations, namely until 2014, asserts that the advancement of the negotiations will be guided by Turkey's progress in converging with the EU. Furthermore, it sets out specific requirements against which such progress will be measured. These include foremost the three 1993 Copenhagen criteria that comprise:

- The stability of institutions guaranteeing democracy, the rule of law, human rights, and respect for and protection of minorities;
- The existence of a functioning market economy and the capacity to cope with competitive pressure and market forces within the Union; and

- The ability to take on the obligations of membership, including adherence to the aims of political, economic, and monetary union and the administrative capacity to effectively apply and implement the acquis.

The Copenhagen criteria have steered EU enlargement since the early 1990s, and Turkey has already met the political criterion sufficiently. The other three measures of progress as defined by the Negotiating Framework will be:

- Turkey's unequivocal commitment to good neighborly relations and its undertaking to resolve any outstanding border disputes in conformity with the principle of peaceful settlement of disputes in accordance with the United Nations Charter, including if necessary jurisdiction of the International Court of Justice;
- Turkey's continued support for efforts to achieve a comprehensive settlement of the Cyprus problem within the UN framework and in line with the principles on which the Union is founded, including steps to contribute to a favorable climate for a comprehensive settlement, and progress in the normalization of bilateral relations between Turkey and all EU member states, including the Republic of Cyprus.
- The fulfillment of Turkey's obligations under the Association Agreement and its Additional Protocol extending the Association Agreement to all new EU member states, in particular those pertaining to the EU-Turkey customs union, as well as the implementation of the Accession Partnership, as regularly revised.

In addition to the above, the Negotiating Framework includes a paragraph stipulating that "in the period up to accession, Turkey will be required to progressively align its policies toward third countries and its positions within international organisations (including in relation to the membership by all EU Member States of those organisations and arrangements) with the policies and positions adopted by the Union and its Member States."[9] This clause, which apparently was inserted by the Greek Cypriots in order to open the way for their membership in NATO, has brought Turkey to the brink of rejecting the entire deal. It was resolved in a binding statement by the EU presidency with the consent of the Council that asserted that the said clause "cannot be interpreted as prejudicing the autonomy of decision-making and rights of any of those international organizations or of their members, or of the Member States of the European Union."[10] This statement, which was agreed to as part of the package containing the Negotiating Framework, was further strengthened by the intervention of U.S. Secretary of State Condoleezza Rice, who also reaffirmed the Turkish position, notably vis-à-vis NATO.

This episode is indicative of a larger point about Turkey's vulnerability in the entire process. Despite the best of intentions, it may be difficult for Turkey to expect an objective progression toward its goal of full membership, as promised in the Negotiating Framework. The process will more likely be laden with subjectivity. Depending on one's particular position vis-à-vis enlargement, this subjectivity is either a design failure in the accession process or a guarantee for members' prerogative.

Obviously the Negotiating Framework is designed to make it as difficult as possible for Turkey to join the EU. It is the most stringent and demanding negotiation process that any candidate to any organization has ever been subjected to. Certainly, it is harsher toward Turkey than for all the preceding candidates.

The document specifies that to ensure the irreversibility of progress in these areas and its full and effective implementation, notably with regard to fundamental freedoms and to full respect for human rights, progress will continue to be closely monitored by the Commission. On that account, the Commission will report regularly to the Council, monitoring the political developments within Turkey. If the EU deems that there is a serious and persistent breach in Turkey of the EU's fundamental democratic values and principles, the Commission by itself or on the request of one-third of the member states can recommend the suspension of negotiations. The decision to suspend would then be taken by a qualified majority among the EU member countries. Once suspended, the reopening of the negotiations would be a hefty affair requiring unanimity. In other words, the negotiations can be suspended by a majority but resumed only by unanimous vote. While the suspension clause appears particularly menacing for candidates, under the Nice Treaty, even the existing members of the EU risk suspension of their EU membership if there is a major derogation from basic democratic standards.

More significantly, even in the absence of such arguably extreme circumstances culminating in the suspension of the negotiations, the framework contains significant checks on opening and closing of the individual chapters of negotiations. Each of the thirty-five negotiation chapters must be opened and closed by the agreement of each EU member state. The EU will not only set out the benchmarks for the provisional closure of each chapter, it will also set such benchmarks for the opening of each chapter "where appropriate."

As if this were not enough, the framework asserts that the capacity to absorb Turkey while maintaining the momentum of European integration is an important consideration for the final decision to let Turkey join the EU.

There being no objective yardstick to measure the capacity to absorb, the EU is thus given subjective leverage to keep Turkey's accession process in check.

Ultimately, people will decide whether Turkey should join the EU. Democratically elected national parliaments will have the ultimate say on the Turkey-EU merger. The European Parliament, whose members are also democratically elected, will also have to extend their assent. What the public will say at the point when the governments have finished their negotiations is premature to guess at this point. The current unpopularity of Turkey's membership cannot be taken for granted ten years down the road, when the EU, Turkey, and indeed the world will be different from today. Most important, by then the public will have had the opportunity to become better informed about what the membership entails, and what it really means for Europe and the Europeans, including the Turks.

A country with Turkey's attributes will always have the option not to join the EU and still thrive. That Turkey will have no alternative to EU membership is a political cliché more than an educated assessment. There is a non-EU option for Turkey, albeit not yet well articulated and probably not able to be truly formulated until the EU track is fully exhausted. President İnönü's statement in 1964 that "a new world would be formed, and Turkey would take its place in it" may have been voiced in a completely different context, but these words reflect the confident side of the Turkish worldview that survives to date. Whether alternatives are better or worse for Turkey or Europe is of course another question. The same is almost equally valid for the EU. It is wishful thinking to assume that the EU would be better off without Turkey. Whether it will be the clash or the alliance of civilizations will be decided in Europe and its neighborhood, and Turkey's membership bid will be relevant to this drama. But in any case, Turkey will remain a critical component of European security, economics, and politics.

Although the effort to spell out an objective short of Turkey's full membership was abortive, the EU did reiterate the wording of the December 2004 Summit in the final Negotiating Framework, which raised the theoretical possibility of an end result different from membership. Thus, the European Union, while declaring in December 2004 the decision to launch negotiations with the objective of accession, has nonetheless stated:

> These negotiations are an open-ended process, the outcome of which cannot be guaranteed beforehand. While taking account of all Copenhagen criteria, if the Candidate State is not in a position to assume in full all the obligations of membership it must be ensured that the Candidate State concerned is fully an-

chored in the European structures through the strongest possible bond. (Article 23 of the Presidency Conclusions)

In this formulation the emphasis is on Turkey's potential shortcomings in meeting the membership requirements, for instance, by failing to adopt the EU legislation. The EU has also asserted in 2006 that the capacity to absorb would also be a consideration in the final decision regarding Turkey. However, if the EU was to shy away from admitting a Turkey that has objectively fulfilled all the criteria and still wanted to join the EU, then there would be ample cause for acrimony. In the final analysis, if Turkey is turned away, ensuring that it is "fully anchored in the European structures through the strongest possible bond" may well be unachievable. How keen a deeply disappointed Turkey would be to settle for such an ambiguous "strongest possible bond" merits a big question mark. At any rate, the Europeans would then hardly be able to offer something appealing enough to Turkey over and above what it already enjoys. There is, therefore, a case for a realistically pessimistic outlook on the whole affair of negotiations.

However, there may also be a more positive outlook that is equally warranted. Leaving aside all the subjectivity that could contaminate the stringent rules and exploitable leverages enshrined in the Negotiating Framework, the end-game defined in the jargon of the document points to a Turkey that is in a multitude of ways better off than it has been hitherto.

The Turkey that would join the EU would necessarily be one that has maintained and even further advanced (1) the stability of institutions guaranteeing democracy, the rule of law, human rights, and respect for and protection of minorities; (2) its market economy and the capacity to cope with competitive pressure and market forces within the Union; and (3) its ability to take on the obligations of membership, including adherence to the aims of political, economic, and monetary union and the administrative capacity to effectively apply and implement the acquis. Abbreviated in the EU terminology as the Copenhagen criteria, these objectives in fact form the basis of Turkish aspirations to reach the highest standards of contemporary governance. A Turkey that has fulfilled these criteria will be a country that the proponents of Turkey's EU membership have been aspiring to bring about. In all areas of the acquis, namely in just about every aspect of governance, the Turkey that would finally be ready to hoist the EU member flag would be a state whose institutions, management capacity, and administrative and judicial systems are up to Union standards. This would mean maintaining the highest standards in its public administration, civil service, and judicial system, not to mention its economic standards. Not even the ardent opponents of EU membership within Turkey would challenge this objective, lest they betray the centuries-old aspirations of the Turkish people.

For many Turks, although not all of them, membership in the EU is the contemporary expression of the grand objective set out by the founder of the modern Turkish state, Mustafa Kemal Atatürk, in the early decades of the last century, which is to reach the level of the contemporary civilization. The contemporary manifestation of this objective is none other than the fulfillment of the Copenhagen criteria. One could argue that once these criteria have been met and Turkish governance has become broadly indistinguishable from the EU, and once Turkey is prospering economically and politically, membership in the EU itself may become a secondary objective for the Turks. The EU membership and the associated process is an instrument toward attaining such standards. From this perspective, the accession negotiations, irrespective of their subjective and likely abusive procedures, can be seen as the necessary training camp to fulfill a national dream.

One should, however, promptly add that both perspectives are valid. They are indeed two sides of the same universe of the EU accession process for Turkey; one dark, the other one brighter. In the long period ahead, politicians, technocrats, and interest groups both in Turkey and in the EU will be immersed in a hectic activity and discussion.

As this tug of war continues, the management of expectations on both sides will be a cardinal challenge. As Heather Grabbe points out, the Turkish government will scramble to explain the short-term costs and long-term gains of adapting to EU standards: "The adjustment to EU standards may well be painful and unpopular. Some Turkish businesspeople may lose their enthusiasm for moving quickly into the EU, because they will want more time to adapt to the EU's requirements and to make the necessary investments," which the consequent increase of costs could negatively impact on their competitiveness.[11] The EU citizens will question the financial burden of preparing Turkey for membership when the EU economies are facing resilient difficulties.

This is expectable, despite the fact that financial support for Turkey will be significantly less than what the previous candidates received. As Kirsty Hughes notes,

> The EU has been decreasingly generous in subsequent enlargements—with Ireland, Greece, Spain and Portugal getting substantially more structural funding per head than the new member states in 2004, and with the budget deal for Bulgaria and Romania also giving them less per head overall than for the new

10 in 2004. With the 2004 enlargement, the amount of structural funds that the new member states could get was limited by introducing a new maximum limit of 4% of GDP. To cope with the costs of Turkish accession, it is quite likely that some new lower limit and other ways of restricting funds will be proposed. Overall, Turkey is likely to get a much lower budget allocation than the estimates . . . of what it might get on unchanged policies—quite possibly closer to €10 billion than €20 billion.[12]

According to the Negotiating Framework, Turkey will not join the EU before 2014. Several EU leaders, and indeed publics, expect and indeed hope for an even longer period. Some mention fifteen years, and of course there are those who say never. A decade of negotiations and adjustment may indeed be needed. In fact, by virtue of the governing framework and current public sentiments, the gear of the accession talks may be adjusted accordingly to delay final accession irrespective of Turkey's own vitality in adopting and implementing the massive provisions of the EU acquis.

Yet previous experience has shown that the accession process develops its own momentum. Turkey may deliver a surprise in terms of how fast it accommodates the EU rules, especially if Turkey feels there is light at the end of the tunnel. In the economic field, its starting point is significantly more advanced than those of most other previous candidates, thanks to the Customs Union in force with the EU since 1996. In the administrative field, that there is tremendous room for improvement should not obscure the fact that the nation has a centuries-long uninterrupted experience in government. While the perceived foreignness of Turkey to other EU members exacerbates the opposition and concern about Turkey's accession for the time being, some of this may change if Turkey succeeds in maintaining the high speed of its modernization and Europeanization. Derided and resented for being poorer, Turkey may turn the tables if it can sustain economic growth, and may instead be regarded as a contributor to Europe's economic vitality. Heather Grabbe confirms this scenario.

When Estonia and Hungary started receiving massive inflows of foreign direct investment in the 1990s, journalists in the EU stopped referring to them as poor post-communist countries and began writing about the Central European tigers. That made a big difference to their accession prospects by turning the arguments about their membership around, from negative to positive. Instead of presenting themselves as potentially unstable countries that needed to join the EU to remain stable, the Central and East Europeans could argue that the EU should let them in because they would give new dynamism to the EU's sclerotic economy. If Turkey can achieve a rise in investment from abroad, it will meet the official economic criteria and also help to relieve the EU's anxieties about how much its accession will cost.[13]

There is no certainty about the coming period of accession negotiations. First of all, Turkey's success in managing reform is not assured. This sizeable country has myriad problems. Whether in terms of its political or economic stability, there have been periods in recent Turkish history when rosy expectations were abruptly shattered. The current outlook may be positive, but the challenges are nonetheless formidable. Turkey will have to sustain its positive course in the period ahead if it is to remain a serious candidate for membership to the rich European country club.

On the EU side, only a self-confident Union will have the vision to include Turkey in its fold. The EU and its member states have their fair share of woes. Several member countries are entangled in a cocoon of faltering economic and social structures and may have grown overly attached to them. The French and Dutch referenda have not debunked or permanently crippled the European project, but it is impossible to overlook the political, and perhaps more profoundly the economic and social, problems they have revealed. If these persist in the time ahead, the allure of the EU will suffer. Obviously, Turkey would face a dilemma if it were confronted with the scenario of joining a failing economic union whose merits its own members question. As in the debate about enlargement, so in other problematic EU issues such as the common agricultural policy—the EU's paralysis damages foremost the EU's image. Countries want to join the EU or have particular relations with it—as the Turkish saying goes—not because of the dark eyes and the eyebrows of the EU, but because the EU is seen to be a succeeding enterprise.

Then, of course, there is the sociocultural question. The problems of integrating and reconciling the hearts and minds of the Muslim immigrant communities with those of the recipient societies bear directly on Turkey's EU membership prospects. The Turks in Europe have had more than their fair share of pain, even before al Qaeda started terrorizing the world. Families were burnt alive in heartland Europe in the 1990s in Mölln and Solingen. The anti-Muslim and anti-Turkish sentiments in Europe run deep in history. But the greater sensitivities and resentments in Europe against Muslim immigrants are also affecting how many Europeans approach Turkey's membership in the EU. It is plausible that a greater Muslim-Christian divide in Europe could hamper Turkey's progress toward EU membership, and stalled Turkish progress toward EU membership could in turn exacerbate this divide in Europe and indeed beyond.

That said, this correlation can also be misunderstood. It is not that Turkey plays a religious card in its EU track. To the contrary, it suffers from the existence of religious and cultural concerns. Similarly, Turks do not vie to represent the Muslim world. Nor have Muslims delegated Turkey to such a role. The issue here is instead that the opponents of Turkey's candidacy to the EU have elevated the relevance of the particular faith of its majority population. Their emphasis in turn has raised concerns that the peaceful European project is under threat from those who resent what Europe has become. Their agenda is thus opposed by other Europeans. And as every action creates reaction, the Muslims of Europe and the world, who had perhaps hitherto regarded Turkey as too Western and too secular, have come to see the case of Turkish accession as a test case for their own future.

This complicated picture of the technical, political, economic, social, and cultural aspects of the accession negotiation period may make foreign and security policy seem like a secondary matter. I would argue that it is in fact not so. Foreign and security policies can multiply both the positive and the negative dynamics that play on Turkey's accession negotiations. Specific economic or social issues may energize and sensitize various segments of the society in Turkey and Europe, and these sensitivities may to a lesser or greater degree impact on the broader Turkish public. However, key foreign policy issues have the potential of tipping balances, if not creating massive reactions, in the opinions of both the general public and the elites. Masses are mobilized when there is a strong sense of shared interest being violated. Strong public sentiments played a considerable role in shaping Turkey's Cyprus policy since the 1960s. The war on Iraq has blotched the American image in Turkey despite a decades-long close partnership and alliance. The suspicions of complicity with PKK terrorists and their financiers in specific European countries has soured Turkish perceptions vis-à-vis not only these specific countries but of the entire EU.

Likewise, Turkey's foreign policies may and do occasionally influence European perceptions of Turkey. Turkey's increasing soft power in the broader Middle East, its stance in the fight against terrorism, improving relations with Russia, and alliance with the United States each have their supporters in Europe. Turkey's continued and even further amplified engagement in regional and international politics, and thus its geostrategic value, will remain the major Turkish trump card in relations with the EU. By itself, however, it will not be sufficient. At the level of public relations, European publics are not so moved by strategic arguments and such positive contributions to their security. Witness European opinion regarding the United States, which has been investing more than anyone in European security and stability, including in

Europe's still unstable periphery and energy supply routes. Yet obviously the United States is not cherished by European publics. Turkey, too, does not score many points in European public opinion for its specific foreign policies. However, like the United States with its invasion of Iraq in 2003, Turkey can easily lose favor due to one or another foreign policy move. Thus, although the Turkish Grand National Assembly refused to endorse the government decree allowing U.S. forces to invade Iraq through Turkey, which was well received by the French and German leaderships, Turkey received no boost in European public opinion, despite the European people's staunch opposition to the war. Habermas and Derrida, while inspired by Europe's public demonstrations against the war in Iraq, did not go so far as to suggest that the simultaneously demonstrating Turks also belonged to this European public space. Therefore, it is hard to cash in foreign policy assets for public support in the EU but easy to further erode public perceptions with controversial policy moves. This, in turn, exacerbates Turkish resentment of what is seen as a no-win situation. It is statesmanship that will be needed in the time ahead, as it was before. Leaders have a better perspective on foreign policy issues and their importance, and they must be able to explain it to their population. This is true as well of intellectuals.

The foreign policy domain is potentially a sensitive one for Turkey's accession period. The negotiation chapter concerning the common foreign and security policy may in itself not be very exacting. As the European Commission submits, there is already great convergence between the Turkish and common EU positions, and more is likely in the time ahead. However, the range of CFSP issues is hardly the full universe of the complex foreign and security policy spectrum touching the EU and Turkey.

The Negotiating Framework document has validated a number of foreign policy issues as part of Turkey's process, although they are not necessarily elements of the CFSP acquis or even subjects of the negotiations. These concern Cyprus and Greece and, to a lesser degree, Armenia.

Indeed, the Negotiating Framework states that Turkey's progress toward economic and social convergence with the EU will be measured inter alia by "Turkey's unequivocal commitment to good neighbourly relations and its undertaking to resolve any outstanding border disputes in conformity with the principle of peaceful settlement of disputes in accordance with the United Nations Charter, including if necessary compulsory jurisdiction of the International Court of Justice."[14]

As general as this may sound, it is in fact shorthand for the problems that exist between Greece and Turkey, although Greece itself is not mentioned in the Negotiating Framework. And as objective as it may read, in reality it reflects the unequal position of the EU member Greece vis-à-vis the candidate Turkey. The inequality between the two is clearly manifest in the fact that this reference levies the burden of resolving the existing Turkish-Greek disputes on Turkey rather than on both parties to the conflict. It implies that it is incumbent on the candidate country alone to make the effort and travel every extra mile. If that reading is true, and time will tell whether it is, then it unrealistically suggests that it takes only one to tango.

Turkey and Greece dispute a number of issues and borders, including most notably the extent of the territorial waters, the airspace, and the continental shelf. Add to those the rights of the remaining Turks in Greece and Greeks in Turkey. Turks also protest the militarization of specific islands in Greece, and Greece disagrees on the interpretation of international legal instruments that imposed the demilitarization requirement when these islands were given to Greece. In the climate of tension, even arguably nonpolitical issues like the Flight Information Regions have become bones of contention. In the tight waterway between Turkey and Greece, both Greece and Turkey have six miles of territorial waters. However, the Greeks assert their right to stretch their territorial waters another six miles, the full extent envisaged under the United Nations Convention on the Law of the Seas. But that convention was not signed by Turkey because it would suffocate the country in a manner that the Turks cannot accept. If the twelve-mile expanse were to be accepted, then Turkish or indeed international maritime vessels would not be able to sail from Istanbul to Antalya without having first to go through Greek territorial waters. While the Greeks maintain six miles of territorial waters, keeping the claim of a unilateral expansion on the table causes a constant unease on Turkey's part and poisons the relationship.[15]

Greece also argues for a ten-mile airspace over six miles of territorial waters, although an airspace routinely extends above the expanse of a given country's lands and territorial waters, not beyond. Turkey does not accept the ten-mile airspace and prevents it from becoming state practice by flying its aircraft beyond the sixth mile. Greece protests this vehemently as a violation of the airspace and sends fully armed fighter jets to intercept the Turkish planes, as if that NATO ally were really going to attack Greece.[16]

Even the mention of referring these issues to the International Court of Justice is inherently misleading, given that Turkey wants to take all the issues to the Court jointly but the Greeks contend that the continental shelf issue is the only dispute, while all the rest are not arguable. There is some inescapable surrealism surrounding the Turkish-Greek disputes. There are incomparable and infinite benefits to finding a negotiated solution to the host of issues dividing the two countries. Many Greek intellectuals and politicians seem to believe that their country has captured the diplomatic high ground due to the fact that it is within the EU, whereas Turkey is trying the get in and will require Greece's endorsement in that regard. However, the atmospherics of the bilateral disputes are significantly different and more benign today than in the period between the 1960s and the end of the 1990s, and the two nations have at least found ways to cooperate in international forums, join regional organizations, increase their trade and social contacts, and participate in exploratory talks to improve the sentiments and perceptions even further. The relations between the leaders on both sides, whether civilian or military leadership, are increasingly friendly. Turks have even consented to the National Bank of Greece's buying the controlling share of a Turkish bank. However, despite all the progress achieved since Greece's involvement in the affair surrounding the PKK terrorist leader's arrest in late 1990s, there is still significant residual negative energy. The good prospects for turning the Aegean Sea into one that unites the two neighbors rather than one that divides them may flounder if Turkey's accession process is seen by Greece as an opportunity to pressure the Turks to "yield" to Greek demands. That would likely be futile as well. At any rate, the Turkish-Greek relationship must be subject to careful handling on both sides of the Aegean in the coming period. The best deal would be one that the two nations have produced through sincere negotiations between two neighboring countries and allies.

The Negotiating Framework's reference to good neighborliness may also concern Turkey's relations with Armenia, although like Greece, Armenia is also not mentioned in the document. Nonetheless, the issue is one that anti-Turkish campaigns in the EU have an opportunity to exploit. There is already evidence on the ground that some in the European Parliament and EU member states may play with this issue in a bid to retard Turkey's membership.

Turkey keeps its borders with Armenia closed because Armenia contests in its constitution the border with Turkey, requisitions foreign parliaments to pass political judgment on the historical record of Turkish-Armenian relations, and still occupies large parts of Azerbaijan, even territories to which it does not lay claim beyond the contested Nagorno Karabakh. And Armenia does these things with no obvious benefit to its state, people, and neighborhood. Armenian diasporas, prosperous and educated as they are, rather than acting as a progressive influence on their kinsmen who have missed the democratic revolution in central and eastern Europe, appear to remain fixated on perpetuating historical quarrels. In the meantime, around one million Azerbaijani people are uprooted from homes they left behind in the occupied territories, and Armenia remains mired in self-imposed economic and political dire straits.

Despite the fact that the Turkish-Armenian border is closed, Armenian diplomats are represented in BSECO in Istanbul, tens of thousands of Armenian laborers work freely in Turkey, and there are flights between Istanbul and Yerevan. The Turkish and Armenian diplomats are reportedly scrambling to find a solution to the anachronistic bilateral disputes. Efforts are also underway to resolve the Azerbaijani-Armenian dispute under the framework of the OSCE's Minsk Group led by three co-chairmen, the United States, France, and Russia.

The leverage of the EU on Turkey in this regard is negligible in Turkish eyes and is secondary to Turkey's own overall strategy to encircle itself with friendly nations. The influence of the EU can, however, be negative, particularly if it tries to put undue pressure on Turkey. That would likely backfire, as it would raise the stakes for the Turkish government vis-à-vis domestic public opinion, while vainly intensifying Yerevan's expectations of gaining unilateral compromises from Turkey. On the other hand, further democratization and greater pragmatism on the Armenian side could help significantly to overcome the current stalemate.

Of all issues, the Cyprus problem may be the most important. Unlike Greece and Armenia, Cyprus is mentioned in the Negotiating Framework. The document mandates that Turkey continue its support for efforts to achieve a comprehensive settlement of the Cyprus problem "within the UN framework and in line with the principles on which the Union is founded." It stipulates that Turkey should continue taking steps to contribute to a favorable climate for a comprehensive settlement and progress in the normalization of bilateral relations between Turkey and the Republic of Cyprus. In so doing, it unduly puts the Greek Cypriot government on a comfortable diplomatic ground—this notwithstanding the fact that the Turkish Republic of Northern Cyprus and Turkey supported the UN sponsored deal in 2004, while the Greek Cypriots overwhelmingly turned it down. By admitting Cyprus before the Cyprus problem was resolved, the EU lost significant leverage, thus missing a historic opportunity to help resolve this long-standing dispute, the first violent interethnic strife in Europe in the post–WWII era, which was prevented by Turkey from deteriorating into something akin to the Bosnian war.

Following the refusal of the comprehensive deal, which would have ended the problem, the European Council stated:

> The Turkish Cypriot community have expressed their clear desire for a future within the EU. The Council is determined to put an end to the isolation of the Turkish Cypriot Community and to facilitate the reunification of Cyprus by

encouraging the economic development of the Turkish Cypriot community. The Council invited the Commission to bring forward comprehensive proposals to this end, with particular emphasis on the economic integration of the island. The Council recommended that the 259 million euro already earmarked for the northern part of Cyprus in the event of a settlement now be used for this purpose.[17]

Once in the EU, however, the Greek Cypriot government led by Tassos Papadopoulos started to impede the European efforts to make good on what the EU has pledged to end the isolation of the Turkish Cypriots. As the EU falters in ending their isolation, the U.S. efforts, although half a step ahead of the EU, also fall short.

The Cyprus problem is obviously not a bilateral issue with Turkey but a problem among the two equal peoples on the island. While not a condition for EU membership, it is nonetheless likely to force both Turkey's and the EU's hand, unless of course a mutually acceptable solution is found in the meantime under the good offices of the UN secretary-general, which remains the only legitimate show in town. However, as long as the secretary-general lacks enthusiasm to relaunch his efforts while the Papadopoulos government remains unrepentant, any hope among the Turkish Cypriots for the reunification of the island may be evaporating. At the same time, the international community is gradually losing faith as well. The Organization of the Islamic Conference already decided as of 2004 to upgrade the representation of the TRNC from "Turkish Cypriot Moslem Community" to the "Turkish Cypriot State." Turkey's traditional allies in Europe and the United States will likely regret their utterly insufficient stances, if the result is the recognition of the TRNC by the Muslim nations as a full-fledged internationally recognized state at some point in time.

In the meantime, the Greek Cypriots, while pursuing a narrow, self-centric agenda oblivious to the big picture of Turkish-EU relations, also provide a useful cover for the others that aim to retard Turkey's membership.

These issues will preoccupy the strategists on all sides in the accession negotiations. The Commission will be obliged to report on the developments regarding these and other issues. Irrespective of how many friends Turkey might have within the Commission, their judgments may over time reflect the Greek and Greek Cypriot vantage points more than those of the Turks. These two parties will also sit at the European Council meetings as full partners and champion their own points of view. Turkey will be outside.

Aegean and Cyprus issues are important, but they are only one part of a much larger foreign policy agenda for Turkey. Positive developments on those issues will surely be important for Turkey and the other countries involved, but as long as the Balkans, the Caucasus, the broader Middle East, Central Asia, and relations between the Muslim and Western worlds remain unstable, there will be other important issues that require Turkish-EU cooperation. It would be a mistake to sap a portion of Turkey's positive energy from these momentous regional and global issues.

There can be no forgone conclusions about the evolution of the dynamic global and regional environment in today's world and how specific international developments could influence Turkey's accession to the EU. The same is true regarding how EU-U.S.-Turkish cooperation could evolve in the time ahead, so laden with significant challenges for each side. The management of this transitory period is a fundamental task that no one should underestimate.

Heinz Kramer argues that "from the very beginning, the negotiations have to be part of a broader process of intensified political contacts, debates, and wherever possible, cooperation between the EU and Turkey."[18] In this regard, without reference to a special status short of membership "issues of the EU's Common Foreign and Security Policy (CFSP), including aspects of European Security and Defense Policy (ESDP), have to be one special focus of negotiations in terms of substance and institutions." Accordingly, "as most of the issues mentioned above are characterized by a high degree of political urgency, they should be addressed early on in the negotiations with the aim of finding some interim framework that would allow the EU to make much better use of the assumed advantages of Turkish membership than could be made by the actual practice of political dialogue or via NATO."[19]

While Kramer's suggestion regarding "a closer and more continuous Turkish participation in CFSP and ESDP along the lines of its former status in the Western European Union, i.e., a kind of special associated membership" might have sounded like music to Turkish ears a few years ago, this has now become a new and controversial territory. There is a vigilant resistance along virtually all sectors of the Turkish political elite and the public to the idea of any divergence from the pledged equal treatment of Turkey with the other accession candidates. Particularly with the calls by skeptics in the EU for a privileged partnership for Turkey short of full membership, there is open opposition to any idea that would seem to reminisce such status. The reference by the European Union to the "open ended" nature of the coming accession negotiations also appears to have inflamed Turkish caution.

It may be comprehensible from the EU point of view to take on board Turkish foreign and security policy capabilities without having to wait a decade until Turkey accedes to the EU. However, while the current capabilities are significant, the real potential lies in their synergy with EU membership.

For Turkey to invest in foreign and security policy without reaping the benefits of EU membership would be hard to justify to the Turks. It is even more difficult, even impossible, to justify concessions when the membership is uncertain. When Turkey entered into a challenging Customs Union with the EU in 1996 before its membership prospects became tangible, it was the one and only aspirant or candidate who had taken that route. A similar incongruent status in the area of foreign and security policy would be hard to market to Turkey.

Furthermore, the notion that accession to the EU is "a process of mostly one-sided adaptation to the EU by a state accepting the EU's demands for accession" cannot be taken at face value in the special field of foreign and security policy, which has not yet been brought credibly into the European integration project. Instead, the coming decade of accession talks between the EU and Turkey should be defined by a renewed vigor in consultations to realize maximum policy convergence in a manner that enables uploading as well as downloading of policy on both parties. Whether this would require additional consultative mechanisms or greater room for Turkish participation in EU foreign and security policy decision shaping during the negotiation period is a separate point.

Currently, the enhanced political dialogue established as part of the accession strategy is the basic consultative mechanism between the EU and Turkey on foreign and security policy. As part of this dialogue, Turkey and the EU also have been exchanging views on international issues such as the Southern Caucasus, Western Balkans, the Middle East Process, the Mediterranean and Middle East regions, Iraq, Iran, Afghanistan, and effective multilateralism. The meetings have been held at political director, European correspondent, and working group levels. Turkey has been actively participating in exchanges with the EU and in meetings of the EU with non-EU European NATO members related with the ESDP.

Although these meetings were most useful from the vantage point of maintaining the steady flow of information between the two sides, it would require a stretch of imagination to consider them an effective Turkish participation in EU decision shaping. Similar meetings are held between Turkey and both the United States and Russia, which demonstrates that the current consultative mechanisms are not of a particularly advanced form and content, as would be expected between the EU and an accession candidate. What makes this observation particularly pertinent is the fact that unlike previous candidates and currently Croatia, Turkey knows it will not join the EU for another decade, presumably irrespective of how fast it adopts the EU acquis.

On the other hand, even with more effective Turkish-EU consultative mechanisms, the indispensable role of the United States cannot be ignored. The Turkish-U.S. partnership is a geopolitical exigency that itself requires more effective consultation.

Turkey needs the breathing space provided by a better transatlantic climate and substantial transatlantic cooperation. A transatlantic rift over a particular issue creates geopolitical distraction for Turkey on the road to EU membership. It thus has a stake in encouraging greater efforts among the transatlantic allies to enliven their cooperation and consultative mechanisms. Against this backdrop, the best way to promote the smooth Europeanization of Turkey's foreign and security policy appears to be one that would engage Turkey in unsurpassed levels of consultation and decision shaping within the EU and between the EU and the United States. Whether this implies, for instance, Turkey's participation in EU-U.S. summits could be given further thought. It is time to think creatively and free of institutional dogmatisms to facilitate Turkish participation in the shaping of EU foreign and security policy decisions even before it joins the EU. Obviously, that needs to be achieved without distracting the parties from the shared objective of the ongoing negotiations, namely full membership. At that stage, the point made by Kramer about engaging Turkey in CFSP and ESDP may become more palatable.

For Turkey and the EU as well as the United States, vision and pragmatism must marry. Whether this is achievable or even realistic is secondary to the understanding of its necessity. European, U.S., and by the same token Turkish acquiescence in greater consultation and a discernible special effort to generate common policies should simply be seen as good policy rather than impractical altruism on all involved parties.

This is not part of the regular negotiation process of an EU candidate. Negotiations are about adopting the EU acquis. While it is mandatory to implement the acquis, Turkey must also feel secure and befriended while making good on its significant potential in foreign and security policy. The EU has tried to make it clear that Turkey is not any other candidate. But negotiating accession must take in the big picture. Its uniqueness should not only be construed and cited against Turkey. Turkey should also be given the benefits of its distinctiveness.

Notes

1. "Turkey Dominates Merkel's Adviser's Maiden Remarks," *Turkish Daily News*, August 19, 2005 (quoting remarks made by Wolfgang Schäuble to Frankfurter Rundschau, August 18, 2005).

2. The full text of the associated documents, namely the EU Opening Statement, Negotiating Framework, and External Arrangements, can be found at the official website of the Turkish Ministry of Foreign Affairs: www.mfa.gov.tr. See also: www .europa.eu.int/comm/enlargement/docs/pdf/negotiating_framework_turkey.pdf.

3. Negotiating Framework for Turkey, Annex.

4. Negotiating Framework for Turkey, Article 12.

5. Fadi Hakura, "Partnership Is No Privilege: The Alternative to EU Membership Is No Turkish Delight" (briefing paper, EPBP 05/02, Chatham House, Royal Institute of International Affairs, September 2005), 3.

6. Katinka Barysch, Introduction to *Why Europe Should Embrace Turkey*, by Katinka Barysch, Steven Everts, and Heather Grabbe (London: Centre for European Reform, 2005).

7. Hakura, "Partnership Is No Privilege," 3.

8. Barysch, Introduction to *Why Europe Should Embrace Turkey*, 8.

9. Negotiating Framework, Article 7.

10. Council of the European Union, document no 12823/05, October 3, 2005. The text can be found at www.mfa.gov.tr.

11. Heather Grabbe, *When Negotiations Begin: The Next Phase in EU-Turkey Relations* (London: Centre for European Reform, 2004), 4.

12. Kirsty Hughes, *The Political Dynamics of Turkish Accession to the EU: A European Success Story or the EU's Most Contested Enlargement?* Stockholm: Swedish Institute for European Policy Studies (SIEPS), 2004, 41–42.

13. Grabbe, *When Negotiations Begin*, 3.

14. Negotiating Framework for Turkey, Article 4, second bullet.

15. In reaction, Turkey states that unilateral expansion of Greece's territorial waters would constitute a *casus belli*.

16. In one such instance in May 2006 a Greek jet crashed into the Turkish aircraft from the rear. ("Greek, Turkish Fighter Planes Collide over Aegean Sea," *USA Today*, May 23, 2006.) The two governments acted in restraint to prevent this unfortunate and avoidable incident from damaging bilateral relations. They also agreed to establish a hotline between military authorities.

17. The European Council of Foreign Ministers Conclusion Statement of April 26, 2004.

18. Heinz Kramer, "Whither Turkey's EU Accession? Perspectives and Problems after December 2004" (paper presented at the conference entitled "Changing Parameters in U.S.-German-Turkish Relations: Future Scenarios," American Institute for Contemporary German Studies, Johns Hopkins University, September 20, 2004, Berlin), 17.

19. Kramer, "Whither Turkey's EU Accession?" 17.

CONCLUSION

The Coming Age of Janus

By opening accession negotiations with Turkey, argued Timothy Garton Ash, the EU has in fact decided that Europe will be a commonwealth, not a dreaded superstate. Accordingly, Turkey being so far to the southeast, the Balkans and the other countries in between will also have to come into the EU. This would bring the total number of the EU's members to thirty-two, or to thirty-seven states, including Switzerland, Norway, and Iceland, by 2015. He contended that "in view of such diversity the EU cannot be a federal, centralized, bureaucratic super-state, but an entity that is beyond a free-trade zone, perhaps a political community that is more like the early modern Polish-Lithuanian commonwealth"[1] If the EU is not going to be a federal state, one should not put the blame or credit on Turkey. The constitution's ambitious integrationist agenda was authored with the participation of Turkey and carried the signatures of the Turkish leaders. Turkey signed up to an EU that was progressing toward a political union with a coherent common foreign and security policy. It has made clear both by its political pronouncements and by contributions to EU military missions that it supports a stronger EU. The constitution's setback was also a setback for the Turkish vision of Europe.

The French and Dutch referenda in mid-2005 applied the brakes on the exuberance of the European elites to develop the precious EU project into a Napoleonic polity of a United States of Europe. At the same time, it is unwarranted to jump to the conclusion that the current confusion with the EU project marks the finality of European integration. The EU will probably look inward for some time to come to grips with its new realities. The current lack of enthusiasm to devolve further powers of common decision making will take its toll on the speed of integration. However, as the leaders and common institutions ponder how to reenergize the EU, neither Europe nor the world will sit still. Irrespective of how much one may strive to wish them away, all the challenges detailed in the European Security Strategy and the overall questions associated with managing Europe's neighboring regions are alive and real.

Therein lies a concrete dilemma for the Europeans. They will have to address the existing challenges, both in the domestic and in the foreign policy domains, but their publics are not ready and willing either to shoulder the burden of greater investment in their capabilities or to return to a higher gear in cooperation with the United States. One may have faith in the EU to overcome this dilemma; at least the EU was ultimately successful in reaching a compromise on the EU budget before the year ended in 2005.

In the current environment of feeble support for EU-wide solutions, there may be a risk of the variable geometry moving toward unhelpful fragmentation through disparate coalitions of the willing. Even granting the view that the EU can avoid deconstruction thanks to the flexibility of its members to go their own ways in foreign policy and even benefit from such flexibility, it is hard to deny that a fragmented Union will be less inspiring even to its own citizens. A fragmented Europe will be a weaker Europe, and at the same time, it would mean a less useful partner for the United States.

The policies of the United States have once again become critical to making a more coherent partner out of the Europeans. The pronouncements from the United States point to a realization that America needs to take a position once again on the side of European integration. In her speech in San Francisco, two days before the French referendum, Dr. Rice acknowledged that the European Union was a source of stability and expressed hope that it could continue its efforts toward integration and unification. Similarly, in the immediate wake of the referenda, Secretary Rice stated at her meeting on June 2, 2004, with the EU Presidency's Jean Asselborn, EU External Relations Commissioner Benita Ferrero-Waldner, and EU High Representative Javier Solana:

> We work hand in hand with the European Union and NATO to provide stable pillars of a transatlantic relationship that I think has demonstrably been an incentive for democratizing states coming out of crisis or coming out of revolutionary situations, as in the case of East Central Europe, to have a kind of lodestar to which they are attaching. And I would hope that that remains an

important goal of the European Union because everybody has a stake in a Europe—which, of course, includes Turkey—a Europe that is united around common values. But, you know, we understand that this has been a difficult period and that there will be some period of reflection going forward, but we continue to hope for an outward looking Europe, not an inward looking one.[2]

The case for Turkey's membership to the EU was strong when the EU had been galloping toward a more integrated and higher-profile common foreign and security policy. There is an overwhelming argument that the EU would need and much benefit from Turkey's membership if it is going to play a more evident role in regional and global affairs. Nonetheless, Turkey's importance for Europe does not diminish due to the current woes of the European project. A less coherent Europe would need Turkey's assets and cooperation as much as a coherent Europe. Such is the reality of Turkey's demographic strengths; strategic location; geopolitical assets; and political, social, cultural, economic, and military attributes. All forecasts of Turkey's diminishing importance have been repeatedly defeated by the facts on the ground. The fact of the matter is that Turkey remains indispensable for the efforts to stabilize and ultimately transform Europe's proximate region and is essentially inextricable from Europe. A privileged partnership, or any other deal that Turkey enters into unconvinced, cannot substitute for a full membership. A permanent rupture of Turkey's EU dream could sooner or later turn into the rupture of the EU's Turkish dream.

Most European wariness against Turkish membership is due to misconceptions, which must be deliberately targeted and corrected. The talk of longer time-lines for Turkey's accession to the EU may be a discourse but it is not a policy, at least not a wise one. The voters want to be reassured that their leaders are following the optimum policies. That reassurance can only come by patiently explaining to the masses why a particular course of action is better than the alternative. As Giuliano Amato has argued, European statesmen must have the courage "to tackle issues that are very controversial and that in some cases raise the same discontent that largely motivated the French and the Dutch Nos: budgets and new allocation of funds to take the needs of the new, poorer member states into due account; a strategy for growth and therefore liberalization; and further enlargement, with the Balkans at the top of the agenda and Turkey immediately after them."[3]

A Turkey that effects reforms and successfully emulates European standards—the expected outcome of successful negotiations—should eliminate many of the arguments against Turkish membership. This would be a Turkey that is more profusely democratic, Europeanized, modernized, and prosperous.

Even regarding migratory pressures toward the EU, Turkey would likely switch from a sending nation to a receiving nation, particularly from its neighborhood. Signs of this happening are already visible. Admittedly, not all of the arguments against Turkey's membership will be nullified. Turkey will continue to be large, populous, and resolutely strong. It will be one of the major nations of the EU. Yet, most important, it will be a European-anchored Turkey. The overwhelming majority of Turks being Muslims will obviously also not change. But Turkey's contributions will be important for the successful integration of the masses of Muslims who are now awkwardly and insecurely cohabiting in European countries. Indeed, in the words of Christopher Brewin, if Turkey is not accepted as a member state, "then second-generation immigrants from the Indian sub-continent or North Africa, who do not identify with Turks, will have more reason to fear that they will remain second-class citizens of the states where they live, and of the EU."[4] Secular and democratic Turkey will be a catalyst for Christian-Muslim understanding and harmony, a strong and credible advocate within the EU to that effect. There is an abundance of tasks that Turkey needs to fulfill in order to join the EU. There are a lot of people who oppose Turkish membership precisely because they are not convinced that Turks can achieve these tasks. The opposition can be marginalized to those who maintain such a stance solely due to narrow domestic agendas and nationalistic or politico-religious fixations.

Many of these points are lost in the debate in Europe regarding Turkey's membership. As Amato underscores, "the xenophobic emotions that animate the jobless and the working poor . . . have been exploited by (part of) the political leadership rather than courageously debated."[5] Just as they are provoked, these misconceptions can also be corrected. However, the incontrovertible requirement to enlighten the European public debate can no longer belong solely to Turkey. The EU political and opinion leaders must also promote this merger in an unprecedented fashion. In the meantime, public perceptions and dialogue will be promoted through joint action under the terms of the agreed framework for the negotiations.

As the accession negotiations proceed and the public debate in the EU countries and Turkey takes shape, developments in the realm of foreign and security policy will exert influence on the atmospherics of the process. The negotiations on the common foreign and security policy chapter may be arguably less contentious than several other chapters that relate to traditionally core EU business, where the EU acquis is more direct and rigid. There is currently far-reaching convergence with the EU on foreign and security policy issues. Whether this will continue and further develop cannot be left to its own devices.

Turks remain suspicious that specific foreign policy issues will be brought to the table to veil the broader resistance to Turkey's membership. Turks have a heightened interest and sensitivity on a particular set of foreign policy issues, and the Turkish Republic has tangible security and foreign policy interests in its neighborhood. Such pressures on Turkey can impact negatively on overall Turkish support for gaining EU membership and the associated reforms. While this may indeed be the calculation of Turkey's opponents in the EU, such an attitude would be too clever by half. A Turkey thwarted in its European aspiration cannot be of benefit for Europe.

On the other hand, it would be wrong to presume that the EU will want to take that road. It would be an injustice to the vast numbers of Europeans who believe in the virtues of Turkey's membership. The most striking attitude vis-à-vis Turkish membership is not being against or in favor; it is instead being undecided which side to take. Beyond the historical duality in European minds regarding Turkey, enlightened European societies must be counted on to tread the path of sincerity and wisdom.

In the intervening time, there must be a dedicated effort to make foreign and security policy convergence and complementarity the positive influence that it promises. For this to proceed at due speed, Turkey will need to be confident that its interests and concerns are duly credited. The absence of this confidence has been a constant problem for Turkish public perception, which continues to display a lack of trust. And at least in recent historical experience, this is not altogether unwarranted. Greater convergence, complementarity, and synergy will not come about only with Turkey's acquiescence to EU policy decisions, necessitated by the accession negotiations. A two-way interaction between Turkey and the EU, involving reasonable levels of policy uploading as well as downloading, is needed to facilitate further convergence and synergy between the parties.

The United States is not extrinsic to the debate about Turkey's EU membership. Naturally, since the United States is not a member of the EU it will not drive the process. Nonetheless, rather than protesting U.S. advice, the EU leaders should be recruiting further U.S. contributions to this historic process. Shoring up U.S. support in the effort to build up the Turkish economy and boost its high-tech industrial base can be a perfect place to start. In the area of foreign policy, the United States is in fact a major player in almost all the issues that the EU and Turkey will discuss in the next ten years of the accession process. At any rate, Turkey cannot be expected to downgrade its partnership with the United States, which will continue to be a key partner in almost every aspect of Turkish foreign and security policy. And the broadening of Turkish-American relations, including in people-to-people contacts, interaction among intellectuals and think tanks, and in the economic and commercial spheres is welcome among the Turks. There is a deep-rooted conviction in Turkey, however, that EU membership and effective partnership with the United States can and must be mutually accommodating. Turkey is neither the first nor the only country in Europe that thinks this way.

Turkey's interests and concerns are inextricably linked to the major enterprise of stabilizing the surrounding regions on a course that is democratic, peacefully interdependent, and reflexively cooperative even if inherently competitive. Turkey's foreign and security policy can be expected to continue to display dynamism in regional affairs, driven by the motivation to promote an environment that is more conducive to economic development, greater security and stability, as well as further democratic progress and indeed consolidation at home. At the same time, when in doubt, Turkey's instincts will be expected to opt for stability, engagement rather than confrontation, and direct negotiation rather than third-party intervention across the slate of regional relations. While cooperation with the EU and the United States will be a reflex, an eye will have to be kept on not upsetting regional connections. Relations with Russia, China, Pakistan, and India will continue to be emphasized, in addition to traditional friendship and relationships in the broad neighborhood. However, this will not be an unconditional deference. The natural limits to collaboration with the regional neighbors will of course be determined by how much they act responsibly in the international scene.

The EU and the United States, not to mention the hundreds of millions of people living around Turkey, share with the Turkish nation a profound interest in managing the positive transformation of the proximate region. Bringing Turkey into the EU is the cornerstone of this sublime project. Turkey's membership in the European Union will be the litmus test for where this vast and diverse region of utmost strategic relevance will go next. It will affect the global tenor of relations between different cultures all belonging to the same human civilization but representing different faiths. Democratic, secular, and strong Turkey will thus be poised to emerge as a figurative Janus, opening new vistas and ensuring good endings. Atatürk's children are capable of assuming this historic role. Now it is time for the EU to seize the opportunity and make it happen.

Notes

1. Timothy Garton Ash, "How the Dreaded Superstate Became a Commonwealth," *Guardian* (Manchester), October 6, 2005.

2. For the full text of Secretary Rice's remarks, see: www.state.gov/secretary/rm/2005/47140.htm.

3. Giuliano Amato, "Après le Déluge," *Internationale Politik* (Transatlantic Edition, Fall 2005): 5–6. Of course, I take exception at his ordering of the line for joining the Union. Candidate countries should join as they become ready. A Balkans-first presumption would again miss the point.

4. Christopher Brewin, "Turkey's Right to a Date" paper for the European Consortium for Political Research, 2nd annual pan-European Conference on EU politics, "Implications of a Wider Europe: Politics, Institutions and Diversity" (Bologna: Johns Hopkins, June 24–26, 2004): 10.

5. Amato, "Après le Déluge," 6.

Selected Bibliography

Adhikari, Gautam. "The End of the Unipolar Myth." *International Herald Tribune*, September 27, 2004.

Akçapar, Burak. "Partnership for Peace's Influence as an Instrument of Continuity and Change in the Euro-Atlantic Region." In *A History of NATO: The First Fifty Years*, edited by Gustav Schmidt. London and New York: Palgrave, 2001.

Akçapar, Burak, and Denis Chaibi. "Turkey's EU Accession: The Long Road from Ankara to Brussels." *Yale Journal of International Affairs* 1, no. 2 (Winter/Spring 2006): 50–57.

Akçapar, Burak, Mensur Akgün, Meliha Altunışık, and Ayşe Kadıoğlu. "The Debate on Democratization in the Broader Middle East and North Africa: A Civic Assessment from Turkey." Istanbul Paper No. 3, TESEV/GMF, June 2004.

Akgün, Mensur, and Sabiha Senyücel. "Reluctant Ally." *Turkish Policy Quarterly* 3, no. 1 (Spring 2003): 59–67.

Altunışık, Meliha Benli. "The Turkish Model and Democratization in the Middle East." *Arab Studies Quarterly* 27, nos. 1–2 (Winter/Spring 2005): 45–63.

Altunışık, Meliha Benli, and Özlem Tur Kavlı. *Turkey: Themes and Challenges*. London and New York: RoutledgeCurzon, 2004.

Asmus, Ronald D. "Rebuilding the Atlantic Alliance." *Foreign Affairs* 82, no. 5 (September/October 2003): 20–31.

Asmus, Ronald D., and Kenneth M. Pollack. "The New Transatlantic Project." *Policy Review* 115 (October/November 2002): 3–18.

Ayata, Ayşe Güneş. "From Euro-Scepticism to Turkey-Scepticism: Changing Political Attitudes on the European Union." *Journal of Southern Europe and the Balkans* 5, no. 2 (August, 2003): 205–22.

Aydın, Mustafa. "Foucault's Pendulum: Turkey in Central Asia and the Caucasus." *Turkish Studies* 5, no. 2 (Summer 2004): 1–22.

———. "Securitization of History and Geography: Understanding of Security in Turkey." *Journal of Southeast Europe and Black Sea Studies* 3, no. 2 (May 2003): 163–84.

Aydınlı, Ersel. "Security and Liberalization: Decoding Turkey's Struggle with the PKK." *Security Dialogue* 33, no. 2 (2002): 209–25.

Aykan, Mahmut Balı. "The Turkish-Syrian Crisis of October 1998: A Turkish View." *Middle East Policy* 6, no. 4 (June 1999): 174–91.

Bağcı, Hüseyin, and Ali Yıldız. "Turkey and the European Security and Defence Policy (ESDP): From Confrontational to Cooperative Relationship." In *The Europeanization of Turkey's Security Policy: Prospects and Pitfalls*, edited by A. L. Karaosmanoğlu and Seyfi Taşhan. Ankara: Dış Politika Enstitüsü, 2004.

Bal, İhsan, and Sedat Laçiner. "The Challenge of Revolutionary Terrorism to Turkish Democracy, 1960–80." *Terrorism and Political Violence* 13, no. 4 (Winter 2001): 90–115.

Baran, Zeyno. "The Baku-Tbilisi-Ceyhan Pipeline: Implications for Turkey." In *The Baku-Tbilisi-Ceyhan Pipeline: Oil Window to the West*, edited by S. Frederick Starr and Svante E. Cornell. Washington, DC: Johns Hopkins University Central Asia-Caucasus Institute & Silk Road Studies Program, 2005.

———. "From the Caspian to the Mediterranean: The East-West Energy Corridor Is Becoming a Reality." *In The National Interest* 2, no. 8 (2003).

Barkey, Henry J. *Turkey and Iraq: The Perils of Proximity*. Washington, DC: United States Institute of Peace, 2005.

Bengio, Ofra, and Gencer Özcan. "Changing Relations: Turkish-Israeli-Arab Triangle," *Perceptions* 5, no. 1 (March–May 2000): 134–46.

Berenskoetter, Felix Sebastian. "Mapping the Mind Gap: A Comparison of U.S. and EU Security Strategies." *Security Dialogue* 36, no. 1 (March 2005): 71–92.

Bilgin, Pınar. "Differences between Turkey and the European Union on Security." In *The Europeanization of Turkey's Security Policy: Prospects and Pitfalls*, edited by A. L. Karaosmanoğlu and Seyfi Taşhan, 25–52. Ankara: Dış Politika Enstitüsü, 2004.

Bir, Çevik, and Martin Sherman. "Formula for Stability: Turkey Plus Israel." *Middle East Quarterly* 9, no. 4 (Fall 2002): 23–32.

Bishku, Michael B. "Turkish-Bulgarian Relations: From Conflict and Distrust to Cooperation." *Mediterranean Quarterly* 14, no. 2 (Spring 2003): 77–94.

Bomberg, Elizabeth, and John Peterson. "Policy Transfer and Europeanization: Passing the Heineken Test?" Paper for the Political Studies Association-UK 50th Annual Conference, April 10–13, 2000, London.

Bostanoğlu, Burcu. "Global Security Calculus: Forcing the Turkish-American Strategic Alliance to New Orientations." *Milletlerarası Münasebetler Türk Yıllığı* [Turkish Yearbook of International Relations] 31, no. 2 (2000): 227–32.

Bremmer Ian, "Would Turkey Split the EU and the US?" *International Herald Tribune*, November 22, 2004.

Brewin, Christopher. "Turkey's Right to a Date." (Paper for the European Consortium for Political Research, Second Annual Pan-European Conference on EU Politics. Bologna: Johns Hopkins, June 24–26, 2004).

Brown, Carl L. ed. *Imperial Legacy: The Ottoman Imprint on the Balkans and the Middle East.* New York: Columbia University Press, 1996.

Brzezinski, Zbigniew. *The Choice: Global Domination or Global Leadership.* New York: Basic Books: 2004.

Çağaptay, Soner. "Where Goes the U.S.-Turkish Relationship?" *Middle East Quarterly* 11, no. 4 (Fall 2004): 1–10.

Çağaptay, Soner (and Cem S. Fikret). *Europe's Terror Problem: PKK Fronts Inside the EU.* Washington Institute for Near East Studies, Policy Watch No. 1057, December 2, 2005.

Çalış, Şaban. "Turkey's Balkan Policy in the Early 1990s," *Turkish Studies* 2, no. 1 (Spring 2001): 135–46.

Calleo, David P. "The Broken West." *Survival* 46, no. 3 (Autumn 2004): 29–38.

———. "Transatlantic Folly: NATO vs. the EU," *World Policy Journal* 20, no. 3 (Fall 2003): 17–24.

Çandar, Cengiz, and Graham E. Fuller. "Grand Geopolitics for a New Turkey." *Mediterranean Quarterly* 12, no. 1 (Winter 2001): 22–38.

Carlsnaess, Walter, Helene Sjursen, and Brian White, eds. *Contemporary European Foreign Policy.* London: Sage, 2004.

Cem, Ismail. *Turkey in the New Century.* Nicosia-Mersin: Rustem, 2001.

Çeviköz, Ünal. "European Integration and New Regional Cooperation Initiatives." *NATO Review* 40, no. 3 (June 1992): 23–27.

Chase, Robert, Emily Hill, and Paul Kennedy, eds. *The Pivotal States: A New Framework for U.S. Policy in the Developing World.* New York: W. W. Norton and Company, 1999.

Cofman-Wittes, Tamara. "The New U.S. Proposal for a Greater Middle East Initiative: An Evaluation." The Brookings Institution, Middle East Memo No. 2, May 10, 2004.

Coker, Christopher. "Globalization and Insecurity in the Twenty-first Century: NATO and the Management of Risk." Adelphi Paper 345, London: IISS, 2002.

Cook, Steven A., and Elisabeth D. Sherwood-Randall, *Generating Momentum for a New Era in U.S.-Turkish Relations.* Council Special Report No. 15, June 21, 2006.

Commission of the European Communities. "Issues Arising from Turkey's Membership Perspective." Commission staff working document, Brussels, June 10, 2004, Sec(2004)1202, Com(2004) 656 Final.

Cordesman, Anthony H. *The Transatlantic Alliance: Is 2004 the Year of the Greater Middle East?* Washington, DC: CSIS, 2004.

Daalder, Ivo H. "The End of Atlanticism." *Survival* 45, no. 2 (Summer 2003): 147–66.

Dannreuther, Ronald, ed. *European Union Foreign and Security Policy: Towards a Neighbourhood Strategy.* London: Routledge, 2004.

Davutoğlu, Ahmet. *Stratejik Derinlik: Türkiye'nin Uluslararası Konumu* [Strategic Depth: Turkey's International Position]. Istanbul: Küre Yayınları, 2002.

Emerson, Michael, and Nathalie Tocci. "Turkey as a Bridgehead and Spearhead: Integrating EU and Turkish Foreign Policy." EU-Turkey Working Papers No. 1, Brussels: Center for European Policy Studies, 2004.

Ergüvenç, Şadi. "The New Security Environment and Turkey's Contribution to European Security." In *Contemporary Issues in International Politics: Essays in Honour of Seyfi Taşhan*. Ankara: Dış Politika Enstitüsü [Foreign Policy Institute], 2004.

Everts, Steven, Lawrence Freedman, Charles Grant, François Heisbourg, Daniel Keohane, and Michael O'Hanlon. *A European Way of War*. London: Centre for European Reform, 2004.

Featherstone, K., and Claudio Radaelli, eds. *The Politics of Europeanisation*. Oxford: Oxford University Press, 2002.

Ferguson, Niall. *Colossus: The Rise and Fall of the American Empire*. New York: Penguin, 2005.

Fırat, Melek M. "Soğuk Savaş Sonrası Yunanistan Dış Politikasının Yeniden Biçimleniş Süreci" [The Process of Reshaping of the Post–Cold War Greek Foreign Policy]. In *Türkiye'nin Komşuları* [Turkey's Neighbors], edited by Mustafa Türkeş and İlhan Uzgel. Ankara: İmge, 2002.

Flournoy, Michele, Julianne Smith, Guy Ben-Ari, David Scruggs, and Kathleen McInnis. *European Defense Integration: Bridging the Gap between Strategy and Capabilities*. Washington, DC: CSIS, October 2005.

Friedman, Thomas. *The Lexus and the Olive Tree*. New York: Farrar, Straus & Giroux, 2000.

Fuller, Graham. "Turkey's Strategic Model: Myths and Realities." *Washington Quarterly* 27, no. 3 (Summer 2004): 51–64.

Ginsberg, Roy. *The European Union in International Politics: Baptism by Fire*. Lanham, MD: Rowman and Littlefield, 2001.

Gnesotto, Nicole. "ESDP: A European View." IISS/CEPS European Security Forum, Brussels, July 8, 2001.

Gordon, Philip H. "One Year On: Lessons from Iraq." In Chaillot Paper No. 68, *One Year On: Lessons from Iraq*, 161–68. Paris: EU-ISS, 2004.

Gordon, Philip H., and Ömer Taşpınar. "Turkey on the Brink." *The Washington Quarterly* 29, no. 3 (Summer 2006): 57–70.

Grabbe, Heather. *From Drift to Strategy: Why the EU Should Start Accession Talks with Turkey*. London: Center for European Reform, 2004.

———. *When Negotiations Begin: The Next Phase in EU-Turkey Relations*. London: Center for European Reform, 2004.

Grgic, Borut. "European Security: A Strategy with No Muscle." *International Herald Tribune*, December 13, 2003.

Haas, Ernst. *The Uniting of Europe: Political Social and Economic Forces, 1950–57*. Stanford, CA: Stanford University Press, 1968.

Haftendorn, Helga. "Ein Koloß auf tönernen Füßen: die NATO braucht eine realistische neue Zweckbestimmung." *Internationale Politik* 60, no. 4 (April 2005): 80–85.

Hickok, Michael Robert. "Hegemon Rising: The Gap Between Turkish Strategy and Military Modernization." *Parameters* 30, no. 2 (Summer 2000): 105–19.

Hill, Christopher. *The Actors in Europe's Foreign Policy.* New York: Routledge, 1996.

Hill, Fiona. "Seismic Shifts in Eurasia: The Changing Relationship between Turkey and Russia, and Its Implications for the South Caucasus." *Journal of Southeast Europe and Black Sea Studies* 3 no. 3 (September 2003): 55–75.

Howorth, Jolyon. "European Integration and Defence: The Ultimate Challenge?" Chaillot Paper 43, Paris: Institute for Security Studies of WEU, November 2000.

———. "Transatlantic Perspectives on European Security in the Coming Decade." *Yale Journal of International Affairs* 1, no. 1 (Summer/Fall 2005): 8–22.

Hunter, Shireen. "Bridge or Frontier? Turkey's Post–Cold War Geopolitical Posture." *International Spectator* 34, no. 1 (January/March 1999): 63–78.

Independent Commission on Turkey. "Turkey in Europe: More Than a Promise?" The British Council, Brussels, 2004.

International Crisis Group. "Iraq: Allaying Turkey's Fears over Kurdish Ambitions." Middle East Report No. 35, January 26, 2005.

———. "Iraq's Kurds: Toward an Historic Compromise?" Middle East Report No. 26, Amman, Brussels, April 8, 2004.

———. "Unmaking Iraq: A Constitutional Process Gone Awry." Middle East Briefing No. 19, Amman, Brussels, September 26, 2005.

International Institute for Strategic Studies. "EU Operational Planning." *Strategic Comments* 9, no. 10 (December 2003).

———. "The European Security Strategy." *Strategic Comments* 9, no. 9 (November 2003).

Jervis, Robert. "The Compulsive Empire." *Foreign Policy,* no. 137 (July/August 2003): 83–87.

Kagan Robert. "America's Crisis of Legitimacy." *Foreign Affairs* 83, no. 2 (March/April 2004): 65–87.

———. *Of Paradise and Power: America and Europe in the New World Order.* New York: Vintage, 2004.

Kaplan, Robert D. *Eastward to Tartary.* New York: Random House, 2000.

Karaosmanoğlu, Ali L. "The Evolution of the National Security Culture and the Military in Turkey." *Journal of International Affairs* 54, no. 1 (Fall 2000): 199–217.

Karaosmanoğlu, Ali L., and Seyfi Taşhan, eds. *The Europeanization of Turkey's Security Policy: Prospects and Pitfalls.* Ankara: Dış Politika Enstitüsü, 2004.

Karmon, Ely. "A Solution to Syrian Terrorism," *Middle East Quarterly* 6, no. 2 (June 1999): 23–32.

Kibaroğlu, Mustafa. "Turkey and Israel Strategize." *Middle East Quarterly* 9, no. 1 (Winter 2002): 61–65.

King, Charles. *The Black Sea: A History.* New York: Oxford University Press, 2005.

Kinross, Lord. *The Ottoman Centuries: The Rise and Fall of the Turkish Empire.* New York: Perennial, 1979.

Kinzer, Stephen. *Crescent and Star: Turkey between Two Worlds.* New York: Farrar, Straus & Giroux, 2001.

Kirişçi, Kemal. "Between Europe and the Middle East: The Transformation of Turkish Policy." *Middle East Review of International Affairs (MERIA)*, 8, no. 1 (March, 2004): 39–51.

Kramer, Heinz. "Whither Turkey's EU Accession? Perspectives and Problems after December 2004." Paper presented at the conference entitled "Changing Parameters in U.S.-German-Turkish Relations: Future Scenarios," American Institute for Contemporary German Studies, Johns Hopkins University, September 20, 2004, Berlin.

Kupchan, Charles A. *The End of the American Era: U.S. Foreign Policy and the Geopolitics of the Twenty-First Century.* New York: Alfred Knopf, 2002.

———. "The End of the West," *Atlantic Monthly*, November 2002.

———. "Resent, Resist, Compete." *World Today* 60, no. 7 (July 2004): 42–44.

Larrabee, F. Stephen, and Ian O. Lesser. *Turkish Foreign Policy in an Age of Uncertainty*, MR-1612-CMEPP. Santa Monica, CA: RAND, 2003.

Leonard, Mark. *Why Europe Will Run the 21st Century.* New York: Public Affairs, 2005.

Lesser, Ian O. "Turkey in a Changing Security Environment." *Journal of International Affairs* 54, no. 1 (Fall 2000): 183–98.

MacMillan, Margaret. *Paris 1919: Six Months That Changed the World.* New York: Random House, 2003.

Mango, Andrew. *The Turks Today.* Woodstock, NY: Overlook Press, 2004.

Marashi, Ibrahim al-. "Middle Eastern Perceptions of US-Turkey Relations after the 2003 Iraq War." *Turkish Policy Quarterly* 4, no. 1 (Spring 2005): 123–36.

Marchetti, Andreas. *The European Neighborhood Policy: Foreign Policy at the EU's Periphery.* Bonn: University of Bonn Center for European Integration Studies (ZEI) Publication, 2006.

Mazower, Mark. *The Balkans.* London: Phoenix, 2001.

Missiroli, Antonio. "The Constitutional Treaty: 'Enabling Text' for Foreign Policy and Defence." *European Voice*, October 21–27, 2004.

Moralı, Turan. "European Security and Defence Identity and Turkey." In *New Trends in Turkish Foreign Affairs: Bridges and Boundaries*, edited by Salomon Ruysdael and Vedat Yücel, 126–31. Lincoln, NE: iUniverse, 2002.

Müftüler-Bac, Meltem. "Turkey's Role in the EU's Security and Foreign Policies." *Security Dialogue* 31, no. 4 (2000): 489–502.

Naumann, Klaus. "What European Defence Capability Requires." *World Security Network Newsletter*, March 21, 2005.

Nye, Joseph S., Jr. *Power in the Global Information Age: From Realism to Globalization.* London and New York: Routledge, 2004.

———. *Soft Power: The Means to Succeed in World Politics.* New York: Public Affairs, 2004.

O'Hanlon, Michael E., and Omer Taspinar. "UN Reform Potential." *Washington Times*, December 17, 2004.

Öniş, Ziya. "Domestic Politics, International Norms and Challenges to the State: Turkey-EU Relations in the Post-Helsinki Era." *Turkish Studies* 4, no. 1 (Spring 2003): 9–34.

Oran, Baskın. *Türk Dış Politikası, Cilt I-II* [Turkish Foreign Policy, Vol. I-II] İstanbul: İletişim Yayınları, 2004.

Orhun, Ömür. "European Security and Defence Identity—Common European Security and Defence Policy: A Turkish Perspective." *Perceptions* 5, no. 3 (September/November 2000).

Öymen, Onur. *Turkish Challenge.* Cambridge: Rustem-Cambridge University Press, 2000.

Özdağ, Ümit, and Ersel Aydınlı. "Winning a Low Intensity Conflict: Drawing Lessons from the Turkish Case." *Review of International Affairs* (London) 2, no. 3 (Spring 2003): 101–21.

Pak, Namık Kemal, "Changing Concepts of National Security in the Post–Cold War Era and Turkish Defence Industry." *Perceptions* 7, no. 2 (June–August 2002): 102–17.

Papagiannidis, A. D. "Greece May Slip Back to 1980s Style Euroscepticism." *Europe's World* 1 (Autumn 2005): 171–72.

Park, Bill. "Strategic Location, Political Dislocation: Turkey, United States and Northern Iraq." *Middle East Review of International Affairs* 7, no. 2 (June 2003): 11–23.

Peterson, John, and Helene Sjursen, eds. *A Common Foreign Policy for Europe? Competing Visions of the CFSP.* London: Routledge, 1998.

Pope, Hugh. *Sons of the Conquerors: The Rise of the Turkic World.* New York: Overlook Press, 2005.

Pope, Nicole, and Hugh Pope. *Turkey Unveiled: A History of Modern Turkey.* New York: Overlook Press, 2000.

Porter, James. *Turkey: Its History and Progress.* London: Hurts and Blackett Publishers, 1854.

Quinlan, Joseph P. *Drifting Apart or Growing Together? The Primacy of the Transatlantic Economy.* Washington, DC: Center for Transatlantic Relations, 2003.

Ramonet, Ignacio. *Wars of the 21st Century: New Threats, New Fears.* Melbourne and New York: Ocean Press, 2004.

Rogers, Philippe. *L'ennemi americain: Genealogie de l'antiamericanisme français.* Paris: Seuil, 2002.

Rubin, Barry, and Kemal Kirişçi, eds. *Turkey in World Politics: An Emerging Multiregional Power.* Boulder, CO: Lynne Rienner Publishers, 2001.

Rustow, Dankwart A. "Turkey's Travails." *Foreign Affairs* 58, no. 1 Fall 1979: 82–102.

Ruysdael, Salomon, and Vedat Yücel, eds. *New Trends in Turkish Foreign Affairs: Bridges and Boundaries.* Lincoln, NE: Writers Club Press, 2002.

Said, Edward. *Orientalism.* New York: Vintage, 1979.

Sasley, Brent. "Turkey Energy's Politics." In *Turkey in World Politics: An Emerging Multiregional Power,* edited by Barry Rubin and Kemal Kirişçi. Boulder, CO: Lynne Rienner Publishers, 2001.

Sayari, Sabri. "Turkish Foreign Policy in the Post–Cold War Era: The Challenges of Multi-Regionalism." *Journal of International Affairs* 54, no. 1 (Fall 2000): 169–82.

Schake, Kori. "EU Should Duplicate NATO Assets." *CER Bulletin,* no. 18 (June–July 2001).

Schäuble, Wolfgang, and David L. Phillips. "Talking Turkey." *Foreign Affairs* 83, no. 6 (November/December 2004).

Schnabel, Rockwell A., and Francis X. Rocca. *The Next Superpower? The Rise of Europe and Its Challenge to the United States.* Lanham, MD: Rowman and Littlefield, 2005.

Settle, Mary Lee. *Turkish Reflections.* New York: Touchstone, 1991.

Sezer-Bazoğlu, Duygu. "Turkish-Russian Relations: The Challenges of Reconciling Geopolitical Competition with Economic Partnership." *Turkish Studies* 1, no. 1 (Spring 2000): 59–82.

Starr, Frederick S., and Svante E. Cornell, eds. *The Baku-Tbilisi-Ceyhan Pipeline: Oil Window to the West.* Washington, DC: Johns Hopkins University Central Asia-Caucasus Institute & Silk Road Studies Program, 2005.

Steinberg, James B. "An Elective Partnership: Salvaging Transatlantic Relations." *Survival* 45, no. 2 (Summer 2003): 113–46.

Steinbrunner, John D. *Principles of Global Security.* Washington, DC: The Brookings Institution, 2002.

Stern, Selma. "Turkey's Energy and Foreign Policy." *Globalization* 3, no. 1 (June 2003).

Sönmezoğlu, Faruk. *Türk Dış Politikasının Analizi.* [The Analysis of Turkish Foreign Policy] Istanbul: Der, 1994.

Taşpınar, Ömer. "Europe's Muslim Street." *Foreign Affairs* 135 (March/April 2003): 76–77.

Torreblanca, Jose I. "Ideas, Preferences and Institutions: Explaining the Europeanization of Spanish Foreign Policy." Arena Working Papers 01/26, 2001.

Türkeş, Mustafa, and İlhan Uzgel, eds. *Türkiye'nin Komşuları* [Turkey's Neighbors]. Ankara: İmge, 2002.

Ulusoy, Hasan. "A New Formation in the Black Sea: BLACKSEAFOR." *Perceptions* 6, no. 4 (December, 2001–February, 2002): 97–106.

Uslu, Nasuh. "The Russian, Caucasian and Central Asian Aspects of Turkish Foreign Policy in the Cold War Period," *Alternatives* 2, nos. 3–4 (Fall & Winter 2003): 164–87.

Vaisse, Justin. "From Transatlanticism to Post-Atlanticism." *In the National Interest* 2, no. 27, July 9, 2003.

Van Ham, Peter. "Europe Gets Real: The New Security Strategy Shows the EU's Geopolitical Maturity." *AICGS Advisor,* January 9, 2004.

Vaquer i Fanes, Jordi. "Europeanisation and Foreign Policy." Observatori de Politica Exterior Europa, working paper no. 21, April 2001.

Vinocur, John, "The Big Winner in the EU Expansion: Washington." *International Herald Tribune,* December 9, 2002.

Wheatcroft, Andrew. *The Ottomans.* London: Penguin, 1995.

White, Brian. "Foreign Policy Analysis and the New Europe." In *Contemporary European Foreign Policy,* edited by Walter Carlsnaess, Helene Sjursen, and Brian White, 11–31. London: Sage, 2004.

Winrow, Gareth M. "Turkey and the East-West Gas Transportation Corridor." *Turkish Studies* 5, no. 2 (Spring 2004): 23–42.

Yeşilada, Birol. "Turkey's Candidacy for European Union Membership." *Middle East Journal* 56, no. 1 (Winter 2002): 94–112.

Zakaria, Fareed. *The Future of Freedom: Illiberal Democracy at Home and Abroad.* New York and London: W. W. Norton & Company, 2003.

Zelikow, Phillip. "The Transformation of National Security: Five Redefinitions." *National Interest* 71 (Spring 2003): 17–28.

Index

Abbas, Mahmoud, 87
acquis communitaire, 164–66; Turkey
    and, 42, 166, 168, 171, 173, 182,
    183. *See also* European treaties
Adhikari, Gautam, 150
agriculture, 36, 164, 166, 167
Ahtisaari, Marti, 44
Akçapar, Burak, 108
Akgün, Mensur, 108
Albania, 134
Altunışık, Meliha Benli, 108
al Qaeda, 174
"Alliance of Civilizations," 108,
    170
Amato, Giuliano, 187, 188
Ankara Association Agreement, 35
Annan, Kofi, 88
anti-Semitism, 29
anti-Americanism, 50, 128
Arab countries, 33, 83, 84, 103, 105,
    107, 108–9, 147
Arab-Israeli conflict, 98, 100, 102, 105,
    107, 147, 155, 158, 159
Armenia, 14, 81, 88, 89, 148, 176,
    178–79

Armenia-Azerbaijan dispute, 79, 102,
    179; Minsk Group, 179
Armenian and Greek lobbies in U.S.
    Congress, 152
Ash, Timothy Garton, 118, 185
Asia, 32, 34, 37, 72, 105
Asmus, Ronald, 114–16, 139, 143, 144
Asselborn, Jean, 186
Atatürk, Mustafa Kemal, 66, 94, 172,
    190; Atatürk revolution, 2
Austria, 14, 15
Azerbaijan, 46, 81, 83, 88, 93, 97, 102,
    148, 178. *See also* Armenia-
    Azerbaijan dispute

Baghdad Pact, 81
Baku-Tblisi-Ceyhan. *See* energy
Balkans, 79, 100, 101, 138, 181; and
    the EU, 44, 129, 185, 186; peace
    operations in, 94, 121, 130; regional
    cooperation in, 86, 92, 111; Turks
    expelled from, 65; Turkish policy
    towards, 43, 44, 69, 72, 73, 80, 81,
    83, 86, 92, 94, 97, 159, 182
Balkanization, 108

Balkenende, Jan Peter, 12
Baran, Zeyno, 48
Barcelona Process, 101, 105
Barchard, David, 65
Barysch, Katynka, 167
Barzani, Mesoud, 113n15
Barzani, Nechirvan, 155
Belgium, 27, 132
Berenskoetter, Felix Sebastian, 127
Bildt, Carl, 108
Bilgin, Pınar, 68, 70
Black Sea, 4, 43, 47, 73, 81, 88, 90, 91,
    93, 100, 111, 147; Maritime Risk
    Assessment, 92; as a region, 91–92,
    101
Black Sea Economic Cooperation
    Organization (BSECO), 81, 86, 93,
    158
BLACKSEAFOR, 86, 92
Black Sea Harmony, 92–93
Bosnia and Herzegovina, 65, 80,
    135
Bowley, Graham, 25
Brewin, Christopher, 188
Broader Middle East and North Africa
    (BMENA), 49, 95, 100, 101, 105,
    107, 181; Democracy Assistance
    Dialogue (DAD), 95, 97, 107, 109,
    158; Foundation for the Future,
    107, 109; Middle East Partnership
    Initiative, 105; transatlantic
    cooperation in, 52, 108, 136, 138;
    Turkish policy toward, 70, 77, 95,
    96, 97, 104, 106–8, 110, 111,
    158
Brzezinski, Zbigniew, 150
Bulgaria, 8, 17 20, 24, 47, 87, 91, 93,
    101, 172
Burt, Richard, 49
Bush, George W., 95, 120, 121, 126,
    127, 151, 157
Bush doctrine, 126, 127. See also U.S.
    National Security Strategy

Cağaptay, Soner, 154, 156
Calleo, David P., 119
candidate countries, 7–9, 15, 17–18, 20,
    35, 58, 61–62, 124, 163, 169,
    172–73, 182; policy converge
    between the EU and, 61–63
caucasus, 79, 100, 101, 138, 181; and
    the EU, 43, 44; and Russia, 90–91;
    and transatlantic cooperation, 52,
    101, 138; Turkish descendants from,
    65; Turkish policy toward, 43,
    48–49, 80, 88–89, 96–97, 147–48,
    159, 182
Cem, İsmail, 85
Central and Eastern Europe, 6, 101,
    109, 137, 178
Central Asia, 79, 89, 90, 101, 181; EU
    and, 24, 44, 102; transatlantic
    cooperation in, 52, 138; Turkish
    policy toward, 24, 48, 49, 73, 80, 83,
    89, 90, 93, 96, 97, 147, 148, 159
Charter of Fundamental Rights, 123
Chase, Robert, 86
Chechens, 102
China, 1, 2, 51, 83, 139, 190
Christianity, 6, 7, 12, 16, 25, 27, 30, 32,
    36, 117; Crusades, 33
Christian-Muslim relations, 2, 4, 12,
    27–29, 32, 34, 106, 174, 188. See also
    "Alliance of Civilizations"; "clash of
    civilizations"
"clash of civilizations," 1, 10, 12, 16, 43,
    106, 108, 119
Cold War, 68, 91, 121; post–Cold War,
    31, 79–80, 122, 129, 135, 136; post-
    post–Cold War, 51; Turkey during,
    48, 70, 71, 78; Turkey after, 69,
    79–80, 89, 91, 111, 148
Combined Joint Task Force (CJTF),
    129
Common Agricultural Policy, 123, 174
Common Foreign and Security Policy
    (CFSP), 8, 52, 60, 61, 117, 123, 124,

125, 140; and Turkey, 49, 73, 165,
176, 181, 183, 185, 187, 188
Constitutional Treaty. See European
Constitutional Treaty
Convention on the Future of Europe,
21. See also European Constitutional
Treaty
Cook, Steven, 149
Cooper, Richard, 3
Copenhagen criteria, 42, 167–68,
170–72. See also Turkish reforms
Core Europe (kerneuropa), 12, 118, 132
counterweight policies, 118, 136–37, 138
crisis management, 61, 69, 70, 71, 140;
non-military, 130, 134, 140
Criss, Bilge, 70
Croatia, 8, 14, 18, 182
Customs Union, 13, 35, 164, 168, 173,
182
Cyprus, 4, 8, 13, 14, 21, 145, 147;
Greek Cypriots, 4, 14, 15, 85, 88,
159, 166, 180; problem of, 4, 72, 78,
88, 140; Turkish membership to the
EU and, 13, 16, 159, 166, 168, 176,
179, 180; Turkish policy toward, 13,
14, 88, 147, 175; Turkish Republic of
Northern Cyprus, 179, 180
Czech Republic, 118

D-8, 65, 75n21
Daalder, Ivo, 121
Davies, Norman, 30
Davutoğlu, Ahmet, 82
De Gaulle, Charles, 123; Gaullism, 128
de Villepin, Dominique, 120
Del Ponte, Carla, 14
Democracy Assistance Dialogue
(DAD), 95, 97, 107, 109, 158
democratization and democracy
promotion, 70, 72–73, 83, 93, 96–97,
100, 106, 108, 109, 111, 149, 179,
186; in Turkish foreign policy, 83,
106–7

Denmark, 118
Derrida, Jacques, 117–19, 137, 176
desecuritization, 68, 70, 112

Ecevit, Bülent, 85
Eco, Umberto, 118
Economic Cooperation Organization
(ECO), 93, 103
effective multilateralism. See
multilateralism
Egypt, 46, 78, 87, 104
Emerson, Michael, 24, 43, 73
energy, 45–48, 53, 147, 148; Blue
Stream pipeline, 47; BTC, 46, 81;
BTE, 47; East-West corridor, 46–47;
Kirkuk-Yumurtalik pipeline, 46, 47,
79; Nabucco, 47; North-South
corridor, 47; security, 2, 126, 147;
Turkey-Greece pipeline, 47
Erdoğan, Recep Tayyip, 82, 107, 157
Erez Industrial Estate, 97
Ergüvenç, Şadi, 45
EU military, 128–30; battle groups in,
134; operational planning of,
132–33; Turkey's contributions to,
49, 68, 69, 185. See also European
Security Strategy (ESS); NATO-EU
relations
Eurasia, 2, 4, 9, 32, 73, 94, 101;
Turkish-Russian cooperation in,
90–91
Euro, 8, 122, 123
Euro-Atlantic Partnership Council
(EAPC), 91, 93, 101, 135
Euro-Mediterranean Partnership. See
Barcelona Process
European Commission, 43, 45, 47, 59,
62, 106, 123; assessments on Turkey,
12, 31, 42, 43, 72, 73, 99; role in the
negotiations process, 164–67
European Constitutional Treaty, 18, 21,
122–25, 132, 185
European Court of First Instance, 165

European Court of Justice, 61, 165
European Defense Union, 123
European Economic Community, 8, 34
European integration, 5, 18, 27, 58, 60,
    61, 62, 79, 122, 124, 182, 186; and
    Turkey, 18, 43, 68, 80, 169; future of,
    2, 41, 140, 185
European Monetary Union, 123
European Parliament, 16, 23, 163, 170,
    178
European Security Strategy (ESS), 6,
    31, 108, 125–28, 186
European Security and Defense Identity
    (ESDI), 68, 129. See also EU
    military; NATO-EU relations
European Security and Defense Policy
    (ESDP), 61, 63, 129, 130, 131, 133,
    137, 181–83. See also EU military;
    NATO-EU relations; Common
    Foreign and Security Policy (CFSP)
European treaties: Amsterdam, 130,
    165; Maastricht, 123, 124, 165;
    Nice, 23, 61, 123, 130–31, 165, 169;
    Rome, 8, 130, 165
Europeanness, 26. See also identity

Ferrero-Waldner, Benita, 186
Finland, 44
Flournoy, Michele, 130
Fortuyn, Pim, 25
Fuller, Graham, 34, 50, 99, 110

G-8, 97, 105, 107, 109, 110, 120, 158
G-20, 65
Gaullism. See De Gaulle, Charles
geopolitics, 43, 45, 48, 51, 82, 100, 111,
    138, 139, 148; "greater Middle East,"
    104; Turkey's, 43, 44, 48, 51, 69, 73,
    82, 89, 100, 148, 159, 183, 187
Georgia, 46, 83, 88, 93, 102, 148
Germany, 21, 23, 36, 63, 87, 91, 120,
    132, 138, 163; and Turkey, 16, 18,
    19, 25–27, 88; reunification, 5, 78

ghettoization, 29
Giscard d'Estaing, Valerie, 21, 23, 24,
    25, 27
globalization, 1, 3, 32, 51, 52, 53, 57,
    63, 67, 69, 119, 128, 151
GNP, 20, 44 53
Gordon, Phil, 137, 148, 149
Greater Middle East, 2, 30, 104, 108,
    110. See also Broader Middle East
    and North Africa
Greece, 8, 36, 67, 72, 93, 108, 172, 176;
    and Cyprus problem, 145; and PKK,
    85; relations with Turkey, 78, 81,
    84–87, 177, 178, 179
Gulf Cooperation Council, 136
Gulf War, 78, 79, 80, 84, 109, 153, 154
Gül, Abdullah, 13, 15, 16, 49, 82, 106,
    146, 157

Habermas, Jürgen, 117–19, 134, 137,
    176
Hadley, Stephen, 95
Hallstein, Walter, 5
Hakura, Fadi, 167
Hamas, 87, 138
Hariri, Rafik, 87, 96, 138
Hickok, Michael Robert, 86, 87
Hill, Charles, 52
Hill, Emily, 86
Hill, Fiona, 91
Hisarcıklıoğlu, Rıfat, 97, 98
Hoffman, Stanley, 3
Howorth, Jolyon, 18, 129
Hughes, Kirsty, 23, 172
human trafficking, 104, 127
Hungary, 36, 47, 118, 173
Huntington, Samuel, 13
Hussein, Saddam, 79, 81, 148, 153, 154

identity: Christian, 6, 27; Eurasian, 90;
    European, 26; politics of, 51, 57, 82,
    101
Ihsanoğlu, Ekmeleddin, 95, 110

immigration, 16, 22, 25, 34, 105
Independent Commission on Turkey, 41, 44, 48
India, 1, 2, 51, 188, 190
İnönü, İsmet, 170
International Criminal Court, 3, 49, 122
International Criminal Tribunal on the War Crimes in Former Yugoslavia, 14
International Crisis Group (ICG), 155
International Court of Justice, 168, 176, 177
International Monetary Fund, 3, 20, 159
International Security Assistance Force (ISAF), 94, 157
Iran, 30, 49, 71, 73, 78, 88, 101; Iran-Iraq war, 81, 153; nuclear program of, 87, 100, 111, 138, 151; Turkey's relations with, 81, 87, 89, 95, 101, 157, 182
Iraq, 21, 30, 46, 79, 100, 102, 108, 109, 112, 135, 136, 154, 155, 156; EU and, 59–60, 120–21, 131; Shiites of, 96, 155, 157; Sunnis of, 96, 98, 154, 157; Turkmens of, 73, 78, 154, 157; Turkish policy towards, 70, 73, 77–79, 81, 87, 95–96, 112, 145, 147–49, 153–54, 157; war (2003), 46, 50, 71, 118–21, 126, 134, 148, 153, 156–57, 175–76. See also Kurds of Iraq
Ireland, 8, 172
Islam, 12, 28, 30, 48. See also Muslim world
Islamophobia, 16, 25, 29. See also Christian-Muslim relations
Israel, 98, 104, 147, 155; relations with Turkey, 47, 83, 84, 87, 88, 95, 97. See also Arab-Israeli conflict
Istanbul Cooperation Initiative, 103, 135. See also NATO

Italy, 47, 63, 85, 107, 118, 123
Ivory Coast, 133

Japan, 119
Jervis, Robert, 120
Jordan, 88, 107
Justice and Development Party, 42

Kadıoğlu, Ayşe, 108
Kagan, Robert, 58, 63, 70, 119, 120
Karaosmanoglu, Ali, 69, 70
Kennedy, Paul, 86
Kenya, 85
kerneuropa. See Core Europe
Khalilzad, Zalmay, 96
Kinzer, Stephen, 9, 33
Kirkuk, 96, 100, 154, 155
Kosovo, 120, 135
Kramer, Heinz, 181, 183
Krueger, Anne, 20
Kupchan, Charles, 137
Kurdish issue, 42, 51
Kurds of Iraq, 73, 78, 84, 96, 153, 154, 157, 156–57; ambitions of, 96, 99, 154–56; support from Turkey to, 79, 81, 156–57. See also Iraq; Kirkuk; PKK terrorism
Kurtz, Stanley, 34
Kuwait, 79, 153
Kyoto Treaty, 3, 122

Laicitee. See secularism
Lamers, Karl, 118
Larrabee, Stephen, 91, 99
Latin America, 24, 25, 62, 63
Leonard, Mark, 3, 4, 58, 122, 123
Lesser, Ian, 83, 99, 148, 149, 153, 154
Livni, Tzipi, 87
Lugar, Richard, 136
Luxembourg, 13, 14, 15, 31,132

Macedonia, 135
MacKinder, Alfred, 104

Makovsky, Alan, 86
Maliki, Nouri al-, 96
Mango, Andrew, 9
Maraishi, Ibrahim al-, 78
Marchetti, Andreas, 6
Mazower, Mark, 34
Mediterranean, 4, 6, 43, 46, 60, 62, 63,
    100, 101, 104, 106, 138; dialogue,
    101, 106, 135, 136; and Turkey, 73,
    92, 182. See also Barcelona Process;
    Broader Middle East and North
    Africa
Merkel, Angela, 120
Middle East, 2, 32, 100, 101, 104, 108,
    154, 181; EU and, 44, 106, 182;
    peace process, 86, 105, 182; Turkey
    in, 4, 34, 43, 47, 49, 73, 78, 83, 86,
    97, 98, 147, 159, 175; United States
    and, 52, 80, 105, 106, 147, 148, 157.
    See also Arab-Israeli conflict;
    Broader Middle East and North
    Africa; democratization and
    democracy promotion
migration. See immigration
Missiroli, Antonio, 124, 125
Monet, Jean, 5
Morris, Jan, 32, 33
Müftüler-Bac, Meltem, 48
multiculturalism, 6, 25, 29
multilateralism, 3, 7, 69, 70, 86, 101,
    112, 126, 127, 147
Musharraf, Pervez, 98
Muslim world, 4, 9, 32, 48, 51, 99, 105,
    106, 107, 110, 149, 175

Nagorno-Karabakh, 65, 92, 178
NATO, 2, 3, 7, 80, 90, 93, 106, 109,
    121, 129, 168, 177; contributions to
    European integration by, 5, 68;
    debate about, 128–29, 132–33,
    135–36, 139; enlargement of, 87, 88,
    90, 91, 102; Istanbul Summit, 95,
    120; Istanbul Cooperation Initiative,
    103; missions and operations of, 92,
    121, 134, 135, 136; NATO-Russia
    Council, 91; NATO-Ukraine
    Commission, 91; North Atlantic
    Council, 121; Prague Summit, 131;
    Turkey in, 8, 36, 69, 71, 79, 84, 91,
    110, 140, 154, 181. See also Euro-
    Atlantic Partnership Council;
    Partnership for Peace
NATO-EU relations, 68, 122, 125,
    129–33, 135, 140, 182; "Berlin Plus,"
    130, 131; "Berlin Plus in reverse," 130
Negotiating Framework, 15, 164–65,
    167–71, 173, 176, 178, 179
Netherlands, 16, 27, 63
Nice Treaty, 23, 61, 123, 130–31, 169
North Korea, 139, 151
Norway, 7, 45, 108, 185
Nye, Joseph, 4, 58, 150

Olmert, Ehud, 87
Organization of the Islamic Conference
    (OIC), 51, 52, 95
Organization for Security and
    Cooperation in Europe (OSCE), 29,
    72, 93, 101, 106, 109, 110, 179
Orhun, Ömür, 29, 131
Ottoman Empire, 9, 19, 33, 34, 36, 51,
    89; legacy, 70, 77; Siege of Vienna,
    14; tolerance in, 27, 34; Treaty of
    Sevres, 66
Özal, Turgut, 19

Pakistan, 51, 98, 104, 190
Palestine, 87, 88, 95, 97, 138. See also
    Arab-Israeli conflict
Palmerston, Lord, 11
Papadopoulos, Tassos, 14, 180
Papandreu, George, 85
Park, Bill, 79
Parris, Mark, 15
Partnership for Peace (PfP), 69, 88,
    101, 135, 136

peacekeeping, 45, 101, 136
permanent safeguards, 167
perpetual peace, Kantian space of, 5
Phillips, David L., 27
PKK terrorism, 19, 41, 50, 64, 68, 70,
    71, 79, 83, 84, 85, 94, 147, 151, 153,
    178; bases in Iraq, 96, 147, 153, 156,
    157, 175
Poland, 8, 63, 118
Pollack, Kenneth, 104
Pope, Hugh, 24
Portugal, 8, 22, 63, 118, 172
post-conflict stabilization and nation-
    building, 134. See also crisis
    management, non-military
privileged partnership, 14, 16, 30, 67,
    181, 187
Provisional Reconstruction Teams
    (PRT), 95, 96

Radaelli, Claudio, 59
Ramonet, Ignacio, 128
regional cooperation, 32, 80, 82, 86, 90,
    92, 93, 97, 101, 102
Rehn, Olli, 16, 17
Rice, Condoleezza, 14, 95, 120, 146,
    151, 157, 169, 186
Robertson, George, 135
Roger, Phillip, 128
Romania, 8, 17, 20, 24, 47, 87, 91, 93,
    101, 172
Russia, 8, 44, 60, 80, 81, 89, 90, 91,
    100, 135, 138, 139, 179, 182; and
    energy, 45–47; relations with Turkey,
    24, 48, 51, 73, 85–86, 89–91, 93, 95,
    97, 175, 190
Rustow, Dankwart A., 32

Said, Edward, 34
Saudi Arabia, 73
Sayarı, Sabri, 83
Schake, Kori, 133, 135
Schäuble, Wolfgang, 118, 163

Schröder, Gerhard, 120, 121
Schumann, Robert, 5
Schwartz, Stephen, 29
secularism, 28, 48, 118; in Turkey, 4, 7,
    9, 11, 28, 33, 48, 52, 65, 77, 95, 110,
    156, 160, 175, 188, 190
September 11, 2001, 29, 52, 68, 108,
    117, 120, 125, 130, 135, 137, 150,
    151
Settle, Mary Lee, 33
Sezer, Ahmet Necdet, 87, 95
Sharon, Ariel, 98
Sherwood-Randall, Elisabeth, 149
Sierra Leone, 133
Simitis, Costas, 85
Slovakia, 63
Slovenia, 101
Smith, Julianne, 130
"soft" power, 4, 53, 58, 63, 150, 159,
    175
Solana, Javier, 125, 186
South Ossetia, 92
Soviet Union, 24, 33, 78, 80, 83, 86,
    89, 90, 93, 94, 122, 128, 145
Spain, 8, 22, 24, 25, 36, 62–63, 108,
    118, 172
Spykman, Nicholas, 104
St. Malo, 129, 130, 133
Steinberg, James, 133
strategic culture, 70, 119, 128, 138. See
    also European Security Strategy
    (ESS); U.S. National Security
    Strategy (NSS)
"strategic depth," 82
strategic medium power, Turkey as, 4
Straw, Jack, 13, 15, 16, 48
Switzerland, 118, 185
Syria, 21, 30, 87, 95, 96, 110, 138, 148,
    151, 157; and PKK, 83–85

Talabani, Jalal, 96
Tarasyuk, Borys, 91
Taşpınar, Ömer, 148, 149

terrorism, 68, 92, 94, 104, 108, 120,
126, 127, 135, 149, 151, 158, 175;
Turkey in the fight against, 64,
69–71, 79, 84, 147. *See also* al
Qaeda; PKK; September 11, 2001
Tocci, Nathalie, 24, 43, 73
Torbakov, Igor, 90
Torreblanca, Jose
transatlantic relations, 5, 52, 100, 104,
119–22, 128, 131, 138–39, 140, 147,
158–59, 183, 186. *See also* NATO;
NATO-EU relations
Trans-Dniester, 92
Turkic world, 24, 51, 73, 80, 83, 140
Turkish armed forces, 45, 71
Turkish reforms, 18, 19, 20, 22, 41–42,
72, 87, 99, 110–11, 174, 187, 189
Turkish Republic of Northern Cyprus.
See Cyprus
Turkish-American relations, 32, 51, 53,
71, 81, 85, 88, 90, 96, 100, 145–49,
152–54, 156–60, 169, 176, 181, 183,
189; public images, 32, 50; strategic
partnership, 146, 147, 148, 158, 159;
"Shared Vision" document, 146–47;
Turkish-Americans, 27; U.S. support
to Turkish EU membership, 49, 50,
147, 189
Turkish economy, 20, 44, 98, 159,
189
Turkmenistan, 93

Ukraine, 60, 91, 93, 95, 100, 102, 135,
138; Orange Revolution, 95
United Nations, 2, 3, 4, 71, 80, 14, 64,
70, 72, 87, 88, 108, 147, 151, 168,
179, 180; Charter, 124, 168, 176;
Development Programme, 105;
General Assembly, 121
United Nations Security Council, 96,
112, 120, 138; Turkish membership
in, 36, 65
United Nations Convention on the
Law of the Seas, 177
U.S. National Security Strategy (NSS),
126–28

Van Gogh, Theo, 25
variable geometry, 100, 186
Voight, Karsten, 137

Warsaw Pact, 5, 78, 79, 90, 91
water, 44, 88
weapons of mass destruction:
proliferation of, 92, 104, 122, 126,
127, 147
Westernization, 70, 112
Wolfowitz, Paul, 52
World Economic Forum, 107
World Trade Organization, 3

Zelikow, Phillip, 57
Ziyal, Uğur, 152

About the Author

For the past seventeen years Dr. Burak Akçapar has been a diplomat, an international civil servant, a professor, and quintessentially a student. He was head of the Policy Planning Department at the Directorate General for Policy Planning of the Turkish Ministry of Foreign Affairs between November 2002 and November 2004. From 1998 to 2002, he served as a member of the NATO International Staff, where he earned the Secretary General's Award for Excellence. Since 1989, his national diplomatic and consular assignments have taken him to Qatar, Germany, and currently the United States.

Dr. Akçapar taught international security at Middle East Technical University in Ankara and lectured extensively on various aspects of international affairs in Europe and the United States. His previous publications include The International Law of Conventional Arms Control in Europe (1996) and "The Debate on Democratization in the Broader Middle East and North Africa: A Civic Assessment from Turkey" (Istanbul: TESEV, 2004) with Mensur Akgun, Meliha Altunisik and Ayse Kadioglu. He also authored a section titled "Partnership for Peace as an Agent of Change and Continuity in the Euro-Atlantic Region" in NATO: The First Fifty Years, edited by Gustav Schmidt (2000). Currently, Dr. Akçapar lives in Bethesda, Maryland.